LEGAL DRAFTING
IN A NUTSHELL®

FIFTH EDITION

GEORGE W. KUNEY
Lindsay Young Distinguished Professor of Law
and Director, Clayton Center
for Entrepreneurial Law
University of Tennessee College of Law

DONNA C. LOOPER
Adjunct Professor of Law
University of Tennessee College of Law

WEST
ACADEMIC
PUBLISHING

444 Cedar Street, Suite 700
St. Paul, MN 55101
1-877-888-1330

Printed in the United States of America

ISBN: 978-1-68467-528-9

PREFACE

Many new lawyers are daunted by the prospect of drafting their first contract. "What do I say first?"

Every lawyer is forced to draft something eventually. And when that document does not precipitate an immediate end to the world, the pendulum often swings to the opposite extreme. Unnecessary fear is replaced by dangerous indifference and unwarranted confidence. Drafting is regarded either as an inherent ability or merely a mechanical function that can be performed by emulating what is contained in form books or found on the Internet.

Discard both misconceptions. Drafting contracts, instruments, or legislation is neither a secret order into which one must be initiated by long and painful steps nor a skill acquired by osmosis from the label "attorney-at-law." It is certainly not a matter of mindless imitation of the past. Drafting is, perhaps, *the* critical lawyering skill, at least when combined with legal analysis. Like other lawyering skills, drafting can be done well or poorly. Doing it well is something that can be taught, learned, and ingrained into one's habits.

This book deals with the process, techniques, and forms of expression used in drafted documents. It focuses on how one drafts private-law documents and legislation, rather than on the details of the substantive law with which the drafter must be concerned. Exactly what should be contained in a will, lease, partnership agreement, construction contract, contract for the sale of residential property, landlord-tenant statute, or any other type of drafted document is determined by substantive law of the jurisdiction, the subject-area expertise of the drafter, and the desires of the client. Books and other reference materials that focus on substance rather than form exist for drafting these specialized documents.

The objective of this book is to enable the reader to produce documents that serve the needs of the client, that solve existing problems efficiently, that foresee and forestall future problems, that make for efficient governance, and that ease the tensions and uncertainties that are inherent in all forms of human social and economic intercourse. The accomplishment of those goals is the lawyer's highest calling.

This book reflects the drafting insights we have gained from our collective experience of practice and teaching legal drafting, both as a stand-alone course and as integrated into substantive courses like bankruptcy, business associations, contracts, legal process, property, secured transactions, and workouts and reorganizations. But in a greater sense, it also attempts to carry forward to a new generation the collective wisdom of the legal drafting community. Over the years, we have taught from or consulted many texts and articles, and those that have contributed the most to our courses and our books include those listed in the acknowledgments at the end of this book, before the index.

For this fifth edition, each chapter has been updated to incorporate the current and developing perspectives regarding subjects like plain English, legal typography, and document preparation in the 21st century. This is especially the case in the sections of the text dealing with contracts and instruments, although it is true throughout the text. We thank David Cantrell, UTLaw class of 2021 for his work on this book and related projects.

This book contains the text of Kuney and Looper's *Legal Drafting: Process, Techniques, and Exercises* (4th Ed. West 2021), omitting the exercises. Some material is also drawn from Kuney's *The Elements of Contract Drafting with Questions and Clauses for Consideration* (5th Ed. West 2020), Readers may find a benefit in these separate titles, which contain additional materials for training in contract drafting, transactional practice, and legislation, but they should be aware of the overlaps.

GEORGE W. KUNEY
DONNA C. LOOPER
Knoxville, Tennessee

October 2020

ABOUT THE AUTHORS

George W. Kuney is a Lindsay Young Distinguished Professor of Law and Director of the Clayton Center for Entrepreneurial Law at The University of Tennessee College of Law. He holds a J.D. from the University of California, Hastings College of the Law, an M.B.A. from The University of San Diego, and a B.A. in Economics from the University of California, Santa Cruz. Before joining the UT faculty in 2000, he was a partner in the Allen Matkins firm's San Diego office. Previously he practiced with the Howard Rice and Morrison & Foerster firms in his hometown of San Francisco, doing litigation and transactional work largely in the context of business restructuring and insolvency. He teaches business law courses including Business Associations, Contracts, Contract Drafting, Commercial Leasing, Commercial Law, Consumer Bankruptcy, Debtor-Creditor, Mergers and Acquisitions, Representing Enterprises, and Workouts and Reorganizations. Kuney writes books and articles about business, contracts, commercial law, and insolvency-related topics. He also advises clients, consults, and serves as an expert witness regarding bankruptcy, contracts, agency and corporate law, restructuring, reorganization, and related subjects. He is admitted to practice law in both California and Tennessee.

Donna C. Looper is an Adjunct Professor of Law at The University of Tennessee College of Law where she teaches Legal Process. She received her J.D. from the University of California, Hastings College of the Law and her A.B. from Barnard College, Columbia University. She clerked for the Chief Judge of the United States District Court for the Eastern District of Louisiana and then for the United States Court of Appeals for the Ninth Circuit. Before teaching at the University of Tennessee College of Law, Ms. Looper was a Senior Attorney for the California Court of Appeal, Fourth District, Division One and, prior to that, was in private practice in San Diego and San Francisco. She is admitted to practice law in both California and Tennessee.

ALSO BY THE AUTHORS

CALIFORNIA LAW OF CONTRACTS (University of California CEB Treatise 2007–2020, Kuney and Looper, updated annually).

A TRANSACTIONAL MATTER (West 2016, Brian K. Krumm and Kuney).

EXPERIENCING REMEDIES (West 2015, Kuney).

BANKRUPTCY IN PRACTICE, 4th Ed. (ABI 2015, Michael Bernstein and Kuney).

A CIVIL MATTER (West 2013, Kuney and Looper).

THE ENTREPRENEURIAL LAW CLINIC HANDBOOK (West 2013, Kuney and Brian K. Krumm).

JUDGMENT COLLECTION IN TENNESSEE (Center for Entrepreneurial Law 2013, Kuney and Wendy Patrick).

BUSINESS REORGANIZATIONS 3d ed. (Lexis 2014, Michael Gerber and Kuney).

BAMBOOZLED? BOWERS V. BAYSTATE AND ITS AFTERMATH (West 2012, Kuney).

THE ELEMENTS OF CONTRACT DRAFTING WITH QUESTIONS AND CLAUSES FOR CONSIDERATION 5th ed. (text and teachers manual, West 2020, Kuney).

CONTRACTS: TRANSACTIONS AND LITIGATION 5TH ED. (West 2020, Kuney and Robert M. Lloyd).

MASTERING ADVOCACY AND APPELLATE PROCESS (Carolina Academic Press 2010, Kuney and Looper, revised printing 2015).

MASTERING LEGAL ANALYSIS AND DRAFTING (Carolina Academic Press 2009, Kuney and Looper).

LEGAL DRAFTING: PROCESS, TECHNIQUES, AND EXERCISES 2D ED (West 2021, Looper and Kuney).

CHAPTER 11–101: THE ESSENTIALS OF CHAPTER 11 PRACTICE (ABI 2007, Kuney with Jonathan Friedland, Michael Bernstein, and John Ayer).

OUTLINE

PREFACE III
ABOUT THE AUTHORS VII
ALSO BY THE AUTHORS IX

PART I. INTRODUCTION

Chapter 1. A Philosophy of Drafting.................... 3
A. The Characteristics of Good Legal Writing.................... 4
   1. Accuracy.................... 4
   2. Clarity.................... 6
   3. Concision.................... 7
   4. Simplicity.................... 9
   5. Tone.................... 9
B. Three Types of Legal Writing.................... 9
   1. Normative Writing.................... 10
   2. Discursive Writing.................... 10
   3. Litigation-Related Writing.................... 11
C. The Ultimate Consequence of Drafted Normative Documents.................... 11
D. Drafting as a Facilitator of Self-Government and Economic Enterprise.................... 13
E. Drafting as a Form of Preventative Lawyering.................... 14
F. Drafting as an Intellectual Exercise.................... 15
   1. Knowledge of the Law.................... 15
   2. Investigation.................... 16
   3. Conceptualization.................... 17
   4. Forethought.................... 19
   5. Organization.................... 19

G. Drafting as a Literary Exercise 20
1. Words 21
2. Sentences 22
3. Other Word Construction Techniques 23
4. Headings 24
H. Drafting as an Ethical Exercise 24
I. The Costs of Bad Drafting 26
1. Social Costs 26
2. Client Costs 27
3. Drafter Costs 27
J. Drafting from Scratch 29

Chapter 2. Contract Drafting 31
A. Basics 31
B. The Context: The Deal Timeline—Whether Big or Little, Deals Follow a Pattern 33
C. The Role of the Contract Drafter 36
D. Recurring Problems in Contract Drafting 38
1. Unintended Contracts 39
2. Documents Intended to Be Contracts That Fail 41
3. Contracts Containing Gaps 43
4. Terms That Are Ambiguous and Terms That Are Unintentionally Vague 44
5. Unanticipated Events 45
E. Types of Contracts 46
F. The Parts of a Contract 47
1. Caption or Heading 48
2. Introductory Paragraph 49
3. Recitals 50
4. Definitions 53
5. Statement of Consideration and Agreement 54

6. Substantive Provisions ... 56
7. Housekeeping Provisions or Boilerplate ... 57
8. Signature Blocks ... 62
9. Date ... 64
10. Notarization ... 65
11. Appendices, Exhibits, Schedules ... 65
G. Exemplar Considerations ... 67
H. Amending Contracts ... 69

Chapter 3. Legislative Drafting ... 75
A. Who Drafts Legislation? ... 75
B. The Function of the Legislative Drafter ... 76
C. Legislation Compared to Private-Law Documents ... 79
1. Nature and Size of the Audience ... 81
2. The Need for Precision ... 83
3. Policy Considerations ... 83
4. The Need for Factual Data ... 84
5. Political Considerations ... 84
6. Fitting the Document into an Existing Body of Law ... 85
7. Legal Limits ... 86
8. Legislative History ... 88
9. Form, Style, and Usage ... 89
D. The Parts of a Statute ... 90
1. Heading and Title ... 91
2. Enacting Clause ... 91
3. Short Title Section ... 92
4. Statement of Purpose or Findings ... 92
5. Definitions ... 93
6. Substantive Provisions ... 94
7. Enforcement Mechanisms ... 94
8. Remedies or Penalties ... 95

9. Housekeeping Provisions 95

E. Amending Statutes 98
1. When Are Amendments Drafted? 98
2. The Parts of an Amendment 99
3. What Amendments Do 99
4. Amendments Changing a Judicial Interpretation or Construction 102

Chapter 4. The Rules of Interpretation 105

A. Statutory Rules 106

B. Common Law Rules 107
1. Intent Controls 107
   a. The Plain Meaning or Four Corners Rule 108
   b. The Mischief Rule and Other Evidences of Intent 109
   c. Effect on Drafters 111
2. The Rule of Strict Construction 112
   a. Criminal Statutes 112
   b. Statutes in Derogation of the Common Law 113
   c. Statutes Depriving a Court of Jurisdiction 113
   d. Statutes in Derogation of Sovereignty 114
3. The Rule of Liberal Construction 115
4. The Rule of *Expressio Unius Est Exclusio Alterius* 115
5. The Rule of *Ejusdem Generis* 117
6. The Rule of *Noscitur A Sociis* 119
7. The Rule of *Reddendo Singula Singulis* 120
8. The Rule of Last Modification 121

9. The Rule That Handwritten Words Prevail over Typed or Printed Words 121
10. The Rule That Written Amounts Prevail over Arabic Number Amounts..... 122
11. The Rule That Specific Language Prevails over General Language or Provisions 123
12. The Borrowed Language Rule 123
13. The Rule Favoring Agency Interpretation 124
14. The Rule That a Document Must Be Read as a Whole 125
15. The Rule of Construing Statutes *In Pari Materia* 125
16. The Rule Disfavoring Repeals by Implication 127
17. The Rule of *Lex Posterior Derogat Priori* 128
18. The Rule of Construing a Document Against the Drafter 128
19. The Rule of Adopting a Construction That Favors Validity 129
20. The Rule Favoring the Construction of Contracts in a Manner Consistent with Public Policy 129

C. Tools for Analyzing and Interpreting Statutes 130
1. Using Tabulation to Explode a Statute ... 130
2. Using the Structure and Other Sections of the Same Statute 132
3. Using Case Law Interpreting a Statute 133

Chapter 5. Drafting Ethics 135
A. Solicitation 136
1. Advertising Specialization or Concentration 136
2. Mass Mailings 136
3. Solicitation of Former Clients, Family, and Friends 137
B. Competence and Diligence 137
C. Scope of Representation 138
1. Objectives and Means 139
2. Criminal, Fraudulent, and Otherwise Prohibited Transactions 140
D. Communication 144
E. Fees 144
F. Confidentiality 145
1. Ethical Requirements 146
2. Attorney-Client Privilege 147
G. Conflict of Interest 149
1. Representation Against a Current Client 150
2. Representation Against a Former Client 154
3. Imputed Disqualification 155
4. Former Government Lawyer-Drafters 156
H. Dealings with Third Parties 157
I. Litigation Ethics 158
J. Aiding the Unauthorized Practice of Law 159
K. Providing Free Drafting Services 160

Chapter 6. Legal Drafting Overview 163
A. Determine the Client's Objectives 163
B. Identify the Audience 165

C. Explore the Broader Legal and Factual Context of the Document ... 165
D. Research the Law ... 168
E. Determine Substance ... 169
F. Get the Facts ... 170
G. Identify the Proper Legal and Factual Concepts ... 171
H. Develop an Organization ... 172
I. Write the Document ... 173
  1. Ambiguities ... 174
  2. Rules of Style and Usage ... 174
  3. Definitions ... 175
  4. Terms Creating Legal Consequences ... 175
  5. Format ... 176
J. Review the Document for Substance and Style ... 176
K. Post-Execution Monitoring ... 177
L. 25 Contract Drafting Considerations That Comprise a Philosophy ... 177

PART II. PREPARATION AND PLANNING

Chapter 7. Getting Started ... 183
A. Determine Client Objectives ... 183
  1. The Basic Questions ... 184
  2. How the Information Is Used ... 185
  3. Objectives from a Variety of Perspectives ... 187
    a. Other Parties to the Transaction ... 187
    b. Scope of Anticipated Use ... 188
    c. Multiple-Client Objectives ... 188
  4. Evaluating Client Objectives ... 190

B. Know the Audience 192
1. Identity of the Audience 192
2. Characteristics of the Audience 193
3. Accommodating the Various Audiences 194
C. Determine the Context of the Document 195
1. Legal Context 196
2. Factual Context 198

Chapter 8. Drafting Within the Law 201
A. Form 201
B. Meaning 203
C. Substance 205
1. Prohibition 205
2. Requirement 206
3. Permission and Authorization................. 207
4. Denial of Permission or Authorization 207
5. Other Consequences 208
6. Implied Terms 208
D. Creating Legal Checklists 209
E. Drafting with Statutory Language in Mind 210
F. Validation Concerns 213

Chapter 9. Determining Substance 215
A. Types of Provisions 215
1. Required by Law 215
2. Going to the Essence of the Transaction 216
3. Extremely Important 217
4. Optional 218
B. Substantive Term Checklists 218
1. Commercially Prepared 218

2. Drafter Prepared 219
C. The Elements of a Legal Rule 229
1. The Person 230
2. The Conduct 230
3. The Object of the Action 230
4. The Circumstances 231
5. The Consequences 231
D. Substantive Gaps 233

Chapter 10. Choosing the Right Concept 235
A. Definition 235
B. The Importance of Concepts in Drafting 236
C. Types of Concepts 236
1. Legal Concepts 236
2. Factual Concepts 238
a. General Versus Specific 239
b. Vague Versus Precise 243
c. Abstract Versus Concrete 249
D. Choosing the Right Word to Reflect the Concept 251

Chapter 11. Organization 253
A. Division 253
B. Classification 257
C. Sequence 259
1. Chronological 259
2. Importance 260
3. Frequency of Occurrence 261
4. Familiar Before Unfamiliar 261
5. Rules Before Exceptions 261
6. What Before How 262
7. Substance Before Procedure 262

PART III. DRAFTING TECHNIQUES

Chapter 12. Avoiding Ambiguities.................. 265
A. Definition.. 265
B. The Consequences of Ambiguity..................... 265
C. Types of Ambiguity.. 267
1. Contextual Ambiguity............................... 267
2. Semantic Ambiguity.................................. 271
a. Homonyms 271
b. "And"... 273
c. "Or" 275
d. "And/Or" 277
e. Specific Dates...................................... 279
f. Time Spans... 281
g. Days, Weeks, Months, and Years 284
h. "Bimonthly," "Biannually," and "Biennially" 286
i. Hours.. 286
j. Relational Words 288
k. Ages 288
l. "Provided That".................................. 289
m. Legalese.. 290
n. Shall, May, Will, and Must 291
o. "Among" and "Between" 293
3. Syntactic Ambiguity.................................. 294
a. Pronoun Reference.............................. 294
b. Modifiers 295
c. Participles 300
d. Chain Prepositions 300
e. Negative Pregnants 300
f. "If . . . Then" Sentences 301
g. "Because" Clauses................................ 302
h. "Unless" Clauses 302

i. "Only" 303
j. Truncated Passive 305
k. "Which" and "That" 305
l. Plural Nouns 307
m. Commas and Semi-Colons 309

Chapter 13. Drafting Style and Usage 315
A. Consistency 315
1. Consistent Terminology 315
2. Consistent Grammatical Structure 316
3. Consistent Document Structure and Approach 318
B. Concision 319
1. Unnecessary Content 319
2. Cross-References and Section/Paragraph References 320
3. Repetitious Substance 320
4. Redundant Couplets, Triplets, and Other Chain Synonyms 322
5. Other Redundant Expressions 329
6. Legalese 332
7. Compound Prepositions and Prepositional Phrases 335
8. "The Fact That" 339
9. Rhetorical and Transitional Words and Phrases 340
10. The Phrase "of the . . . " 341
11. Unnecessary "Who's," "Which's," and "That's" 342
12. Substantive Numbers and Redundant Numeration 343
13. Expletives 344
14. Nominalizations 346

15. Passive Voice ... 347
16. "To Be" Verb Forms ... 348

C. Clarity and Simplicity ... 350
1. Short Sentences ... 350
2. Simple Sentence Structure ... 351
3. Present Tense ... 353
4. Simple, Ordinary Words ... 354
5. Terms of Art ... 359
6. Technical and Trade Terms ... 360
7. Foreign Words and Phrases ... 360
8. Words Ending in "-ee" and "-or" ... 361
9. Compound Adjectives and Noun Phrases ... 362
10. Unconventional Capitalization ... 363
11. Positive Versus Negative Expression ... 363
12. Exceptions ... 364
13. Personal Pronouns ... 365

D. Some Basic Rules of Grammar Relevant to Drafting ... 366
1. Forming the Possessive ... 366
   a. Form the Possessive Singular of Nouns by Adding " 's" ... 366
   b. Form the Possessive Plural by Adding an Apostrophe ... 366
   c. Its, It's, His, and Hers ... 366
2. Use of the Semicolon Versus the Colon ... 367
   a. The Semicolon ... 367
   b. The Colon ... 367
3. Slashes ... 368
4. Subject and Verb Agreement ... 368
5. Parentheses ... 369
6. Quotation Marks ... 370
7. Spacing After Sentences ... 372

E. Misused and Abused Words and Expressions 372
F. Gender-Specific Language 374

Chapter 14. Definitions 381
A. General Principles of Usage 381
  1. Terms with Established Meanings 383
  2. Terms of Art and Technical Terms 384
  3. Humpty-Dumpty Definitions 384
  4. Circular Definitions 386
  5. One-Time Definitions 387
  6. Definitional Mazes 389
B. Substantive Matters 390
C. Definitions Incorporated by Reference 392
D. Types of Definitions and Terminology 394
  1. Defined Terms 394
  2. Full Definitions 396
  3. Partial Definitions 398
    a. Enlarging Definitions 399
    b. Limiting Definitions 399
  4. Combining Full and Partial Definitions 400
  5. Examples 401
E. Methodology 402
  1. Use Familiar Terms 403
  2. Use Precise Terms 403
  3. Identify Components 403
  4. Identify Specific Referents 404
  5. Indicate Relationship to a Larger Unit ... 404
F. Location of Definitions 405
G. When to Draft Definitions 406
H. Testing Definitions 406

Chapter 15. Terms Creating Legal Consequences 409
A. The Importance of These Terms 409
B. Identifying and Creating the Appropriate Legal Consequences 409
C. The Suggested Conventions 410
1. Duties 411
a. Statutory Duties 411
b. Privately Created Duties 413
2. Negation of Duties 413
3. Rights 415
4. Negation of Rights 416
5. Surrendering Rights or Causes of Action—Waiver and Releases 417
6. Privileges 418
7. Negation of Privileges 420
8. Immunity 420
9. Conditions 421
a. Definition and Types 421
b. Terminology 428
c. Objective Versus Subjective Conditions 430
D. Covenants 431
E. Representations, Warranties, Releases, Guaranties, and Indemnities 432
1. General Rules and Techniques: Typical Representations and Warranties 433
2. Representations 435
3. Warranties 438
4. Guaranties and Indemnities 439
5. Indemnities 439
6. Releases 440
7. Conclusion—Cautionary Procedures 440

F. Exceptions 443
G. Events of Default and Remedies 444
H. When Not to Follow These Conventions 448

Chapter 16. Document Typography and Layout 451
A. Physical Appearance 451
   1. White Space 451
   2. Type Size and Font 452
   3. Limited Use of All Capitals and Underlining 454
   4. Line Length 455
   5. Justification 456
   6. Line Spacing 456
   7. Blank Spaces 457
   8. Sections and Paragraphs 458
B. Text 458
   1. Table of Contents 458
   2. Numbered Pages 459
   3. Hierarchical Paragraph Headings 459
   4. Lists and Enumerations 461
   5. Tabbing 464
   6. Charts and Graphs 465
   7. Computations 466

Chapter 17. Reviewing and Revising 469
A. Prepare a Flowchart 469
B. Document Review 472
   1. Review by the Drafter 472
      a. Review for Content—a Ten Point Checklist 473
      b. Review for Style and Usage 478
      c. Prepare a Summary 482

2. Review by Other People 482
   a. Your Colleagues and Supervisors 483
   b. Review by the Client 486
   c. Review by Opposing Counsel 488

C. Proofread the Document 492

Appendix 493

INDEX 497

LEGAL DRAFTING
IN A NUTSHELL®

FIFTH EDITION

PART I
INTRODUCTION

CHAPTER 1

A PHILOSOPHY OF DRAFTING

The goal of all legal writing is to communicate clearly and concisely. Too often, however, briefs, office memoranda, client letters, and especially contracts and instruments are drafted in ponderous, repetitive, and pretentious language that undermines this goal. The objective of this book is to provide you with comprehensive processes and techniques to identify common problems in legal drafting and to produce documents that clearly and concisely communicate substance to their audiences. In short, we believe there is no reason that legal drafting cannot be elegant, utilitarian, and efficient in achieving its purposes.

Before we begin, you should know that every rule stated in this book is subject to exceptions. Legal drafting, like so many things, is subject to trends and fashion. Reasonable minds may differ on many of these matters. As with all legal writing and drafting, the purpose is communication. Remember, it is easier to tailor the form of your message to your audience than to try to force your audience to enjoy the form of your message. Use the rules, principles, and methods in this book as a default guide to legal drafting, but modify them to fit your audience and surroundings. It is best to remain flexible at all times.

A. THE CHARACTERISTICS OF GOOD LEGAL WRITING

The goal of the drafting process is to produce documents that can be easily understood by the legal and lay audience involved in the matter. Legal drafting is different from other forms of writing. It is purposeful writing meant to inform, persuade, and memorialize events, agreements, and legal analysis.

Good legal drafting features use of plain English and possesses five basic characteristics.

As a starting point, the basic characteristics of plain English are:

- Short sentences;
- Definite, concrete, everyday language;
- The active voice;
- Separate paragraphs and sections with headings, for separate concepts;
- The absence of overly legal jargon, highly technical terminology, Latin, or other foreign terms.

In addition, the five characteristics of good legal drafting are (1) accuracy, (2) clarity, (3) concision, (4) simplicity, and (5) a professional tone.

1. ACCURACY

The most inexcusable inaccuracies in legal drafting are those that result from carelessness, like writing "employee" when the drafter meant "employer," thus radically shifting the duty from one party to another. But accuracy involves more than careful proofreading. Unless the words are chosen with care and assembled into proper sentences and paragraphs, the safe and accurate communication of ideas will fail. For example, "My client has discussed your proposal to fill the drainage ditch with her partners" is, hopefully, not an accurate expression of the idea. Presumably, the drafter meant: "My client has discussed with her partners your proposal to fill the drainage ditch."

Lewis Carroll fully understood the need for accuracy in communication.

> "You should say what you mean," the March Hare went on.
>
> "I do," Alice hastily replied; "at least—at least I mean what I say—that's the same thing, you know."
>
> "Not the same thing a bit!" said the Hatter. "Why, you might as just as well say that 'I see what I eat' is the same thing as 'I eat what I see.'!"

Meaning what you say but not saying what you mean can have devastating consequences. The poor selection and arrangement of words can prevent a letter from accurately advising a client what to do. It can prevent a contract from accurately expressing the intention of the parties. It can prevent a statute from accurately reflecting the legislative purpose. Accuracy is critical to everything a lawyer does.

Certainty is a component of accuracy; ambiguity is the opposite of certainty. Put differently, an ambiguous expression is capable of two or more accurate interpretations, depending on the perception of the reader. For example, if a will gives the executor authority to "pay Thomas and Megan $10,000," this can be interpreted as an instruction to pay each of them $10,000, construing the "and" in its several sense. It can also be integrated as an instruction to give only a total of $10,000 to Thomas and Megan, jointly. Which interpretation prevails is said to depend on the intent of the testator, but the drafter of the will should have reflected that intent with more certainty. After all, by the time the will "speaks" (during probate), the testator is no longer with us to make his or her intent otherwise known.

2. CLARITY

Uncertain references, homonyms whose meaning must be determined from context (*e.g.*, "plain" versus "plane"), dangling modifiers, convoluted sentence structures, and stream-of-consciousness prose create an impenetrable swamp through which the reader must slog. These are examples of bad legal writing. The reader should be able to move rapidly and confidently through the document, understanding immediately the meaning of each word, phrase, sentence, and paragraph—and how they all tie together into a coherent whole. If the reader is puzzled about what the writer intended and has to go back and parse a sentence or ponder a paragraph, the legal writer has failed to communicate clearly.

Using the active voice promotes clarity. This is also accomplished by use of short sentences, writing with verbs instead of nouns or nominalizations, and keeping subjects close to verbs and verbs close to direct objects. Wherever possible, make the subject a person or entity that can act, rather than a concept. Hence, the subject of a provision or sentence should be "doing" [verb phrase] something to an object and, often, the provision or sentence should also address what happens if the subject does not. It also helps to make the elements of a sentence parallel in structure, to be careful in word choice and usage, and to punctuate correctly.

3. CONCISION

Being concise means saying all that needs to be said with the fewest number of words. Concision should not be confused with brevity. It is important for the legal drafter to avoid jumping to conclusions. Outside of the legal profession, being able to reach the right answer or course of action quickly, even instinctively, is rewarded. Although these abilities have a place in legal work, in law and legal drafting you need to *slow down and show your work.* Each step in the analysis should be explicitly stated, and no assumptions beyond a common understanding of American English usage and style should be presumed. A document can be concise, but not brief, if the document covers substantive terms that are both numerous and complex. And a document can be brief but not concise, if it omits necessary clarification and detail.

True concision is an essential element of good drafting. Lawyers, judges, clients, and other readers of legal writing are generally very busy people. They are not reading for pleasure. They have neither the time nor the patience to plod through page after page of excess in a brief or a contract. Nor do they need to be given information that is irrelevant to the purpose for which they are reading the document. As is true of all writing, legal writing must be done with the needs of the intended audience well in mind.

If a word can be eliminated or if three words can be replaced by one without sacrificing the meaning of the sentence, do it. Similarly, if a sentence has effectively communicated the idea, then delete the second sentence that merely restates the idea in different words. Redundant paragraphs and provisions are an even greater shortcoming.

Concision is most easily achieved through judicious self-editing. At the initial stages of the writing process, the writer should focus primarily on substance and organization. After the document has matured into the passable draft stage, the writer should put on an editor's hat and approach the document with a critical eye and a red pen. The length of a document can often be reduced substantially by editing out wordy idioms, compound prepositions, expletives, nominalizations, redundant couplets, and passive voice constructions. The result will be a work product that is concise, crisp, and to the point. These attributes are particularly important in drafted contracts, instruments, and legislation.

4. SIMPLICITY

To be "concise" means to say it in the fewest necessary words. Simplicity, in contrast, relates how those words are put together. The more substantively complex a document is and the greater the number of truly necessary words, the more important it is that they be presented in a straight-forward, simple manner. A drafted document can and should emulate the simplicity of a good set of instructions: "Go to Lake Road. Turn left. Drive 3.5 miles. The house is on the right."

5. TONE

Good legal drafting has a direct, professional tone. The opposing evils in legal drafting are folksiness and pompousness. The object is to steer a course between the two. Legal documents are about serious matters. They should not read like social media—with contractions, colloquialisms, sentence fragments, or editorial comments. Nor should lawyers ignore the conventions about what is offensive to the community, such as the use of gender-specific language. On the other hand, a legal document should not be written in stuffy, pretentious language.

B. THREE TYPES OF LEGAL WRITING

Though all good legal writing possesses the attributes of plain English—accuracy, clarity, concision, simplicity, and a proper tone, differences exist between the various forms of legal writing.

1. NORMATIVE WRITING

Contracts, leases, wills, trust agreements, waivers, releases, by-laws, statutes, ordinances, and regulations all serve to establish, define, and regulate legal relationships. These documents are forward-looking and normative in character—meaning they provide the rules that will control the behavior of the parties in the future.

Private documents like contracts, and public documents like statutes, differ from each other in some respects. The differences, however, are mainly cosmetic. The process and the necessary skills are basically the same, regardless of whether one is drafting an apartment lease or a noise ordinance. This book focuses on normative writing.

2. DISCURSIVE WRITING

In the legal context, "discourse" means speaking or writing authoritatively about a topic. The lawyer's discourse serves two different purposes—to inform and to persuade. Most legal documents contain an element of both. Client letters, legal memoranda, and judicial opinions are designed primarily to inform, presenting an accurate statement of the law and its application to the facts at hand. Although these documents have a persuasive component, they manifest largely in the form of correct data and reasoning. On the other hand, briefs, memoranda in support of motions, and settlement letters are primarily intended to persuade someone to do something.

In either event, the literary form of legal discourse is that of an analysis or argument, consisting of premises from which a certain conclusion is drawn. In addition to being logically structured, this form of legal writing must also be easily readable and possess some degree of eloquence. Word choice, sentence structure, diction, cadence, and the smooth flow of ideas are all of critical importance.

3. LITIGATION-RELATED WRITING

Complaints, answers, motions, interrogatories, discovery requests, and the like are designed to satisfy both the formalities and the substantive ends of litigation. Statutes and court rules often dictate the exact form, order, and wording of litigation related documents.

These documents function primarily as triggering mechanisms, setting into motion the various phases of litigation. However, if done properly, these documents also inform, persuade, and channel the litigation to the writer's advantage. Although federal and many state rules of civil procedure allow for a highly abbreviated form of notice pleading, a good pleader will use every filed document to educate the court—each provides an opportunity to introduce or reinforce the theory of the case that is meant to drive the decision on the merits beneath the doctrine.

C. THE ULTIMATE CONSEQUENCE OF DRAFTED NORMATIVE DOCUMENTS

One of the highest aims of government is to structure societal relationships that are fair and just through laws that preserve individual rights and promote the common good.

Drafted normative documents play a major role in this endeavor by creating and evidencing legal obligations and remedies for those to whom a duty is owed that is unperformed. The law operates on the assumption that most people will honor their legal obligations most of the time. If the county enacts an ordinance (a public law) prohibiting the burning of leaves, we may grumble over the passing of a cherished rite of fall, but we haul our leaves to the landfill like everyone else. If Sam contracts to sell an orange to John at a fixed price (a private law), Sam will probably honor that obligation even if he later discovers that he could have sold the orange to Sharon at a higher price. If not, the law should provide a remedy or a penalty—there is no right without a remedy.

The potential for serious, unintended consequences should always be in the back of the mind of every legal drafter because its realization will instill a strong sense of duty to be diligent, careful, cautious, thorough, and correct. A badly drafted leaf-burning ordinance, whose overly broad language makes it applicable to conduct that was not within the contemplation of the city council constitutes the threatened imposition of a penalty against anyone who fails to comply. A badly drafted contract of sale, which omits a significant condition subsequent that would have cancelled the transaction, will allow a seller or a buyer to petition a court to force the transaction to close.

D. DRAFTING AS A FACILITATOR OF SELF-GOVERNMENT AND ECONOMIC ENTERPRISE

In a political society, especially a democracy, the laws are expected to be easily understood by citizens, applied in an even-handed manner regardless of one's status or class, and to operate consistently with both substantive and procedural due process. The government needs individuals with the training and aptitude to produce such laws. When one considers the chaos that results when a legislature enacts a poorly drafted law, it boggles the mind to think of the result that would inure if all laws were similarly flawed.

Similarly, a sophisticated and complex economy would be impossible without documents that provide for the future exchange of goods and services, and a legal system that makes the promises contained in those documents legally binding. A contractor would never build a house on the mere promise of future payment by the owner. Likewise, an owner would never pay the price of the home's construction in the mere expectation that the house would eventually be built. Commerce and enterprise could not exist. The legal drafter produces the documents that are the necessary conditions of a viable economy. It is said that our economic system depends on investors to provide the capital, workers to perform the labor, and managers to coordinate this combination of capital and labor. None of this would be possible without the drafter's assistance. The drafting skill and diligence that is required of the transactional lawyer is enormous, perhaps more than what is required of the legislative drafter.

E. DRAFTING AS A FORM OF PREVENTATIVE LAWYERING

Lawyers are primarily in the problem or problem-solving business. The buyer of a house has a problem with the condition of the house and the seller has a problem with the buyer's refusal to close. The lawyers on both sides will attempt to resolve these problems, first by amicable negotiation, then, if that fails, through litigation. The value of the lawyers' involvement in this problem-resolution process cannot be ignored.

While the litigator is a backward-looking problem-resolver, the transactional drafter faces perhaps a more difficult task, that of the forward thinking problem-preventer. Although the peaceful resolution of an existing problem is a worthy endeavor, the often more challenging goal of the lawyer is to prevent problems from occurring in the first place. If done well, drafting helps accomplish that goal. If done poorly, it only creates more problems. Suppose that a manufacturer wants to retain a contractor to build a new production facility. This will be a massive, complex, expensive, and lengthy undertaking. If the drafter of the contract anticipates the problems and disagreements that are likely to arise during the course of construction and deals with them intelligently, the project will go forward to completion without difficulty. But if the contract is incomplete, ambiguous, unnecessarily vague, or unfairly favors one side, then the parties are likely to end up in litigation—while the partially constructed new plant sits in the middle of a muddy field.

F. DRAFTING AS AN INTELLECTUAL EXERCISE

Drafting is one of the most intellectually demanding of all lawyering skills. It requires knowledge of the law, investigative instincts, the ability to deal with abstract concepts, an extraordinary degree of forethought, and organizational skills.

1. KNOWLEDGE OF THE LAW

Drafting presupposes an extensive knowledge of both substantive and procedural law. The drafter of normative documents uses the law in a manner unlike that of the brief writer, the memorandum writer, or the litigator. The brief writer uses the law to challenge or justify what has already happened. The memorandum writer uses the law to predict the legal consequences of what may happen. The litigator uses the law to determine how to characterize what has happened in its proper legal form and to then present it in court.

The drafter of normative documents uses the law affirmatively, to accomplish the client's objectives. The client wants to ensure that a sales representative will not go to work for a competitor after her employment with the client is terminated. This is not an especially easy objective to achieve. The law dealing with a covenant-not-to-compete is complex, and the drafter must work through the intricacies to produce an agreement that is both effective and enforceable. Or, the drafter may discover that a living will, in its mandated statutory form, will not accomplish all the client desires. The drafter may thus supplement it with a durable power of attorney.

In sum, the drafter must know how to use legal rules to meet the needs of the client. Although Chapter 8 more fully discusses how the drafter uses law in the drafting process, the basic principle is to harness the law by drafting clearly into or around existing legal rules and precedents.

2. INVESTIGATION

The client rarely comes to the drafter with an already prepared, comprehensive list of facts that the drafter will need to prepare the document. In part, this is because the client usually does not know what the document must contain to serve its desired purposes. The drafter must ferret out these facts through investigation.

The investigation usually begins with asking the client questions. The drafter must know what questions to ask. Checklists are an invaluable tool. In addition, the drafter must know how to ask the question so that the response provides an accurate reflection of what the client truly wants or needs. For example, "Do you want to impose any conditions on your duty to purchase this house?" might elicit a negative response. But the client is likely to respond favorably to, "Do you want to require the seller to provide a "free from termites" inspector's letter as a condition of your duty to purchase this house?"

The drafter's investigation, however, cannot be limited to the information provided by the client. The client may not know if the property being purchased has had environmental pollution problems or even realize that this should be of concern. The drafter must anticipate this as a problem, discover the information from other sources, and draft accordingly.

The investigation required of a legislative drafter may be even more extensive. One cannot attempt to regulate a complex facet of human behavior, such as the issuance of corporate securities, without fully understanding the factual context and the problems that the legislation is designed to correct. Drafters of federal legislation usually have the luxury of committee hearings, where the facts are fully ventilated. And state legislative drafters are sometimes similarly fortunate. But city ordinance drafters are often left to their own resources in the development of the facts that are necessary to produce legislation that accomplishes its purposes. These matters are discussed more fully in Chapter 9.

3. CONCEPTUALIZATION

Another fundamental intellectual skill required of the drafter is the ability to conceptualize—in terms of both law and facts. Simply put, conceptualizing involves knowing exactly what you are talking about and finding the right words to express it.

Legal conceptualization is the easiest to understand. Legal concepts, for the most part, come prepackaged. Negligence, agency, incorporation, consideration, and a host of other legal concepts have fairly fixed meanings. The task of the drafter is to choose the concept that will accomplish the client's desires.

Occasionally, the statutory drafter is compelled to create a new legal concept. Often, this is caused by new technologies. In the nineteenth century the advent of the railroad required the creation of many new tort concepts. Today, the information technology evolution has spawned many new forms of misbehavior—such as unauthorized access and theft by computer—that require careful conceptualization. Or, a form of previously unregulated conduct is recognized as unacceptable, like sexual harassment. It could not be addressed legally, however, until it was first reduced to a concept with identifiable dimensions.

Factual conceptualization is a bit more difficult to understand. Briefly, it involves envisioning and expressing the facts with the proper degree of generality/specificity, vagueness/precision, and abstraction/concreteness. Choosing between these alternatives is an intellectually demanding and difficult task for the drafter.

Conceptualization is discussed more fully in Chapter 10.

4. FORETHOUGHT

Most drafted normative documents deal with events that will occur at a future date. The circumstances existing at the time the document is drafted and the circumstances existing at the time of actual performance may be radically different. The drafter must try to anticipate those changes and deal with them appropriately. The fundamental question of drafting is, "But what if . . . ?" A good drafter is like a chess player who sees three moves in advance. Anticipating the future, however, must also be tempered with common sense.

Hence, the drafter must not only anticipate what might happen, but also make a judgment about whether the contingency is likely and important enough to be dealt with in the drafted document.

5. ORGANIZATION

Contractual and legislative precision is achieved through good organization. Within a document, each section should address a specific subject or aspect of the transaction. Within each section, each subsection or paragraph should carry out one function. Within each subsection, each sentence should perform one subtask. Do not hesitate to subdivide sections, subsections, paragraphs, and sentences as needed to break them into meaningful, digestible chunks that each accomplish a single task.

The drafter's job is to create order out of chaos. Doing this requires a certain kind of intellect. A disordered document is often the product of a disordered mind. The skillful drafter must take the mass of information that is to be incorporated into the drafted document and divide it up into logically related and properly sequenced units.

Good organization is essential in making a document functional—that is, capable of being used easily by the intended audience. A tenant who wants to know their landlord's various maintenance and repair duties should be able to find that information in one place in the lease agreement, not scattered throughout six provisions. Or, consider the confusing disorganization of a criminal statute that states the prohibition in one section and a critical exception some sixteen sections later.

The organization of normative documents is discussed more fully in Chapter 11.

G. DRAFTING AS A LITERARY EXERCISE

Drafting not only requires exceptional thinking abilities, it also requires exceptional writing abilities. Drafting involves a combination of architectural (design) and construction (assembly) skills, albeit of a linguistic variety. The basic units are words and punctuation, instead of bricks and mortar. The words and punctuation must not only be selected with care, they must also be carefully assembled so that the document does not fall into incoherence. All legal analysis and writing should be concerned with explicitly identifying every link in a chain of reasoning. As was the case with long division in grade school, even if you get the right answer, you are not awarded points if you do not show your work.

1. WORDS

Lawyers are "word people." Words, phrases, sentences, paragraphs, sections, contracts, and briefs are their stock in trade. The contracts, instruments, and legislation that you draft must be clear, practical, and focused so that they work by guiding the course of performance or providing the foundation for a successful lawsuit. All of that is for your client's sake.

The legal drafter should be very particular about words. At the thinking stage, the drafter has clarified the concepts that the client wants to deal with in the document. Then, the drafter must find exactly the right word or set of words to mirror that concept. The drafter must know the standard dictionary meaning of words, the conventional and specialized usages, and how they have been construed by the courts—all of which may be different. Avoid legalese—lawyer sounds and words or phrases you would normally not use. This sounds easy enough, but beginning legal drafters tend to use words that they think sound "legal" or sophisticated but merely sound obtuse or pompous. A primary goal in legal drafting is to ensure that readers easily understand the words.

Unlike most writers, however, the drafter is not limited to the existing storehouse of words with fixed meanings. Drafters have the extraordinary liberty of creating new words or giving old words new meanings. New words are the corollary of new concepts. A contract, for example, might empower the buyer to do A, B, and C—the combination of which has no given name. For ease of reference, the drafter thus creates a new word, Z, which is defined in terms of A, B, and C in combination. Unfortunately, some drafters abuse this liberty and use definitions to create a new and incomprehensible vocabulary unique to the document in question. Such documents could just as well have been written in code. The use and misuse of defined terms is discussed more fully in Chapter 14.

The drafter must also choose words that will promote the objectives of good writing discussed earlier, especially those of accuracy, clarity, simplicity, and tone. Words that create legal consequences are particularly important, because this goes to the essence of the function of a drafted document. If the drafter uses "may" (which merely creates a discretionary authority to act), when the drafter really intended to create an absolute duty (requiring the use of either "shall" or "will"), the drafted document will be flawed. This is discussed more fully in Chapter 15.

2. SENTENCES

Sentences in legal writing should be as clear, direct, and concise as possible. Always looks for ways to use fewer words and to eliminate unnecessary words. In a brief or office memorandum, a dangling participle may merely mark the writer as a poor wordsmith. But in a drafted transactional document this may produce an ambiguity or vagueness that cannot be resolved short of expensive litigation. The drafter must have a thorough knowledge of grammar, syntax, and punctuation. These are the nails that hold the individual words together and allow them to function as a sentence.

Where possible, always make your subject a person or entity rather than a concept. Generally, avoid the passive voice as it obscures the action and sounds weak and uncertain. The exception is made when one is seeking to conceal an actor's identity or it is unknown, which is fairly rare in transactional documents. If you use the passive voice, make it a conscious decision.

In legal drafting, you are competing for the reader's time and attention; therefore, do not use more words than necessary to clearly and accurately communicate the information. Put yourself in the position of the distracted, unfamiliar reader. Are any of your sentences too long or hard to follow? Three lines on the page is stretching the limit. In reviewing long sentences, ask yourself if you can use fewer words and clearly communicate the same idea; if you can, do so. If not, it is likely you have packed too much content into one sentence and should break it up into more than one sentence. Legal drafters should do everything needed to make their documents easy to follow and readily accessible to readers.

3. OTHER WORD CONSTRUCTION TECHNIQUES

The legal drafter is not limited to sentences and paragraphs and can also use devices like lists, enumerations, charts, and tabbing to achieve greater clarity and readability. These are discussed in Chapter 16.

4. HEADINGS

A drafted normative document is typically organized in outline form. Each major division and sub-division has a heading. The heading describes the substance of that portion of the document at a very high level of generality. Headings enable the reader to easily find in the document—whether a statute or a contract—the exact provision the reader wants to consult.

Writing an appropriate heading is a vastly under-appreciated skill. The heading cannot be over- or under-inclusive. If a heading carelessly refers to a class of entities that is broader than those that are specifically referenced in the substantive provision itself, this will produce a contextual ambiguity. The inclusion of matters that have nothing to do with the stated subject of the heading may also be legally ineffective—the misplacement of warranty disclaimers, for example. And notwithstanding the sometimes applicable rule that headings are not part of the contract or statute, courts have been known to explicitly resolve uncertainties in the text by reference to the wording of the heading.

H. DRAFTING AS AN ETHICAL EXERCISE

The drafter is faced with many ethical dilemmas. Whether it is solicitation, scope of permitted representation, conflicts of interest, confidentiality, destruction of documents, or some other aspect of professional ethics, all of the rules have special applications in the drafting context. But what the rules require is not always clear. Legal ethics operate principally from the perspective of the lawyer as a confrontational advocate of a single client. The manner in which these rules are applied in the context of the lawyer as a problem-preventer and facilitator of agreement is a matter of considerable dispute among the bar.

Even if what the client wants the drafter to accomplish is not illegal or fraudulent, it may offend the drafter's sense of morality, ethics, and common decency. The lawyer is not expected to accept representation of everyone who requests it. And, contrary to the popular image of lawyers as scavengers and sharks, most lawyers do exercise discretion over the kind of client and the nature of the representation they will accept.

The drafter-lawyer has an opportunity that the litigator-lawyer often lacks. The litigator-lawyer is usually faced with conduct that has already occurred, and that lawyer's decision is between representation or not, to defend the conduct or challenge it. In contrast, the drafter-lawyer is usually brought into the process before the conduct occurs. This gives that lawyer the opportunity to suggest to the client that what the client proposes to do, while not illegal, may be questionable. And even if the client lacks even a shred of ethics, a realization that the behavior would not enhance his or her reputation and standing in the community may be sufficient, from a strictly pragmatic point of view, to deter the client from acting in that fashion. The drafter-lawyer's function as counselor cannot be underestimated. These matters are discussed more fully in Chapter 5.

I. THE COSTS OF BAD DRAFTING

A badly drafted document may impose tremendous costs on society, on clients, and on the drafter. All documents that go out over your name should be proofed, spellchecked, substantively correct, neat, and well organized. Each error that slips out can and most-likely will have a damaging effect upon the way others judge your professional competence, prudence, and attention to the matter at hand.

1. SOCIAL COSTS

A badly drafted document is an invitation to litigation. Litigation is not just a private undertaking, fully funded by the participants. Everyone pays for it. Providing judges, clerks, staff, and courtroom facilities is a fundamental function of government funded by taxpayers. In addition, contract litigation caused by bad drafting clogs the dockets. Bad drafting contributes enormously to that litigation and the resulting social cost. A high percentage of all contract cases involve issues that could have been avoided by more careful drafting.

Statutory litigation provides an even more damning testament to the social costs that flow from bad drafting. Purely factual disputes are unavoidable. But the critical issue in statutory litigation is often not what the facts are, but whether the law as drafted applies to those facts or what the statute really means. Such litigation is evidence of bad drafting and the social cost of it is enormous. Further, poor drafting, especially of criminal statutes, leads to harms not effectively prevented as well as the unintentional criminalization of behavior that, in a free society, should go unregulated.

2. CLIENT COSTS

People want lawyers to forestall or solve their problems, not to create them. If a document does not accomplish the client's objectives, this could be a very expensive drafting mistake indeed. A badly drafted contract will inevitably produce misunderstandings and ill-feelings that poison the relationship between the contracting parties. It may even prevent the relationship from arising again, causing the loss of an otherwise valuable customer, client, tenant, supplier, or subcontractor. Worse yet, a badly drafted document is an invitation to litigation, and litigation is extremely expensive for the parties. Someone always loses in litigation and often it can be said that all the parties have, in some sense, lost, no matter who wins. Damages can impose a significant and sometimes crushing financial hardship on an individual or business entity.

For the prevailing party, it is often a pyrrhic victory. The costs and attorneys' fees of prosecuting a valid claim may equal or sometimes exceed the recovered amount. For the prevailing defendant, it is simply the minimization of loss, but a loss nonetheless.

3. DRAFTER COSTS

The drafter who produces unworkable or litigation-producing documents will eventually pay for this ineptitude and sloppiness. At best, the attorney will suffer the loss of a client. Beyond that, upon discovering that their travails are the drafter's fault, many clients not only terminate the relationship, they also refuse to pay the bill and adopt a decidedly hostile "so sue me" attitude. There is also the spectre of a successful malpractice suit, especially if the lawyer does sue to collect the bill. The disappointed client will usually spread the word among friends, business associates, and even casual acquaintances.

Beyond the client, however, lawyers need to pay close attention to detail and take pride in all their written work product for their own sake. Each document you create—your work product—is your calling card. It is on this that you will be evaluated by your colleagues, clients, opponents, and others. Documents, including correspondence and emails that contain typos or substantive errors, that are badly formatted, or that do not convey an appearance of well-thought-out precision and accuracy will be held against you in the court of professional reputation.

All documents that you work on or that go out over your name should be proofed, spellchecked, substantively correct, neat, and well-organized. This requires a level of attention to detail that few people other than lawyers, accountants, editors, and publishers give to writing. Each error that slips out can be damaging to your professional reputation. The effect is cumulative. At some point—reached fairly quickly—mistakes add up to the reader, who assumes that the author is (a) not very smart, (b) not very careful, or (c) not paying attention. None of these impressions will advance your legal career.

J. DRAFTING FROM SCRATCH

Few documents are truly drafted from scratch. Rather, the drafter will rely on something from the firm's document files, a form book, or legislation from another jurisdiction, modified only with respect to the specific details of the transaction or regulated activity. These documents may not, however, conform to the style, usage, and terminology that modern drafting practice attempts to use and may contain provisions that are inappropriate for the matter at hand. Some of the substantive provisions of the prior contract may have been included because of a specific and unique aspect of that transaction.

What can happen is the current drafter is unaware of the purpose of the original provision, but includes it in the new contract on the assumption that it is probably essential, although the drafter could not possibly explain why to the client. The drafter then adds some provisions unique to the immediate transaction, and these in turn become part of the collective wisdom for that particular type of document. The one-size-fits-all documents often found in formbooks or produced via Internet document assembly programs suffer from similar problems.

Hence, when using precedent documents, it is necessary to critically evaluate their structure and provisions to determine if they are appropriate for the current matter. The drafter must "reset" the document's provisions. Better still is the ability to craft a document from scratch, after reviewing multiple precedent documents and understanding the context in which they were produced. Often, however, this is an unattainable luxury due to constraints of time and expense.

CHAPTER 2
CONTRACT DRAFTING

A. BASICS

The words of a contract will govern the parties' relationship, rights, and duties. They will be considered the primary, and often only, evidence of the parties' intentions. Thus, documentation that clearly communicates its meaning to the parties, their counsel, and enforcing courts is the ideal end result. Good contract drafting is marked by precision, exactitude, lack of ambiguity, and an absence of unintended vagueness.

A document can be drafted in plain English and still satisfy the requirements of the law and the purposes of the client. Avoid being a drafter who relies on less-than-plain language to achieve transactional ends. The plainer the language and the clearer the drafting organization, the more likely it is that the parties will not have differing interpretations of the contract. This should minimize the potential for litigation, or at least the risk of loss in litigation caused by a court adopting a different interpretation.

A contract drafted in this manner has at least four salient characteristics:

(1) It is accurate, meaning it correctly expresses the deal.

(2) It is complete, meaning all possibilities have been addressed. Look down the road,

determine the range of different contingencies, and provide your client with rights and remedies to address contingencies if they occur. Focus on what could occur if one party fails to perform and is insolvent, injured, or dead. Include protections for your client addressing these possibilities.

(3) It is exact, meaning it lacks ambiguity and unintended vagueness.

(4) Finally, it is able to withstand hostile, critical review. More likely than not, after the contract is executed, the next thorough review of its provisions will be by someone trying to break the contract or sue over the transaction. That person will focus on interpreting the document in a vacuum, ignoring any evidence of the parties' intent not found within its four corners. Edit your contract with an eye to identifying and fixing unclear pronoun references, modifiers that may relate to one or all of the terms in a series, conjunctions that make a list conjunctive or disjunctive, introductions that make the list exclusive or inclusive, and classification or categorization systems that do not accurately reflect hierarchical relationships.

To address these elements, some drafters tend to be long and wordy. They use overlays of multiple synonyms, qualifying phrases, and arcane or legalistic prose in an attempt to be accurate, complete, and exact. All too often, the work product collapses under the weight of these techniques. It becomes filled with ponderous, repetitious sentences, paragraphs, and sections.

Rather than using as many words as possible—the shotgun approach—strive to find the right word or words. This will involve considering the level of detail and generality of the words involved, as well as their potential multiple meanings and connotations.

B. THE CONTEXT: THE DEAL TIMELINE—WHETHER BIG OR LITTLE, DEALS FOLLOW A PATTERN

A transaction generally follows a standard timeline or chain of events: (1) negotiations, (2) due diligence (detailed factual and legal investigation), (3) preparation of interim transactional documents, (4) definitive transactional documents are finalized and signed, (5) further due diligence and other pre-closing activities, and (6) the closing.

First, the parties make contact and negotiate. A preliminary agreement is reached and they contact their lawyers, if they have not done so already. Although the key business issues have probably been addressed by the parties, there will often be significant issues left open, some of which will only become apparent to the client after consultation with counsel.

If possible, it is helpful for clients to meet with counsel prior to negotiating the basic business deal to explore the possible issues and structures for the contemplated transaction. A well prepared client can then bargain for an issue or structure with the other party from the very beginning. This may result in key issues being resolved in your client's favor with little or no discussion or quid pro quo. This might not be the case if the opposing party was just as prepared, left the issue open, followed up with his or her own counsel, and then negotiated the point.

As the parties proceed with full, formal documentation, due diligence—detailed factual and legal investigation—begins. Usually one party will produce documents and information relevant to representations and warranties that are being negotiated. It is important to realize that transactional documents reflect the stage of the relationship to which they relate. Therefore, the legal drafter must keep in mind the present stage of the relationship as well as those stages that are to come in the future.

The next step is the preparation of interim transactional documents, such as term sheets or letters of intent. The key issue at this stage of the relationship is to determine whether or not the interim transactional documents are meant to be binding or if they are simply tentative reflections of the terms and deal structure that the parties have been discussing and are intended to promote clarity and understanding, but not to bind the parties. Often, even the most tentative term sheets contain provisions that are intended to be binding, such as confidentiality provisions and covenants to return documents and other things if the contract is terminated. Whatever the degree of bindingness intended, the preliminary documents should make that intent explicit in their provisions. Due diligence—the process of factual and legal verification of things like parties' due formation, their capacity to contract, the legal stat of title to assets, the number, amount, and status of claims against a party or its assets, and the like—usually begins at this stage of the process.

The definitive transactional documents are then finalized and signed, and further due diligence and other pre-closing activities take place. Then the closing occurs. This is the point at which all (or the majority) of the consideration changes hands. Payments or deliveries may be made directly, party-to-party, or through an escrow (the preferred route for all but the most basic transactions). Escrows provide the parties with the security of knowing that although they have parted with their consideration, it will not be delivered to the other party until that party's deliveries are complete. In case of a dispute, the escrow agent can hold all consideration already delivered and maintain the status quo pending the dispute's resolution. There may be a post-closing adjustment period as well.

Contract negotiation and documentation is an exercise in *selling*. In the process, you are selling three things. You are selling:

(1) the parties on executing the documents at the present time;

(2) the parties on voluntary performance, after the document has been executed; and

(3) a later court or other entity on enforcement, after voluntary performance has ceased.

These three sales goals undermine each other to some extent. Consider the tension between selling the parties on execution, which tends to imply documentation with few, if any, teeth, and selling the parties later on voluntary performance, which is furthered by fairly detailed documents that contain both "carrot" and "stick" provisions tailored to the particular parties. Balanced documents that accomplish all three sales goals require careful consideration before and during the negotiating and drafting processes.

In the private law context, contracts are probably the most common form of drafted document. Wills, trust agreements, and various corporate and business documents—all of which are very substantive-law specific—comprise the remainder. Within the contracts sub-category, various types of contracts also tend to be very substantive-law specific. The desired substance of any particular type of document is beyond the scope of this book. Nevertheless, some generalizations are possible about contract drafting.

C. THE ROLE OF THE CONTRACT DRAFTER

Being a transactional lawyer involves a mode of analysis different from the litigation model that traditionally dominates law school, especially the first year curriculum. In the litigation model, one extracts rules of law from cases or statutes, examines a given set of facts, spots the issues, applies the law to the facts, and reaches a conclusion. (IRAC: Issue, Rule, Analysis, Conclusion). At every step of the way, one is dealing with "givens": facts that have already happened, laws that have already been made by legislatures and courts (even when one is arguing for a change in law). This is not to say that they cannot be argued, emphasized, or shaded in the advocacy process, but, at their core, they are fixed.

Transactional practice is different. It involves understanding the parties' deal and then translating the business terms into a transactional structure that uses contract, commercial, and other business law principles to govern the parties' relationship. It also involves making an appropriate record along the way as negotiations and documentation continue so that, should the deal break down and litigation ensue, litigation attorneys can present the case in the light most favorable to the client. Transactional documents create a record of the parties' deal while simultaneously creating mechanisms to foster agreement, encourage performance, and provide for enforcement and dispute resolution. The key here is that nothing, or at least very little, is a "given." There are notions of what is customary or what is the "market" approach or rate, and regulatory systems may affect what is possible to achieve with a given transactional structure. But the attorney is creating the structure and the provisions along the way in a manner that creates the most benefit for the client by harnessing applicable law and allocating risk and reward. This means determining what facts or states of nature should form the basis of conditions precedent to the transaction moving forward; what factual matters should be the basis for representations and warranties; when and how the transaction should terminate, if needed; and what sources of recovery should be available in the event of loss.

This is not to say that an attorney cannot be both a transactional lawyer and a litigator. Rather, the attorney should be conscious of which role is being played, and adjust his or her mode of thinking accordingly. Too often, especially with new attorneys, there is a tendency to look at transactional law and deal documents with the eyes of a litigator rather than a transactional planner. The transactional focus is on constantly improving the structure and utility of the documents.

D. RECURRING PROBLEMS IN CONTRACT DRAFTING

Transactional documents are an opportunity to prevent and plan for future litigation. You should think about how to integrate concepts from other sources and experiences into contracts. Transactional lawyers draft to fall within or to avoid the ambit of particular statutory or case law. What contract remedies would be available under the common law if the contract makes no provision for them? How can this common law result be altered in the contract? What is the evidentiary significance of various parts of the contract in later litigation? What can be done to render these portions admissible evidence? How can they be drafted so that they are favorable evidence for either party? Contract drafting provides an opportunity to use and reinforce a full range of substantive legal skills.

A review of the case law shows that contract litigation centers around the following problems, most of which are a result of poor drafting: (1) unintended contracts, (2) documents intended to be contracts that fail, (3) contracts containing gaps, (4) terms that are ambiguous and terms that are unintentionally vague, and (5) unanticipated events. If contract drafters consistently avoided these problems, contract litigation would diminish significantly. A great deal of this book is about the avoidance of these problems.

1. UNINTENDED CONTRACTS

Contract formation often begins with something that might appear to be an offer or even a full contract, but the originator intends it only to be a preliminary negotiation or an inquiry. The other party also frequently responds with something that is in appearance one thing, in intent another. Later, when it is to the advantage of one of the parties to do so, that party will claim that the correspondence was an offer/acceptance or a counter-offer/acceptance, thus creating a binding contract. Usually, objective appearance will prevail over subjective intent.

Drafters working with a client at the preliminary stages of a transaction should, if this is the client's intent, expressly indicate in the document itself that the letter or proposal is merely a preliminary inquiry, counter-inquiry, or an invitation to entertain offers and that the author reserves the right to terminate the negotiations at any time without prejudice. In other words, the terms stated in these documents are not necessarily intended to be the final terms of any agreement.

Often, however, even after the parties have agreed on all the principal terms, they still do not intend for their agreement to be binding until these agreed-upon terms are reduced to writing, the document is signed by both parties, and copies are exchanged. This preliminary document is sometimes referred to as a letter of intent. It should be conspicuously captioned as such and contain a comprehensive disclaimer of contractual intent. That disclaimer should indicate that the document is neither a contract nor the memorial of an oral contract, and that the parties do not intend to be bound until the designated formalities are followed. Even with these drafting safeguards, letters of intent are a minefield for the unwary. Many lawyers try to avoid them altogether. Others advise their clients never to sign them to prevent them from being construed as an agreed upon set of terms.

An even more dangerous form of letter of intent is one that does contain some binding promises, such as maintaining the status quo, keeping the negotiations secret, and not negotiating with anyone else until all the details are worked out. Here, the drafter must take particular care to indicate which provisions are binding and which are not. The better practice may be to make these two separate documents, one expressly binding, and the other not.

2. DOCUMENTS INTENDED TO BE CONTRACTS THAT FAIL

Regardless of the intent of the parties, the law will not necessarily enforce every promise that a person makes. Often the parties will sign a document intending to be bound by it, one of them will have a change of mind, and the other will discover that the promise is, indeed, unenforceable. The primary problems here are the lack of any recited or provable consideration and the incompleteness of the document.

With limited exceptions, for a contract to be enforceable it must be supported by mutual consideration. There must be a bargained-for benefit conferred or a detriment suffered by each party to the contract. Consideration takes a number of forms, including cash, promissory notes, letters of credit, transfers of property, services, transfers or surrender of rights, assumption of another's duty or liability, or mutual promises. Generally, lack of consideration is not an issue in real life, especially as the modern conception of consideration focuses on the "bargain test" rather than on notions of sufficiency or adequacy, yet it bears remembering. In some jurisdictions there are presumptions of consideration that arise when a written contract recites that consideration has been "had and received" or similar formulations.

Consideration is also an issue when one party's contractual obligations are supported by a third party's guaranty of payment or performance. In this circumstance, the guarantor may not appear to be receiving consideration for the guaranty as the only parties receiving benefits are those to the contract being guaranteed; the guarantor appears merely to be gratuitously sticking its neck out for another. Some transactional lawyers put their minds at ease over the guaranty/consideration issue by ensuring that the guaranty states that it is being given by the guarantor to induce one or both of the parties to enter into the primary transaction and having the guarantor sign the guaranty *before* the parties execute the primary transactional documents.

The drafter can easily resolve consideration problems. Either ensure that the contract contains mutual promises, or recite that consideration has been paid to support the one-party promises contained in the contract. Do not leave it up to the courts to imply the return promise that is necessary to make the express promise enforceable. Consideration recitations should also be considered more than a formality. In some jurisdictions, proof that the consideration was not actually paid may defeat the contract. The drafter should ensure that it is paid. Similarly, if the promised exchange is one that might be construed as a gift, and the recited consideration is very small, then a court might regard it as nominal consideration—consideration in name only—which is to say it is not consideration at all.

Also, to be an enforceable contract, the document must also contain all terms that courts in that jurisdiction regard as essential. Because of the liberality with which modern courts supply missing terms, few contracts fail completely for this reason anymore. But any contract that has to be salvaged in this way reflects poorly on the drafter.

3. CONTRACTS CONTAINING GAPS

A document may contain all of the essential terms of the transaction, thus qualifying as a contract, and yet be incomplete with respect to what turns out to be important details. Often, if the omission was unintentional, the parties acting in good faith can resolve these matters as the need arises. But sometimes, at the time of contracting, the parties will consciously decide to defer agreement on some matters and thus include an agreement-to-agree provision. To prevent such an agreement from being regarded as illusory, the drafter should either impose a good faith bargaining requirement, identify an objective basis for supplying the terms, or provide for mediation or binding arbitration.

In the absence of a later agreement between the parties, the missing terms must be supplied by a court. Extrinsic evidence may show that the parties had a contemporaneous understanding about this term that simply did not make it into the written contract. This presents a parol evidence problem. The UCC gap-fillers (found in article 2, part 3 of the UCC) are available to supply some missing terms in commercial contracts. Beyond that, there are course of performance, course of dealing, and usage of the trade provisions that provide possible terms. And, there are some common law rules about what a court should imply if a contract is silent on a particular term, generally revolving around the notion of reasonableness.

So, the missing term can usually be supplied one way or another. However, it may be a term that one or even both of the parties would never have agreed to originally; and it nearly always comes only after expensive litigation. This is a result the contract drafter must seek to avoid.

4. TERMS THAT ARE AMBIGUOUS AND TERMS THAT ARE UNINTENTIONALLY VAGUE

The object of good drafting is to communicate clearly the meaning and legal significance of the provisions of the document, thus reflecting the purposes and intent of the parties. Both ambiguity—when a term is susceptible to more than one meaning—and unintentional vagueness—when a term is imprecise—cloud a document's ability to achieve this goal. If the parties have honestly agreed in substance but the document does not reflect that agreement because of ambiguous or unintentionally vague terms, these drafting flaws may provide a way out when circumstances change to the disadvantage of one of the parties. In this way, ambiguity and unintentional vagueness are common causes of contract litigation. Avoiding ambiguities is discussed in Chapter 12, and vagueness versus precision is discussed in Chapter 10.

5. UNANTICIPATED EVENTS

Transactional documents are documents that speak as of one particular time—in the case of most, the date of their execution. This means they are intended to capture the agreements of the parties, to set out their respective rights and obligations, and to establish rules that will—govern future dealings. They must provide for substantially all of the details of the parties' future dealings or they fail in their job.

Almost all contracts deal with what will happen at some future time, ranging from one day to many years. For the drafter, this causes two related problems. First, at the time of contracting, the parties may be operating on a set of assumptions that later turn out to be incorrect. The parties assumed the subsoil was sandy loam, when it turns out to be solid rock. Second, at the time of contracting, the parties may have assumed something was going to happen in the future, an assumption that turns out to be false. The parties assumed the government would not impose an oil embargo, but the government did.

The contract law doctrines of mutual mistake, impossibility, commercial impracticability, and frustration-of-purpose allocate the risks of these unforeseen events, but they are a poor substitute for conscious risk-allocation by the parties themselves. Neither the parties nor the drafter can anticipate and address every possible contingency that might arise later. A surprising amount of contract litigation, however, deals with events that could have been anticipated, but were not. The conscientious contract drafter must always draft with the all-important "but what if. . . ?" question in mind.

E. TYPES OF CONTRACTS

From the drafter's perspective, contracts come in three basic types. In the first, offer, acceptance, and performance are virtually simultaneous—buying an orange at Sam's fruit stand, for example. Drafted documents are often not used here, because no need exists for them. If, however, there are representations, warranties, covenants, or conditions that survive beyond the initial exchange, then drafted documents are appropriate for what is termed a "sign and close" deal.

In the second type, the contract is formed but performance is delayed. These transactions are said to be "delayed and closing" deals. The performance is still of a discrete variety. Once the transaction is complete, the parties generally have no further dealings with one another. In simple, day-to-day transactions, the contract is often oral and the professional drafter is not even involved. Bill agrees to sell Jane his used legal drafting book at the end of the fall semester. But quite apart from the requirements of the Statute of Frauds, contracts calling for the future performance of complicated and expensive obligations, like the sale and purchase of a corporate subsidiary, cannot safely be predicated on an oral agreement and a handshake. The drafter plays a critical role in the formation of this type of contract.

The third type of contract involves an ongoing relationship between the contracting parties, either for an extended or an indefinite period. Installment sales, requirements contracts, employment contracts, collective bargaining agreements, partnership agreements, joint ventures, and major construction contracts are examples of this type of contract. The skills of the drafter are acute in this type of contract, mainly because of the possibility of unexpected events. In deciding how many of an infinite number of contingencies should be dealt with in the contract, the drafter must assess the nature of the relationship between the parties, their past transactions, their reputations in the business community, and either count on the parties being able to resolve unforeseeable problems or provide an alternative mechanism, such a mediation or arbitration. The objective is simple: make it work, by whatever means are necessary.

F. THE PARTS OF A CONTRACT

Regardless of type or subject matter, the typical contract consists of the following parts:

1. Title.

2. Introductory paragraph that includes the parties and the date of agreement.

3. Recitals or a Statement of Background Facts.

4. Definitions.

5. Core substantive provisions, including consideration, conditions, and closing.

6. Representations, warranties, covenants, indemnities, guaranties, and releases.

7. Events of default and remedies.

8. Boilerplate.

9. Signature blocks.

10. Exhibits and attachments.

The overall organization of a transactional document or group of transactional documents follows a group of rules:

- General provisions before specific ones.
- Important, central provisions before others.
- Rules before exceptions.
- Separate provisions or sub-sections for each concept.
- Technical, boilerplate, housekeeping, and miscellaneous provisions located last, before the signature blocks.

1. CAPTION OR HEADING

Generally, begin the first page of any transactional document with a title in all caps, centered, and in bolded type. The title should identify the type of contract using a generic term, such as "Lease," "Prenuptial Agreement," or "Asset Purchase Agreement." For example, **RESIDENTIAL LEASE**,

CONTRACT OF SALE, or **EMPLOYMENT CONTRACT**.

2. INTRODUCTORY PARAGRAPH

The first paragraph of the agreement identifies the parties by their full legal names and the type of transaction they are documenting, indicates the defined term names that will be used later when referring to both the document and the parties, and provides a reference date for the document. Ensure that all parties' names and other information (such as state of incorporation) are correct—using defined terms means they will not come up again until the signature blocks. Beyond these items, there is no need for further detail. Leave that for the recitals and the body of the contract.

The introduction paragraph is not numbered. It should be in this form:[1]

This [Agreement, Lease, etc. as appropriate] ("[Defined Term]") dated [as of], 20xx, is between, [a Corporation, Limited Liability Company, General Partnership, an Individual, etc., as appropriate] ("[Defined Term]") and, [a Corporation, Limited Liability Company, General Partnership, an Individual, etc., as appropriate] ("[Defined Term]") [add additional parties as needed].

---

[1] Bracketed—[ ]—text in examples is optional language or language needing replacement when drafting a specific provision. Brackets should be deleted when using these provisions.

For example:

> *This asset purchase agreement ("APA") dated September 21, 2020, is between Mayfield & Associates, LLC, a Delaware limited liability company ("Buyer"), and Bronson Construction, Inc., a California Corporation ("Seller").*

Note the form used to define a term. These defined terms should be used consistently throughout the document. For ease of future use of this agreement as an exemplar for future transactions, choose generic defined terms like "Buyer," "Seller," "Landlord," "Tenant," etc. This allows a change of party name in the first paragraph to ripple or flow through the document automatically when the document is used as an exemplar in a subsequent matter. The use of the "as of" form for dates avoids the need to make sure dates are updated or changed when negotiations take longer or shorter than expected.

3. RECITALS

Preambles or recitals set the context for the agreement and are useful in later interpretation. They also provide a place to list related transactional documents and other things that may be part of the transaction as a whole but are otherwise not referenced in the particular agreement itself. Preambles or recitals do not need to be preceded by the word "whereas" and it is not necessary to title the section "Recitals," although you will no doubt run into those forms (and those who aggressively adhere to them) in practice.

The recitals section provides the premises on which the contract is based. Some courts have stated that recitals are not part of the contract. This is not correct. Recitals are as much a part of the contract as everything else in the document. The difference is that recitals are not promissory in form; they are statements of fact or belief. However, they serve other important functions and should be drafted with care. Each recital should be written in plain English and should be preceded by a capital letter, numbering, or ordinal system—just like this section of this text. In the recitals, include facts that will help a later reader grasp the nature, purpose, and basis for the agreement.

A recital might explain the purpose of the contract. This could be important if one of the parties later tries to avoid the contract under the doctrine of frustration of purpose. Or, a recital might state a mutual understanding of fact. This could later pave the way for avoidance of the contract under the doctrine of mutual mistake. Facts stated as a recital might also be relevant to whether a breach qualifies as a material breach, since the recital will establish what is important to the parties. For example, if a particular brand of pipe is important to the owner of a house being constructed, then the recital should indicate this and, to further ensure that a court will strictly enforce the contract, explain why. If the body of the contract contains a "time is of the essence" clause, include a recital that demonstrates why time is so important. Neither the clause nor the recital will ensure that courts treat lateness as a material breach, but these provisions will certainly help.

Recitals are powerful medicine. Some courts have held that recitals are conclusive evidence of the facts they state. Recitals often provide background information that becomes relevant in the computation of damages. For example, a contract recital might list the profits that the enterprise has enjoyed over a certain period, thus easing proof of damages in the form of lost profits. Examples of appropriate facts for recitals include: (1) the relationship and goals of the parties, (2) the nature of the transaction, and (3) other transactional documents and things associated with the transaction. Take care to be accurate and not to include unnecessary facts in the recitals—they may be used later in litigation to prove that which they state. When in doubt, be more general than specific in the recitals. Avoid the temptation to recite everything.

An appropriately drafted recital may also prevent a contract from being declared unconscionable for either procedural or substantive reasons. If a particular provision could appear to a court to be harsh or unfair to one of the parties, and thus subject to a later unconscionability challenge, the recital should explain why the provision was included and indicate that the apparently disfavored party fully understands its implications.

Recitals, like definitions, should not contain obligations or promises. If an assertion of fact is unilateral, and is in essence a warranty by one of the parties, then it should be in the substantive sections of the contract with other warranties and be correctly labeled.

4. DEFINITIONS

Defined terms are powerful tools that can decrease the length and increase the readability of substantive provisions. They allow you to lay out the full meaning of a complicated concept that must be addressed without cluttering the substantive provisions with litanies of near-synonymous terms. At the same time, they increase the readability of your document by unpacking your provisions. In the same way that nicknames can make it easier to refer to a person, defined terms simplify references to longer, more detailed concepts.

For example, one definition of the word "claim" might be: "Any right to payment, whether or not such right is reduced to judgment, or is liquidated, fixed, contingent, matured, disputed, legal, equitable, or secured, or a right to an equitable remedy for breach of performance whether or not such right to an equitable remedy is reduced to judgment, fixed, contingent, matured, disputed, or secured." If this definition is provided for separately in the document, the single word "Claim" can be used when needed in the contract's substantive provisions and its broad meaning is included without need for the litany.

This example raises another issue because this definition was taken from the Bankruptcy Code (specifically 11 U.S.C. § 101(5)). If there is a body of law that covers the concept you are trying to express, consider incorporating this law into your contract. In doing so, you must consider the effects of future amendments or repeals of the statute. Should you define the term with a reference to the citation of the statute alone? Or would your contract be more effective with a recitation of the current statutory definition because the citation will likely change? In any event, should you include the phrase, "as it may be amended from time to time"?

Terms may be defined throughout the contract "on the fly." This is especially appropriate for terms that are used only in one section or group of sections. If they are used more widely or if there are many of them, provide a defined term section at the beginning of the contract, after the recitals and statement of consideration, rather than at the end. For easy reference, put definitions in alphabetical order.

Beware of overly broad or narrow definitions that can inadvertently introduce ambiguity or reallocate beliefs and burdens. If you define a term, it must *only* be used in the defined sense in the document. If not, ambiguity crops up. To prevent against inadvertent ambiguity, many drafters adopt a standard form of defined terms that varies the normal rules of format or capitalization, such as: Initial Caps, ALL CAPS, *italics,* **boldface**, or <u>underlining</u>.

5. STATEMENT OF CONSIDERATION AND AGREEMENT

Most contracts include a statement of consideration near the beginning of an agreement. Examples of statements of consideration include the following (which range from archaic and legalistic to plain English):

> *NOW, THEREFORE, premises considered and in consideration of the mutual covenants and agreements hereinafter set forth and in consideration of one dollar ($1.00) paid by Seller to Buyer, the receipt and adequacy whereof is hereby acknowledged, the Seller and Purchaser hereby covenant and agree as follows:*
>
> *—or—*
>
> *In consideration of the mutual promises set forth in this Agreement, the parties agree [as follows]:*
>
> *—or—*
>
> *[Accordingly] The Parties agree:*

The second formulation is preferable to the first or third, as it retains the notion of agreement and bargain and transitions a reader from the recitals to the main body of the agreement. Further, it strips out all the excess verbiage that seems to elevate form over substance by suggesting that this recital of consideration will make the contract enforceable even if it is not true. Although this may be correct in limited circumstances—option contracts, for example—the law is not uniform in this regard, and the lengthy chant about consideration may give false courage. Better is the short statement of agreement that describes the transaction, including the bargained-for nature of the exchange of covenants and other provisions that can aid in interpretation or demonstrate consideration.

6. SUBSTANTIVE PROVISIONS

This is the main body of the contract. The provisions should be tightly organized, so that everything dealing with a particular aspect of the transaction is brought together in one place. It should contain informative headings and sub-headings, using proper outlining techniques.

Substantive provisions are constructed out of five basic types of provisions: (1) covenants or promises, (2) conditions, (3) representations, (4) warranties, and (5) waivers or releases. These basic building blocks of contracts, covered in depth in Chapter 15, are the mechanisms that give all the substance to the contract. Covenants establish rights and duties of the parties; conditions trigger, excuse, or modify those rights and duties; representations and warranties capture statements of fact made by one party and relied upon by another party; and waivers and releases extinguish rights and duties.

Notes, leases, and other contracts that govern continuing relationships feature specific sections that delineate events of default, procedures for declaring a default, and the remedies available to a non-defaulting party upon declaration of default. These provisions are the special concern of the lawyers because, at the front end of the deal—the negotiation and documentation stages, the clients are primarily focused on performance, not on default.

7. HOUSEKEEPING PROVISIONS OR BOILERPLATE

These provisions deal generally with the administration of the contract. Some, but not all, are what is known as boilerplate. In the early days of newspaper syndication, the term "boilerplate" was used to describe the plates of non-movable type that publishers delivered to local newspapers and which contained the syndicated text and advertising that the local paper would adopt in full, adding its own stories and advertising to supplement the syndicator's standard material. The term was first used in the legal context in the mid-1950s, as a reference to standard clauses found in most contracts. That is the salient characteristic of good boilerplate—it contains language that allows it to be used in a variety of documents. Unfortunately, many people, lawyers and non-lawyers, similarly believe in the inviolability of the wording of whatever boilerplate they are familiar with, however hoary with age the verbiage might be. This is nonsense. Boilerplate terms can be worded in a variety of ways. There is no reason why these provisions cannot be as well drafted as the rest of the document.

These provisions are routine but very important. To refer to these provisions as "housekeeping" provisions (as we do here), as when labeling anything "miscellaneous," tends to denigrate their importance. The term "boilerplate," when understood, reflects their fundamental importance as well as their routine nature.

Thoughtless boilerplate can be an enormous problem if the deal goes south. Boilerplate provisions commonly come into effect when there is a problem or disagreement between the parties, so they must be carefully considered and drafted to ensure that they work correctly when they are needed most. They represent another opportunity for prelitigation planning, something that every lawyer must keep in mind when drafting documents.

Although it is fine for a lawyer to prepare boilerplate in advance that can be inserted without change into almost any document, the lawyer should always consider whether the needs of the client would be better served if the provision in question were individualized. The standard no-assignment clause, for example, could be modified to allow assignments under certain conditions or to a designated class of potential assignees.

Never take boilerplate for granted or simply incorporate standard provisions without thought and analysis. When reviewing contracts drafted by others, do not just skim the boilerplate: Much mischief can be hidden there. Students and lawyers that do not have a transactional practice sometimes claim that this advice is hypertechnical and exaggerated. But transactional lawyers confirm the import and potential mischief of boilerplate. Just as beginning litigators are advised never to agree to the "standard stipulations" in a deposition without knowing what those stipulations are, transactional attorneys are cautioned against taking the other side's boilerplate for granted.

The more common housekeeping provisions include the following:

Severability Clause. This clause states that if a court declares any part of the contract void, the remainder of the contract is unaffected. The converse of a severability clause is a prohibition against severance and partial enforcement. Whether the clause allows or prohibits severance, in most cases it simply mirrors the contract law default rule that would be applied even in the absence of a clause. That is, if a court has declared one provision void or unenforceable, the court will usually treat the other provisions of the contract as still in force unless doing so would destroy the purpose of the contract or create unfairness. If, however, there is any question about how the default severability rule would be applied if a particular term in the contract is declared void, then the drafter should, by all means, make this express.

Choice of Law. This identifies which state or national law the parties want the court to use in construing and enforcing the contract. Conflicts law provides a default choice. Before deciding whether to alter that, the drafter should carefully compare the law in the various jurisdictions that might qualify. Although courts generally defer to the desires of the parties on this matter, choice-of-law provisions are subject to certain limits. Since a court might refuse to defer to the parties choice of law, the drafter should always draft with the default choice in mind.

Modification. Most written contracts require that any changes, amendments, or modifications also be in writing. Although UCC § 2–209(2) recognizes the efficacy of these no-oral-modification (NOM) provisions, courts in both sales and non-sales contract contexts are often quite liberal in finding a waiver of the provision. This notwithstanding, NOM clauses may serve a useful prophylactic effect.

No Waiver. The contract may provide that the failure of a party to insist on strict performance in one instance does not constitute a waiver of the right of that party to insist on strict performance if another default occurs. Again, although these provisions are useful in some situations, courts often circumvent them by finding that the parties implicitly modified the contract through a course of performance. The duty of the drafter here is to advise the client of the possible consequences of non-enforcement, the contract language notwithstanding.

Merger Clause. This clause indicates that the contract is the final and complete agreement of the parties with respect to this transaction. If properly drafted, a merger clause will prevent a party from alleging that the agreement also includes some additional or different terms from another source—usually oral. The common law parol evidence rule performs the same function, but to prevail under that approach usually requires litigation, while a merger clause may forestall such litigation.

Assignment and Delegation. The parties may want to expressly prohibit or permit the assignment of contract rights or the delegation of contract duties to a third party. Dealing with the issue in this manner is much easier than litigating it under the murky common law rules on assignment and delegation. Although a reference to an assignment of the contract is frequently construed as referring to both rights and duties, the drafter should deal separately with the assignment of rights and the delegation of duties.

Survivability. This provision deals with the effect the incapacity or death of one or more of the parties will have upon the continued validity of the contract and who may enforce it.

Notices. If the contract requires notices, this provision will describe to whom the notice must be sent, where, and by what means.

Liquidated Damages. This is one of the most important of the various boilerplate provisions. Some drafters prefer to put liquidated damages provisions in their own section, along with other remedy provisions such as one expressly stating that a decree of specific performance is appropriate and consented to. Liquidated damages clauses, however, may not be viewed with favor by all courts and the drafter should review the controlling law of the jurisdiction to ensure that the provision is enforceable and will not be construed as a penalty. It should also specify whether or not the liquidated damages are the parties' sole remedy in case of default or breach.

Force Majeure. This clause will excuse delay or discharge the duty of performance altogether if certain extraordinary events occur. Natural disasters, pandemics, war, governmental actions, labor disputes, and unavailability of transportation are commonly included in the list. Formbook *force majeure* clauses vary enormously, however. Before borrowing a *force majeure* clause from a commercial formbook, the drafter should carefully review each item on the list to ensure that excusing delay on that basis is consistent with the intent and objectives of the client and that nothing has been omitted.

The drafter should also ensure that the list is consistent with other provisions of the contract. For example, the *force majeure* clause must be consistent with the liquidated damages clause or a cost-overrun provision. The contract cannot simultaneously provide for liquidated damages per day of delay or an enhanced fee while also excusing the delay entirely.

Other Matters. In specialized contracts, the housekeeping section might include some other matters. This section, however, should not be used as a catch-all for provisions that do not fit anywhere else. A housekeeping section that is full of miscellaneous substantive matters is evidence of poor conceptualization and organization. Either create a separate section for these other substantive provisions or include them in the section that relates most closely to their substantive content.

8. SIGNATURE BLOCKS

This provides a place for the parties and witnesses to sign. Type the name and title below the signature line. Signatures should not be on a separate page if possible; include some of the text of the contract on the page on which the signatures appear. In addition, on extremely important documents, the parties should initial each page at the bottom.

Before the signature blocks, there is usually some introductory language. Like other standard provisions in agreements, there is a tendency for this language to become ossified and to exhibit dated legalese. It is better to delete phrases such as "In Witness Whereof" and "as of the date that first appears above" and use a modern, plain English provision.

> *The Parties agree to the terms of this Agreement, above.*
>
> *—or—*
>
> *To show that they have agreed to the terms of this Agreement, the Parties have executed this Agreement below on [the date stated on page 1* or *the date(s) indicated below].*
>
> *—or—*
>
> *Agreed.*

To avoid inconsistent dating of documents, the introductory language to a signature block often refers to a date appearing on the first page or paragraph of the document. This is fine, as long as that date is filled in. Too many times, in the heat of closing, the parties simply flip to the last page of the agreement (which they have already reviewed many times before in negotiations), and fail to note that the date on page 1 has been left blank. In another form that is common in practice, the agreement is dated "as of" a date contained on the first page (filled in early in the drafting process) and the signature blocks are undated or contain the dates of execution by the parties. In such a case, it is a good idea for the contract to specify which date is the effective date.

Take care with party names and make sure you get them *exactly* right. Especially easy to miss are issues of punctuation, such as commas and periods, and descriptors of limited liability status, such as "LLC" or "Inc." For example "Allen Bates & Lebowitz LLP" could be a limited liability partnership that is the successor to "Allen, Bates & Lebowitz" a general partnership and is legally distinct from the former entity, a general partnership including professional corporations. Many jurisdictions do not prohibit the formation of entities with very similar names, which might differ only by a comma or spelling out the word "and" rather than using an ampersand (&). Train your eye to notice details of this nature. It is embarrassing when the client catches the mistake at the closing. It is even worse when the error is not uncovered until it is the subject of later litigation. When a subsidiary of a larger company is signing an important contract, consider attempting to require the parent company to also be a party to the agreement.

9. DATE

If the date was not included in the lead paragraph, include it here with the signature blocks.

10. NOTARIZATION

If the contract is to be notarized, the notary's statement or "jurat", signature, and seal come last, before any appendices, exhibits, schedules, or other attachments.

11. APPENDICES, EXHIBITS, SCHEDULES

Many complex commercial, financial, and corporate contracts include an appendix containing exhibits and schedules. An exhibit usually consists of a document that is relevant to, but not a part of, the agreement itself. In a multi-party transaction, the contract between Acme Corporation and Beta Corporation may build on or interface with the contract between Beta Corporation and Gamma Corporation, which could be attached as an exhibit to the Acme/Beta contract. A schedule, on the other hand, is properly a part of the agreement. It may consist of a list of persons to whom certain notices must be sent, list of contracts, leases, or other assets, important but tedious technical data, computation formulas, and even standard boilerplate provisions promulgated by government regulation or industry trade groups.

Certain sections of agreements are designed to elicit information from the parties to the agreement, such as lists of existing indebtedness, contracts, subsidiaries, etc. Those items should be included as a schedule to the agreement or identified as having been delivered under the agreement. Identification of the schedules can be by sequential numbering or lettering, or may correspond to the numbers of the sections addressing this information in the agreement. Rather than leaving the form of schedules as an open issue to be resolved after the parties have signed the main transactional documents, negotiate and agree to them up front. This will avoid later disputes when one party will have gained or lost negotiating leverage. This establishes that everyone knows what is expected and helps to avoid later, disruptive disputes.

Where an agreement requires the delivery of *existing* documents or certificates, copies of the documents do not need to be attached to the agreement as long as it states that the documents will be delivered prior to closing. Often, the attorney will also want the representations and warranties of the party to apply to these documents. The documents should be accurately identified and incorporated into the agreement with a specific reference in the representations or warranty section.

Where an agreement calls for the execution and delivery of instruments or other related documents, consider attaching forms of these documents as consecutively numbered or lettered exhibits ("in substantially the form of Exhibit A to this Agreement.") As with schedules to an agreement, it is the best practice to negotiate the form of supplemental documents up front, rather than leaving them for negotiation and preparation after execution of the main agreement. Among other things, this will force the parties and counsel to think through all aspects of the deal and make appropriate arrangements for all foreseeable contingencies. This practice can make for bulky documents. However, the benefits generally outweigh the extra work and paper expended on the front end to prevent disputes later.

Consider including complicated provisions dealing with special aspects of the transaction (complex valuation or pricing formulas, for example) as exhibits. This is common practice in real estate transactions, where a metes and bounds description of property can be long and cumbersome. It is often used in purchase contracts, where pricing formulas and worksheets can be complex, but its use can be expanded into many other areas of practice. Another popular use for exhibits is to provide the form of various instruments and other documents that may be needed in the course of performance of the contract. Examples include bills of sale, assignments of contracts, deeds of trust, security agreements, and the like. By providing these forms of these instruments, drafters avoid any later dispute as to whether the form selected by a party is sufficient.

Reference appendices, exhibits, and schedules in the table of contents in any agreement of more than ten pages. Consider doing so even with shorter documents. The appendix itself should have its own table of contents and be consecutively paginated, even if some of the enclosed documents have their own internal pagination.

G. EXEMPLAR CONSIDERATIONS

To save time and expense, maintain exemplars from prior deals so that they can be quickly accessed and tailored for a new transaction. This is most easily accomplished by maintaining files in word processing format in separate folders on your computer system along with an index listing file names, document title, and comments (*e.g.*, "LeaseLL.txt, Lease of Real Property, Landlord Oriented"). When a similar matter arises, you will be able to consult the index, pull up the exemplar, and proceed to tailor the document to the specifics of the new deal. This technique will greatly expedite your revision of the document. If your agreements use generic defined terms for parties and other deal specifics you can then change these items in the preamble and definitions sections, and proceed to review and modify the substantive provisions. Remember, laws and practices change, exemplars do not. Always understand what substantive provisions and legal phrases mean. Do not simply parrot a document. It may be outdated.

Finally, remember that an exemplar from a prior transaction was, at best, right for that transaction, not the current one. It represents a negotiated compromise of issues that were in play in that prior deal. Said another way, it represents an allocation of risk and reward, benefit and burden, between those parties at that time. This being the case, it is best to view the exemplar with a critical, not an accepting, eye and reset the provisions to a neutral position or one that favors your client before proposing the document to the other side. Pay particular attention to the qualifications, carve-outs, materiality thresholds, and the like in the representations and warranties; they were negotiated for the prior deal and may need to be deleted or modified for the current transaction.

H. AMENDING CONTRACTS

Often, contracts and other transactional documents require amendment after they have been executed. There are three basic methods of amending a contract.

The first is crude but effective: the parties manually change the provisions by hand, striking out or inserting text on the original document and then initialing each change. It may be a good idea to add new signature blocks at the end of the document, or on a separate sheet, where the parties re-execute the agreement as amended.

The second method is to prepare a second document, entitled "Amendment [Number] to [name original document]," and then to specify the amendments that are being made, perhaps including recitals that give context to the amendment for later use in understanding what went on and why the document was amended. In essence, this sort of amendment acts as an instruction sheet for later use in virtually cutting and pasting the two documents together into the new, resulting agreement.

The third method is called "amending and restating" the document. Using this method, the original contract terms, as amended, are set out fresh as a new contract. The contract can be prepared to reflect the original contract date, the amendment date, or both. This is the best method for situations where there are many amendments to be made at once. Sometimes, an original agreement has been amended piecemeal many times using the second method described above, and it may make sense to amend and restate the amendments. This would result in the original agreement accompanied by a consolidated, amended, and restated set of amendments.

In choosing the method used, consider how often the document will be referred to by the parties for guidance. If the answer is seldom, then either of the first two methods may be used effectively. If it will be reexamined often, amending and restating, or restating amendments is appropriate. The major risk in embarking on a complete restatement of a document is that it may reopen issues for negotiation that had been previously settled.

Amending an existing contract can require as much care, thought, and skill as drafting one. First, if the existing contract has a clause that not only prohibits oral modifications but also dictates the form of any modification, then those form requirements must be satisfied.

Second, the drafter must ensure that the modification is either supported by consideration or, if the modification affects UCC Article 2 goods, that it meets the "good faith" test of UCC § 1–203. Contract modification is perhaps the most important instance when the issue of consideration comes up. A contract to modify an existing contract must generally be supported by mutual consideration. It is good practice to make sure this is the case by providing for consideration on both sides of the deal (the one-dollar-had-and-received formulation of yore), even if your jurisdiction has done away with the common law pre-existing duty rule (requiring more than a pre-existing duty to support a contract). *See, e.g.*, UCC § 2–209(1) (preexisting duty rule repealed by UCC for sales of goods).

Third, the drafter must consider how changing one part of the contract may affect other parts. If paragraph 6(a) is changed from "January 15, 2015," to "January 15, 2020," and if an unmodified paragraph 67(c)(iii) still refers to "the date provided in paragraph 6(a)" as the triggering date for something else, does the amendment of paragraph 6(a) operate as an implied modification of the second provision as well?

Fourth, the amendment should identify exactly what in the existing contract is being modified and what the change is. An amendment should *not* merely say:

> *The contract dated October 23, 2018, between Able and Elizabeth is amended to provide as follows:*
>
> *(a) Roger will deliver the Series 7 drill presses on January 15, 2020.*
>
> *(b) Roger is not required to ship the drill presses using the Seattle Kluless Trucking Company.*
>
> *(c) If Elizabeth requires any additional drill presses meeting the Series 7 specifications for a*

period of one year following delivery, Elizabeth will purchase those presses from Roger.

Rather, the amendment should specify what is being changed, what is being added, and what is being deleted.

The contract dated October 23, 2018 between Roger and Elizabeth, is amended to provide as follows:

(a) The "January 15, 2019," date in paragraph 6(a) is changed to read "January 15, 2020." [changing the date]

(b) Paragraph 10 is deleted in its entirety. [deleting the mode of delivery requirement]

(c) Paragraphs 11, 12, and 13 are renumbered 10, 11, and 12 respectively.

(d) A new paragraph 13 is added, as follows:

If Elizabeth requires any additional drill presses meeting the Series 7 specifications, for a period of one year following delivery Elizabeth will purchase those presses from Roger. [adding a new provision]

When the amendment is complete, ensure that it is distributed to all those that have or had the original document and ask them to include the amendment with their copy of the original document. When amending documents that have been filed or recorded with governmental offices, it is probably necessary for the amendments, an amended and restated document, or, at a minimum, an abstract of them, to be filed with the same office to be perfected or "good against the world." This is generally the case with recorded deeds, encumbrances, lease abstracts, UCC–1 financing statements, and the like. In refiling, thought must be given to the effect of intervening filings by the parties or third parties, and the effect of those filings and the new filings on lien priority and similar issues. Title policy endorsements are available to provide "no loss of priority" protection in some cases.

CHAPTER 3

LEGISLATIVE DRAFTING

Public law documents—broadly referred to as "legislation"—include codes, statutes, ordinances, regulations, rules, and anything else of a command nature that emanates from an agency of government.

In 2010, Congress passed the Plain Writing Act of 2010 (Pub. L. 111–274, 124 Stat. 2861, 5 U.S.C. § 301 note) which requires federal agencies use clear, plain language in public law documents and public communications.

A. WHO DRAFTS LEGISLATION?

Legislation comes from several classes of drafters, with varying degrees of expertise and competence. Federal and most state legislative bodies have full-time staff attorneys who do nothing but draft and revise proposed legislation on behalf of the elected representatives. The President and most governors have staff members whose sole job is to draft legislation for the administration. Administrative agencies within the executive branch nearly always have a section in the legal department that does nothing but draft agency regulations. Cities and counties usually rely on their appointed or elected attorneys, for whom drafting is only one of a myriad of duties and who sometimes work on a part-time basis. Unfortunately, some legislators and other officials, many of whom are not lawyers, think that because they were elected to enact laws they are also competent to draft them.

In recent years, there has also been an increase in the amount of legislation that was initially drafted by private sector attorneys. Trade associations and labor unions frequently use experienced in-house drafters to prepare legislation favorable to their special interests. Law firms that provide lobbying and legislative oversight services nearly always have attorneys who are competent to translate a client's desires into proper statutory form.

Those are the people who may initially draft a piece of legislation. At this stage, drafting can be a thoughtful, reflective, careful, and painstaking process. Lawmaking, however, is not very tidy; the results of this initial drafting process rarely survive intact. Typically, a bill will be sent to a committee, where the amending and rewriting process begins. Whatever emerges from committee is subject to further tinkering by the full legislative body. As a matter of both style and substance, the drafting that is done at this stage is often—but not always—inferior to the initial proposal.

B. THE FUNCTION OF THE LEGISLATIVE DRAFTER

Legislation starts with an idea and ends with words on paper. The legislative drafter's primary function is not to come up with the idea. Lawyers working for a legislative drafting service are almost never expected to produce the idea; they draft what they are asked to draft. But many of the other classes of drafters discussed above do play an integral role in the development and formulation of the client's policies—whether it is those of the President, the governor, the Securities and Exchange Commission, the AFL-CIO, or the Chamber of Commerce.

On the other hand, even if formulating the idea is not within the drafter's expertise, the legislative drafter does more than merely ensure compliance with the technical composition and formatting rules of drafting. In between the idea and the legislation attempting to implement it lies a long and complex period of gestation. The idea or policy usually exists initially only as a vague generality; making it clear requires a host of subordinate policy choices. Even if the original idea is generally a good one, bad choices with respect to the details and implementation can quickly convert well-intentioned legislation into an instrument of oppression.

The primary function of the legislative drafter is to be instrumental in promoting good rather than bad choices at this critical stage of the process—realizing that the ultimate choice is the client's. Thus, the legislative drafter must thoroughly understand the problem being addressed, its sources and impact, and the alternative techniques and approaches that are available for addressing it. More specifically, the legislative drafter should usually consider, in consultation with the sponsor or client, some or all of the following:

- Is the legislation really needed; or can social and market forces deal with it more quickly and efficiently?

- Will the legislation deal with the problem or simply drive it underground?
- What will be the secondary effects of the legislation? For example, what will people do instead of the prohibited conduct? It could be as bad or worse.
- What will be the long-term effects of the legislation?
- Exactly who will benefit or be harmed, and how?
- Can the law be enforced as written?
- If so, what are the costs of that enforcement in time, money, and personnel? Are those resources available?
- What is the fundamental philosophical premise of this legislation and can it withstand the test of general application?

If the legislative client has thought through the hard questions and is determined to proceed in a particular manner, then the legislative drafter should effectuate that intent. Subverting the intent through subtle drafting techniques is one of the most unethical things a legislative drafter can do. Unfortunately, it does occasionally occur.

One of the best strategies for an industry or interest group that is or is likely to be the target of legislation or regulation is *not* to oppose that trend once it is clear that legislative regulation is inevitable. Rather, the better course at that juncture may be for the industry or interest group to strongly support the process, advancing its own legislation and regulation and even the creation of an agency to provide oversight. In doing so, the affected group can draft legislation and regulations that are not too burdensome and that contain exceptions, appeals, and other mechanisms to allow the affected group to grind down the efforts of those that would seek to affect its behavior through the legislative and regulatory process. At the far end of this strategy is what is called "agency capture"—where an interest group infiltrates an agency's leadership and technical staff with its own expert representatives and also telegraphs that availability of future employment opportunities to agency officials and employees, the so-called "revolving door" of the agency who may then be more apt to become prospective employers and benefactors. In carrying out this strategy, as well as in seeking to oppose it, a sense of proportion and balance is essential to preserve what political scientists would term "legitimacy"—once that quality is lost, "reform" is the next step, often reversing the balance of power between the regulated and the regulators, with unpredictable results for all concerned. These dynamics often lie behind the legislative process and should not be ignored by the legislative drafter.

C. LEGISLATION COMPARED TO PRIVATE-LAW DOCUMENTS

All drafted documents serve essentially the same function. They establish the rights, duties, privileges, immunities, and other legal relations of and between the parties that are subject to the jurisdiction of the document. This is as true of a criminal code as it is of a construction contract. Moreover, the investigatory and thinking process of creating drafted documents is basically the same, as are the rules of organization, style, and precision that are used in contract drafting.

Thus, the preparation, form, and content of the portions of a condominium lease dealing with limits on the use of the leased premises might not differ appreciably from the comparable regulations of a county housing authority. Both are law. The lease represents the private law between two parties who have consented to its terms. The regulation represents public law between the sovereign and its subjects, whether they specifically consent to it or not.

Private law documents that are in the form of rules likewise bear a striking similarity to statutes—an employer's work rules or condominium homeowners association rules, for example. Indeed, many regard private law documents of this type as being essentially legislative in form. This chapter, however, uses the terms legislation and legislative to refer to public-law documents exclusively.

Although they share basic similarities, legislation differs from private law documents in several material respects. This difference affects how each is drafted.

1. NATURE AND SIZE OF THE AUDIENCE

Most private law documents have a relatively limited audience. They address the relationship between a limited number of people or entities with other users being secondary. This means that the drafter needs to focus only on the identity, objectives, and circumstances relating to these particular people, or entities and need not worry about others, their objectives, or their circumstances.

Legislation, however, typically applies to very large classes of persons or entities. It may include everyone in the country, the state, the county, or the city. Even a limited class including only the registered owners of handguns living in incorporated areas is larger than the class directly affected by the typical private law document.

To accommodate this larger audience, the legislative drafter may do one of three things. The first option is to draft at a higher level of generality than is customarily used in a private law document. This is necessary to ensure that the broad harm to be prevented or the good to be promoted, varying only in its factual detail, is covered by the legislation. This approach, however, may fail to recognize that while the intended audience shares a primary characteristic, important subsidiary differences also exist. A one-size-fits-all piece of legislation inevitably encounters difficulties of enforcement, efficacy, and fairness.

The second option is to draft a complex set of rules or exceptions to deal with these differences. It is almost impossible, however, to get all of these details right in the first instance. Experience and a better understanding of the problem and the various possible solutions frequently suggest the need for alterations. However, the legislative process is cumbersome; amendments fine-tuning the legislation may be impractical.

The third option is to draft in fairly general terms, but also to empower an administrative agency to fill in the details with regulations, which are much easier to enact and change than the legislation itself. The drafter following this alternative, while giving the agency sufficient discretion to deal with the complexities of the problem, must also provide guidance to prevent the agency from taking the legislation beyond its intended limits.

Legislation also has an audience that private-law documents lack. The parties to the transaction usually initiate the enforcement of private law documents by filing a lawsuit; a court or arbitrator then makes the enforcement decision. This is also true of some legislation, such as a statute establishing a tort unknown to the common law or one creating additional damages for some types of contract breach. But, the enforcement of most statutory law is initiated by a third party—either a police officer, a government official, or an administrative agency. Legislation must be drafted with this audience in mind. If a criminal statute is so complex and obscure that a police officer cannot understand it, the statute may end up being enforced in a draconian fashion or not at all.

In addition, many administrative agencies not only initiate the enforcement process, through the filing of a charge or complaint; they also adjudicate it in the first instance, with limited judicial review. Although this involves some technical separation-of-powers problems that the drafter must also address, the point is that the view of an agency's administrative law judge may differ from that of a court. The drafter, thus, must understand and draft with that audience characteristic in mind.

2. THE NEED FOR PRECISION

Vagueness can be a viable technique in drafting private law documents. The transaction costs of being completely thorough on every detail may outweigh the advantages. The parties may be content to rely on each other's good faith and their ability to work out details and disagreements later. The legislative drafter does not, or should not, enjoy the same degree of latitude. Whether civil or criminal, a statute is a command by the sovereign to do or refrain from doing certain things, with sanctions for noncompliance. Fundamental fairness requires that a citizen be on notice of what is required. Criminal statutes that do not meet this test may be void-for-vagueness. Courts are more tolerant of civil statutes that are unduly vague; but such statutes reflect both poor drafting and poor governing.

3. POLICY CONSIDERATIONS

The drafter of private law documents has a limited duty to discuss the broader social and policy implications with the client. Serving the client's interest is the primary concern. The legislative drafter's involvement in policy is usually somewhat broader. In a sense, the public is that drafter's ultimate client. The legislative drafter, however, can assist the proximate client—whether it is an individual legislator, a committee, or the head of an administrative agency—in making the correct policy choices.

4. THE NEED FOR FACTUAL DATA

Because of the wider audience, the more precise focus, and the policy considerations, the legislative drafter usually requires more facts than the average private law document drafter does. Often, this factual data is developed in legislative hearings, which the drafter must then study and assimilate into the drafting process. At lower legislative levels, the drafter is often the one who does the investigation.

5. POLITICAL CONSIDERATIONS

The legislative drafter working for a specific legislator, committee, or agency cannot ignore the political opposition. The drafter must assess what they are likely to object to, how strong the objections are, and what they might compromise on. The ultimate decision will be made by the client. But, the drafter can assist by suggesting alternative provisions that basically meet the client's objectives, but that are also more palatable to the opposition.

The drafter should warn the client about crippling amendments. Complex legislation involves an interaction between the various provisions. Section 2 may be essential to the structural integrity of the statute. If it is deleted by floor amendment, this might render the entire statute incoherent. Thus, if Section 2 is likely to have significant opposition, then that opposition should be accommodated before the bill is introduced, if possible. Alternatively, the drafter should have a substitute bill prepared that both accommodates the opposition and still advances the objectives of the client, albeit perhaps to a lesser degree.

Sometimes, political pressures will force the drafter to employ ambiguity to reach finality in the legislative process. This occurs, for example, when the opposing political factions are at deadlock over a particular provision but agree in principle on everything else. The drafter is thus instructed to draft an ambiguous provision that could be construed either way, leaving it to the courts to sort out.

6. FITTING THE DOCUMENT INTO AN EXISTING BODY OF LAW

Sometimes, the parties to a private law document will have other existing relationships (also created by private law) that the drafter must take into account and accommodate to ensure consistency in the legal relationship. Similarly, some of the rights and duties that will inure to the transaction may have already been the subject of statutory regulation—a landlord-tenant statute, for example. The private law drafter must take that into account and draft accordingly.

This task of accommodating the new document with existing documents and laws, and making sure they all fit together, is much more difficult for the legislative drafter, because there is so much more to consider. The drafter must take into account everything touching on the proposed legislation—constitutional provisions, existing statutes, administrative regulations construing that legislation, court opinions (on that and related subjects), attorney general opinions, existing statutes in other jurisdictions, common law rules, and even scholarly treatises and law review articles.

7. LEGAL LIMITS

Distinct from "making it all fit together" is ensuring that the newly drafted document is within the limits imposed by superior law. The private-law document drafter is bounded by numerous legal constraints with respect to substance. A waiver of rights under the Age Discrimination in Employment Act must contain certain things to be effective. The inclusion of some provisions in a consumer loan agreement may render it void.

For the legislative drafter, the principal limits are those imposed by the hierarchy of legal authority and the scope of delegated powers. Federal and state constitutions are the highest legal authority. In addition to establishing the structure of government, their principal function is to limit legislative and executive authority. The most important limits are those contained in the Bill of Rights. No conscientious drafter should draft legislation that patently infringes upon an individual's freedom of speech. Other constitutional provisions are more technical in nature. State constitutions, for example, often prohibit statutes dealing with more than one subject. Although the concept of a subject virtually defies definition, the legislative drafter should be cautious before including in an ordinance on the location of mobile homes a provision also dealing with the tax consequences of certain municipal bonds. The more important constitutional limits are the substantive ones. Unfortunately, legislative clients often instruct the drafter not to worry about possible constitutional limits, erroneously believing this to be an exclusive function of the judiciary.

Similarly, within the hierarchy of authority, federal law generally overrides inconsistent state law and state law controls over inconsistent local law. Drafters working at one of these subordinate levels of government must draft with the superior law in mind.

At the federal level, a great deal of legislative law is not in the form of statutes; it is in the form of administrative rules and regulations. State administrative law is also fairly extensive. Administrative agencies, however, do not have inherent power to enact law. The existence and scope of their authority depends on a delegation from the legislature. The administrative drafter must always keep the scope of that delegation in mind, because rules that go beyond it will be declared void.

The administrative drafter must also comply with administrative procedure acts that dictate the procedure an agency must follow when promulgating a rule or regulation. The statute that created the agency may impose additional procedural requirements. And since administrative agencies are generally considered a part of the executive branch of government, they are often subject to executive orders as well. In sum, the administrative drafter must be aware of a myriad of both substantive and procedural limits.

Courts and their administrative offices are a final source of legislation-like rules. Here, the principal limits flow from the doctrine of separation of powers. The question is whether the court has the authority—constitutional, inherent, or statutory—to promulgate a particular rule or whether this is exclusively a legislative function. The judicial rule drafter must draft within those often uncertain constraints.

8. LEGISLATIVE HISTORY

Bargaining history is sometimes used in contract litigation to determine the intent of the parties. So, too, with legislation. The person who drafted the legislation will frequently write the committee report or a summary explaining the bill. If the drafter is a part of a legislator's staff, the drafter may also prepare the remarks the sponsor will make when introducing the legislation. These reports, comments, and speeches can put a gloss on the legislation that may not be apparent from the words themselves.

Because of the fictional nature of legislative intent and its capacity for abuse, many courts take a decidedly jaundiced view toward this manufactured evidence of intent. Nevertheless, it remains an important part of the legislative drafting function.

9. FORM, STYLE, AND USAGE

This book follows the accepted form for federal statutes in terms of formats and nomenclatures for their parts. Under that system, the first divisional unit of a statute is generally the "section," which is numbered with an Arabic numeral.

Sections may be divided into subsections, if the division is a complete sentence and a standalone idea unto itself, which are designated by lower case letters in parentheses: (a), (b), (c), etc.

(1) This is sub-idea one,

(a) Which has two parts, this one, and;

(b) This one.

(2) This is sub-idea two.

(3) This is sub-idea three.

If the section is divided into statements that are not complete sentences but, rather, phrases or clauses, they are called "paragraphs" and are designated with Arabic numerals in parentheses: (1), (2), (3), etc. (Ignore the fact that these "paragraphs" are not paragraphs of English grammar and style—it is just a name for them).

The next division of the statute is typically called a "clause" (they need not be clauses in the sense used in discussions of English grammar and style), designated with a lower case roman number in parentheses: (i), (ii), (iii), etc. These are followed by sub-clauses, designated with upper case roman numbers in parentheses: (I), (II), (III).

When statutes are passed as bills that cover myriad different topics, as is the case in so-called omnibus bills or Christmas-tree legislation, they may be divided into titles, chapters, and subchapters, grouping similar topics together, all above the section level.

Within limits, the private law document drafter is free to adopt whatever conventions of form, style, and usage that meet that drafter's fancy. A failure to follow sound drafting principles may cause difficulties in interpretation and enforcement; but it generally is not going to disqualify the document. The legislative drafter does not enjoy that freedom. Legislatures, legislative drafting services, administrative agencies, and even the various court systems frequently use drafting manuals and rules that explicitly dictate the form, the style, and the usage that must be adhered to when drafting legislation.

D. THE PARTS OF A STATUTE

Statutes typically consist of several discrete parts, as follows:

1. HEADING AND TITLE

Statutes and constitutions frequently require that legislative enactments contain a title that describes the purpose of the legislation.

The heading of a bill contains information regarding before what legislative body and session the bill is presented, the date of its introduction, and the legislators that introduced the bill.

The title of the bill is generally formal and may be long and serves to both describe the legislation's purported purpose and identify the statutes, if any, that are to be affected by it.

> A BILL TO AMEND CHAPTER 3, TITLE 16, CODE OF LAWS OF SOUTH CAROLINA, 1976, BY ADDING SECTION 17 SO AS TO PROHIBIT HARASSMENT AND STALKING, TO PROVIDE DEFINITIONS, TO PROVIDE PENALTIES, AND TO AUTHORIZE TEMPORARY RESTRAINING ORDERS; AND TO REPEAL SECTION 16–3–1070, RELATING TO THE CRIME OF STALKING.

As in this example, titles may be fairly long and typed in all-caps, which makes them difficult to read. The title of a bill, however, is not to be taken lightly. Legislation without a proper title may be void.

2. ENACTING CLAUSE

Constitutions or statutes also often prescribe the exact language of enacting clauses. Under federal law, legislation must be introduced with the following:

> *Be it enacted by the Senate and House of Representatives of the United States of America in Congress assembled.*

The exact wording of enacting clauses varies from state to state. Legislation that does not contain these magic words is void.

3. SHORT TITLE SECTION

This indicates how the legislation is to be referred to colloquially.

> *This chapter may be cited as the "Fair Labor Standards Act of 1938."*

4. STATEMENT OF PURPOSE OR FINDINGS

Comprehensive enactments frequently contain a section outlining the legislative body's findings. These may consist of specific facts, an identification of the problems to be corrected or purposes to be served, the underlying policy, how the law is to be construed, and other matters of a general nature.

Some findings are of critical importance. For example, if a bill states that Congress has found a particular type of transaction to impose a burden on interstate commerce, then courts are likely to accept that finding without further proof in any individual case. In the absence of such a finding, however, a court might resolve the issue differently.

Legislative findings are also relevant to the question of intent, which determines how courts will construe the substantive provisions. If the literal words of a section are capable of two interpretations, then the stated purpose or policy of a statute may determine which controls. The legislative drafter, however, should not rely on the findings section to salvage what is an otherwise poor job of drafting.

5. DEFINITIONS

As in private law documents, definitions in statutes are usually consolidated into one section. However, in a statute with many chapters, if a term is used in only one chapter, that is probably the best place to put the definition. Five key principles apply to defined terms:

1. Do not define terms that are used in the ordinary sense of the word.
2. Do not define terms in a way that is contrary to their ordinary meaning
3. Do define terms to broaden or narrow the scope of the terms as used in their ordinary sense.
4. Once you have used a term as a defined term, eliminate all other uses of that term to avoid confusion.
5. Do not include substantive obligations within defined terms; those provisions belong in separate, substantive sections of the bill.

6. SUBSTANTIVE PROVISIONS

The core of a statute is an identification of the conduct that is prohibited, required, allowed, disallowed, or made a condition of a particular entitlement. The substance of the bill should be organized according to three general principles within each group or subdivision (section, subsection, phrase or paragraph, clause, or sub-clause):

1. Assume the reader will read the provisions in the order they appear. As a result, do not put one provision before another that is necessary to understand it. In other words, put the context before the details.

2. Provisions should be arranged in declining order of importance, with general rules before special ones or exceptions.

3. Group provisions dealing with the same subject matter together.

Note that headings may be used to further clarify these provisions by providing sign-posts along the way for the reader. Generally, headings are not used at the level of the clause or sub-clause.

7. ENFORCEMENT MECHANISMS

Unless it is a criminal statute, where enforcement is presumed to be by the attorney general or district attorneys, a statute will generally contain a provision indicating who may enforce it, how, where, and under what time limits. If enforcement is primarily by a government official or agency, the statute should indicate whether it also creates a private cause of action and, if so, on whose behalf. A statute should contain a limitations period and indicate whether the limitations period is jurisdictional and thus not subject to waiver, estoppel, and tolling. It should indicate whether jurisdiction lies in federal court, state court, or both. If an administrative agency will be involved in the application or enforcement of the statute, then the statute will need to contain provisions dealing with its establishment, powers, duties, and procedures. The statute should also indicate, directly or indirectly in the provision dealing with civil suits, whether plaintiffs are required to exhaust these administrative procedures. Of increased importance is whether alternative dispute resolution mechanisms, if agreed to, must be used to enforce the statute.

8. REMEDIES OR PENALTIES

Whether criminal or civil, the penalties, sanctions, and other remedies that are available for violations of the statute are usually contained in a separate subtitle or subchapter. The availability of an award of attorney's fees, punitive damages, damage multipliers, and the like should also be dealt with here.

9. HOUSEKEEPING PROVISIONS

These typically include the following:

Effective Date. This presents a more complicated drafting problem than might appear at first. A provision simply stating that the statute is effective when signed is inadequate, since it does not indicate what the consequence of effectiveness is. For example, a change in procedural law could be construed (1) as applying only to cases that are filed after the signing date; (2) as applying also to cases that are pending and have not gone to final judgment at the time of signing; or (3) as even applying to cases that are already on appeal or still subject to appeal.

Similarly, a change in substantive law could be construed as applying (1) only to operative events that occur after signing; (2) to all operative events, regardless of when they occurred, except those on which the statute of limitations has run or which have already been litigated and are barred by the doctrine of *res judicata* or collateral estoppel; or (3) to operative events that occurred prior to signing that are, however, subject to pending litigation at the time of signing.

Courts have construed the effective date of statutes in all of these ways. Whatever the legislative intent with respect to retroactivity, that intent should be made express.

Savings Clause. A savings clause preserves rights and duties that have matured and proceedings that have begun before the effective date of the statute. A cause of action that has accrued or a crime that has been committed remains actionable, even if the underlying statute is being repealed by the new one.

Repeals. If one statute is replacing another, the existing statute must be repealed—subject to a savings clause discussed above. Older statutes sometimes contained a general repeal: "All laws that conflict with this law are hereby repealed." This is sloppy drafting because it suggests that the drafter does not know what existing laws are in conflict. It is also dangerous. It presents courts with the difficult task of determining when a conflict exists. If the two statutes can be reconciled by giving each of them a particular construction, should the court to do that? Or should it declare a conflict and treat the earlier statute as repealed? The drafter should not leave these matters to chance. If a proposed statute conflicts with a prior statute, the legislative client should decide whether to amend the proposal, modify one or both of the statutes to resolve the conflict, or repeal the prior statute in whole or in part.

Termination Date. Occasionally, a statute will contain a date certain for termination. More common are specific provisions stating that particular sections lapse after a certain period of time.

Severability. These provisions state that if any part of the statute is declared void, the remainder of the statute is unaffected. As is true with private law document severability provisions, these are generally unnecessary in legislation because courts already have the inherent power to sever illegal provisions and enforce the remainder. Conversely, courts also have the power to ignore a severability provision and to declare the entire statute void if severance of a key provision would render the statute arbitrary or unenforceable. Nevertheless, most statutes contain a severability clause.

Appropriations. This provision will indicate the amount, the source, and the recipient of any monies necessary to enforce the statute. Unfortunately, it is a trick of the political process to conspicuously enact a popular piece of legislation but quietly fail to include any money for implementation.

Preemption. Although general rules exist for determining when a federal statute preempts a state statute or a state statute preempts a local ordinance, an express provision will help avoid litigation over the issue.

E. AMENDING STATUTES

1. WHEN ARE AMENDMENTS DRAFTED?

Often drafters will be asked to draft amendments to an existing statute. Here, there is no reason why they cannot devote as much time and effort to the planning and investigating functions as is spent in drafting a statute in the first instance. As a matter of substance, the drafter should also be sensitive to the broader ramifications of the amendment. Will it create internal inconsistencies? To make it workable, will other provisions also have to be amended? Will it create insurmountable enforcement problems? These and other problems of this type should at least be brought to the attention of the sponsor.

The professional drafter may also be called upon to prepare an amendment to proposed legislation when the bill is either in committee or is to be proposed as a floor amendment. Time and sponsor demands permitting, the drafter should again take as much care in the wording and content of the amendment as the original drafter did. This is not always possible. Legal drafters are often asked to prepare amendments during the heat of battle, as it were, while the legislation is being actively considered by committee or the legislature itself. These "yellow pad" amendments are rarely great examples of the drafting art—but that is not the fault of the drafter.

2. THE PARTS OF AN AMENDMENT

Amendments consist of two parts. The first part contains what is called "vehicular language." This simply indicates that the bill is amending an existing statute.

> *Section 1. The Fair Labor Standards Act is amended by adding the following new section*:

This is then followed by the substance of the amendment, with the new section being put in quotes:

> *"Section 405. An enterprise located in the District of Columbia that is engaged in the manufacture of. . . ."*

3. WHAT AMENDMENTS DO

An amendment generally does one of three things: (1) add or insert language, (2) delete language, or (3) both add and delete language.

First, an amendment may add language to an existing statute. This may consist of an entirely new section, as in the above example (called "*adding*"), or merely a word or phrase in a particular section (called "*inserting*"), as in the following:

*Section 1. Section **15–4–2006(c)** is amended by inserting "or mules" after the word "horses."*

Second, an amendment may delete a word or phrase or an entire section (called "*striking*"), as in the following:

*Section **16**. Section **401(k)** is amended by striking the words "unless otherwise provided for by state law."*

—or—

*Section **16**. Section **401** is amended by striking subsection (k).*

If Section 401 contains sub-sections following (k), these will have to be redesignated, as follows:

*Section 17. Section **401** is amended by redesignating subsections (l) through (t) as subsections (k) through (s) respectively.*

If an entire title, chapter, or major portion of a statute is going to be deleted by an amendment, this is usually dealt with in terms of repeal.

*Section 7: Title V of the Livestock Inspection Act of **1943** is repealed.*

Third, an amendment may both add and delete, as in these examples:

*Section 3. Section **499(c)(4)** is amended by striking the word "children" and inserting "dependent minors."*

> *Section **10**. Section **15–678–2000** is amended by striking subsection (4) and by inserting the following:*
>
> *"(4) Homestead property that is located in a Class IV city is subject to a tax rate of. . . ."*

It is unnecessary to add "in lieu thereof" or "in its place" since it is assumed that the insertion will replace the deleted material.

Amendments that deal only with the specific language that is being added or deleted can be very confusing since the reader must constantly move back and forth between the original text and the amendments. An alternative approach, and one that is most appropriate when numerous changes are being made to a particular provision, is to present the amendment in the form of a complete restatement of the amended section.

> *Section **13**. Section 647 of the Livestock Inspection Act is amended to read as follows:*
>
> *"Section 647. . . ."*

Although this gives the reader a clear understanding of what the amended section will do, it does not put the reader on notice of the specific changes that have been made. Thus, some legislative rules require that amendments be in both the specific and the restatement form.

4. AMENDMENTS CHANGING A JUDICIAL INTERPRETATION OR CONSTRUCTION

Decisions by a court of last resort construing a statute may precipitate an amendment if the legislature disagrees with the court's interpretation. Some of these disagreements are fairly technical in nature, with the amendment resolving the matter cleanly and clearly.

But corrective legislation is far more difficult to achieve, and the end result more problematic, when the court's interpretation (often reflected in a series of decisions) radically alters the meaning or scope of a significant piece of social legislation. This requires the legislature to re-determine its own policy and find ways of expressing that policy in ways that the court cannot ignore. If the matter is of widespread public concern, the legislature must also accommodate the political demands of the public—which can produce all kinds of strange outcomes. It is not surprising that amendments of this type are often poorly conceptualized, obtusely worded, and thus the source of a whole new generation of litigation designed to determine exactly what the new law means.

Ideally, a legislative body that is attempting to enact this kind of amendatory legislation should, through its drafting staff, do several things. First, if the alleged objective is to codify the law as it was before the offending decision, then a legislature and its drafters must have a thorough understanding of what the law was generally thought to be before the decision in question. But frequently there will have been a variety of views among the various courts of appeals, with the court of last resort taking its own approach. Congress must decide which, if any, of the other views it wants to codify and find words that will do that accurately.

Second, drafting this kind of amendatory legislation requires a thorough understanding of what the court did in its offending decision. Congress and its drafters must know exactly what the problem is before they can purport to correct it.

Third, watershed decisions by courts of last resort not only affect the meaning of the specific statute before the court, they nearly always have a ripple effect on similar statutes, with the lower courts assuming that the court was articulating a broad principle of interpretation. The legislative drafter, thus, must determine the scope of this ripple effect and deal with it. Suppose, for example, that the court determines that Provision A in Statute 1 means X-Y. But before the legislature can gear up for an amendment, which may take several years, the lower courts felt compelled to construe provisions of substantively related statutes in a similar fashion. If the legislature, in specific response to the court decision itself, later amends Provision A in Statute 1, what effect does this have on that kind of provision in the other statutes? Some courts will say that if the legislature wanted to amend these other statutes, it could and should have done so expressly. Other courts will imply an intent that the amendatory language to Statute 1 also applies to these other statutes.

One familiar with statutory law does not have to look far to find amendatory statutes that were enacted by legislatures without a sufficient amount of the understanding referred to above. Inevitably, this results in enormous legal confusion and years of clarifying litigation.

CHAPTER 4

THE RULES OF INTERPRETATION

The rules of interpretation have two sources: statutory and common law. Some rules of statutory interpretation imposed by statute are quite specific. Other statutory rules of interpretation, like common law rules of interpretation, are general principles or presuppositions. Moreover, many of these interpretive admonitions are capable of canceling each other out. For example, if one rule favors the statute dealing with a problem specifically over a statute that deals with the problem only generally, and another rule favors the most current statute, how should the courts deal with a general statute that is, however, more recent than the specific statute? Indeed, the invocation of a particular rule of interpretation often merely serves to justify an interpretation reached on a different basis; and sometimes the courts ignore the rules altogether when it suits them.

Still, the drafter cannot totally ignore these various rules of interpretation. They are, however, something to be drafted around rather than tools for achieving a particular result. Put differently, if a document is properly drafted, then a court will probably not need to rely on these rules when construing the document.

Most of these rules are applicable to both statutory and contract interpretation, although some are unique to a particular type of document. The rules of interpretation have two sources: statutory and common law.

A. STATUTORY RULES

Many codes contain an umbrella interpretation or construction provision that applies to all the statutes within the code. For example, Chapter 1 of Title 1 of the United State Code provides, in part, as follows:

> *In determining the meaning of any Act of Congress, unless the context indicates otherwise—*
>
> *words importing the singular include and apply to several persons, parties, or things;*
>
> *words importing the plural include the singular;*
>
> *words importing the masculine gender include the feminine as well;*

Some of the state statutory rules of interpretation are modeled after the Uniform Statutory Construction Act. Often, these rules are in the form of mandated definitions. For example:

> *The term "person" includes corporations, companies, associations, firms, partnerships, societies, and joint stock companies.*
>
> *A "quorum" of a public body is a majority of the number of members fixed by law.*
>
> *Words importing the singular include the plural.*

A legislative drafter in a jurisdiction with such a statute must draft with these rules and definitions in mind. Sometimes, a statute itself will expressly dictate how it is to be construed.

> *The rule that statutes in derogation of the common law are to be strictly construed does not apply to this Act.*

Perhaps the most bizarre example of a legislatively mandated judicial rule of interpretation is contained in the Civil Rights Act of 1991. It provides:

> *No statements other than the interpretive memorandum appearing at Vol. 137 Congressional Record S 15276 (daily ed. Oct. 25, 1991) shall be considered legislative history of, or relied upon in any way as legislative history in construing or applying, any provision of this Act that relates to Wards Cove-Business necessity/ cumulation/alternative business practice.*

Not surprisingly, the referenced memorandum is unenlightening on the issue—which apparently was the intent of Congress.

B. COMMON LAW RULES

The more frequently used rules of interpretation are those that have been fashioned by the courts themselves.

1. INTENT CONTROLS

This is the cardinal rule of interpretation. Intent controls, whether it is the intent of the legislature in passing a statute, the intent of the testator in writing a will, or the intent of the parties in making a contract. But intent is really a conclusion, not a fact. The question is: How should a court determine intent? The courts follow two radically different approaches in answering that question.

a. The Plain Meaning or Four Corners Rule

Under this rule, a court must interpret a document by the plain meaning of the words that lie within the four corners of the document. Common words are given their ordinary dictionary meaning, technical words are given their specialized meaning, and sentences are construed by reference to the rules of grammar and punctuation. Under this approach, a court construing the words of a statute will not look at the legislative history, the purpose of the statute, the harm to be avoided, the good to be achieved, or any other extraneous evidence of legislative intent. Similarly, a court construing a contract or other private-law document will not look at the negotiating history, statements either party may have made, the course of performance under the contract, course of dealing under other contracts between these parties, usage of the trade, or other evidences of intent (sometimes referred to as a "textualist" approach as contrasted with the "contextual" approach, which involves considering extra-contractual evidence of what the parties intended). Although courts frequently acknowledge the plain meaning or four corners rule, they rarely apply it so strictly.

Moreover, the rule has two exceptions—ambiguity and absurd results. The first of these is not so much an exception as it is a corollary of the rule. If a statute or contract is ambiguous—which is just another way of saying that it has no single plain meaning—then courts have no choice but to look to external sources to determine intent and thus resolve the ambiguity.

Similarly, if the plain meaning of a provision would lead to what the courts regard as an absurd result, then the courts will ignore that interpretation and adopt a more reasonable one. Suppose, for example, a city ordinance requires all bars to close at midnight. Sam closes his bar at midnight and then opens five minutes later. The bar is closed at midnight. Sam has not violated the statute, literally construed. This, however, would be an absurd result.

The trouble with this rule is that one person's absurdity may be another person's reasoned judgment. For example, in one case the lower court had held that a particular construction of the statute was "unthinkable." The court of appeals disagreed and proceeded to adopt that construction: "Quite obviously, the result we reach cannot be unthinkable; we have thought it." *Simmons v. Robinson*, 399 S.E.2d 605, 611 n. 5 (S.C. Ct. App. 1990).

b. The Mischief Rule and Other Evidences of Intent

Justice Oliver Wendell Holmes once noted that a "word is not a crystal, transparent and unchanged, it is the skin of a living thought and may vary greatly in color and context according to the circumstances and the time in which it is used." Justice Holmes and judges like him did not think much of the plain meaning rule. Rather, they believed that if intent is the controlling consideration, then everything relevant to determining that intent should be considered. As the Restatement of Contracts (Second) puts it, "Words and other conduct are interpreted in the light of all the circumstances. . . ."

Chief among the circumstances this school of interpretation relies on in construing statutes is the harm or mischief the legislation was intended to correct or the good it was designed to achieve. An extreme variant of the mischief rule goes beyond direct purpose and looks at the spirit of the legislation. This approach is sometimes referred to as the "Holy Trinity Church Doctrine," named after a case involving a New York City church that retained the services of a new rector and prepaid his passage from England to the United States, in violation of the literal words of a federal statute that was apparently intended to stem the tide of immigration. The Court dismissed the indictment, holding that "a thing may be within the letter of the statute and yet not within the statute, because not within its spirit. . . ." *Holy Trinity Church v. United States*, 143 U.S. 457, 459 (1892).

Courts construing contracts and other private law documents also frequently go beyond the plain meaning and four corners of the document in search of intent, looking at the purpose of the document, bargaining history, contemporaneous memoranda, and other matters. This is, again, sometimes referred to as a "contextualist" approach to contract interpretation. Indeed, under the Uniform Commercial Code, usages of the trade, prior dealings, and course of performance are themselves a part of the contract and can be used to determine intent even under the textualist approach.

c. Effect on Drafters

The drafter should keep in mind both the plain meaning rule (with its exceptions) and the mischief rule and recognize that it is impossible to predict which approach a court might take in any particular case. The drafter's object, however, is to control the outcome. This has several consequences.

First, the plain meaning rule imposes an obligation on the drafter to use language that does in fact have a plain meaning.

Second, if the drafter intends the courts to take a plain meaning approach in the interpretation of the document, then the drafter should consider using express words to that effect. This can be done with a simple statement that the words of the document are to be given their ordinary meaning and by specifically excluding other possible evidences of intent.

Third, the drafter must try to imagine every possible situation that the literal words of the statute might encompass. A drafter should never count on a plausible linguistic interpretation being discounted merely because of its apparent absurdity to the drafter. Conversely, if the drafter is dealing with something in a novel manner, producing a result that might appear absurd to someone who disagreed with it, then the drafter should take special care to ensure that the client's intent is clearly and unequivocally expressed.

Fourth, if the drafter intends courts to have broader discretion in the interpretation of the document, then the drafter should consider providing the resources for the exercise of that discretion within the document itself. This can often be done in the preamble of a statute or the recitals of a contract.

2. THE RULE OF STRICT CONSTRUCTION

Courts traditionally construe certain kinds of statutes strictly or narrowly, as follows:

a. Criminal Statutes

The reason for strict construction of criminal statutes is that citizens are entitled to have advance notice of the government's commands. In one case, for example, an individual had been convicted of interstate transportation of an airplane known to have been stolen under a federal statute that referred to a "motor vehicle," which was defined as "an automobile, automobile truck, automobile wagon, motor cycle, or any other self-propelled vehicle not designed for running on rails." Justice Holmes opined that although an airplane fit within the literal words of the "or any other" clause of the statute, an ordinary citizen would not normally think of an airplane when pondering the meaning of a "self-propelled vehicle not designed for running on rails." *McBoyle v. United States*, 283 U.S. 25, 26–27 (1931). The drafter of criminal statutes thus needs to operate at an elevated level of clarity and precision.

b. Statutes in Derogation of the Common Law

One reason for the rule of strict construction of statutes in derogation of the common law dates back to the time when most law was judge-made rather than statutory, and courts were jealous of their law-making prerogatives. The common law does not enjoy the same prominence today and judges are less inclined to resent legislative intrusions into the law-making process.

A less partisan reason for the continued vitality of the rule relates to the nature of the common law itself. Common law rules operate at a very high level of factual generality, and are relatively unstructured and interconnected—the so-called "seamless web" of the common law. A carelessly drafted statute that alters one common law rule may have unanticipated effects on other common law rules, unless the alteration is narrowly construed.

The drafter of statutes in derogation of the common law needs to fully understand the common law rule the statute will affect and draft with a pin-point focus.

c. Statutes Depriving a Court of Jurisdiction

Here, judicial prerogatives continue to assert themselves. The courts are an equal branch of government and do not look kindly upon legislative encroachment. Indeed, the United States Constitution and state constitutions define the jurisdiction of courts. As Chief Justice John Marshall established early on, what those provisions mean is a matter for the courts to decide.

The drafter of a jurisdictional statute must be aware of both the constitutional limits and the proclivity of the courts to protect their respective jurisdictions. And even if the constitution, state or federal, does allow the legislature to allocate jurisdiction, the drafter should draft limiting statutes with special care and precision.

d. Statutes in Derogation of Sovereignty

Sovereignty—the power to issue and effectively enforce commands within a given geographical area, is the factual predicate on which all law is based. Take it away, and no law exists. In the United States, this sovereignty is divided between state and federal governments and, within each, between the three branches of government. The courts, as one branch of the larger sovereignty, are thus suspicious when an equal branch purports to surrender some of that sovereignty. Alternatively, the surrender of sovereignty is regarded as an extraordinary occurrence. Thus, for either reason or both, courts construe statutes in derogation of sovereignty strictly and narrowly.

State and federal tort claims acts are a typical example of the operation of this rule. Under the notion of sovereignty, it is axiomatic that "The King can do no [legal] wrong" and thus cannot be sued. Statutes allowing tort suits against government agents are thus narrowly or strictly construed. The drafter of these statutes must again take extra care to be specific and precise.

3. THE RULE OF LIBERAL CONSTRUCTION

Courts frequently state that a remedial statute must be liberally construed, so as to effectuate its object and purposes. Remedial statutes include any statute that creates or improves a remedy for an existing or newly created wrong. Most civil statutes are remedial in this sense. Thus, unless a statute falls within one of the categories covered by the rule of strict construction, the courts will liberally construe it. If that is what the legislative client desires, then everything is fine. Otherwise, the drafter must work with extraordinary precision to limit the scope of the enactment to its truly intended boundaries.

4. THE RULE OF *EXPRESSIO UNIUS EST EXCLUSIO ALTERIUS*

"The expression of one thing is the exclusion of another." This rule creates a negative inference that when a document lists certain things, the list is exclusive. Suppose, for example, that a county ordinance gives park directors general powers to enact rules affecting the use of their parks. The ordinance also specifically provides:

> *A Park Director may prohibit motorcycles, mopeds, go carts, and other motorized vehicles on park trails that are within **100** yards of a camping area.*

Does a park director also have the power to prohibit non-motorized trail bikes on these trails? By implication, the answer might be no. The drafters of the ordinance appear to have gone out of their way to define what the park director may prohibit on certain park trails. Arguably, this was intended to be an exclusive list, despite the existence of the park director's general power to regulate.

In the statutory context, at least, the United States Supreme Court has limited the application of the *expressio unius* rule so that it can no longer be applied simply because something was omitted from a list. Rather, the nature of the omitted item must itself suggest that the omission was intentional. In the words of the Court, "The canon depends on identifying a series of two or more terms or things that should be understood to go hand in hand, which are abridged in circumstances supporting a sensible inference that the term left out must have been meant to be excluded." *Chevron U.S.A. Inc. v. Echazabal*, 536 U.S. 73, 81 (2002) (citing E. Crawford, *Construction of Statutes* 337 (1940)).

In that case, a disability statute had expressly authorized employers to establish qualification standards. It stated that " 'qualification standards' may include a requirement that an individual shall not pose a direct threat to the health or safety of other individuals in the workplace." Using the *expressio unius* rule, some courts had read this as a prohibition against the exclusion from the workplace of an individual whose disability posed a risk only to that individual. The Supreme Court disagreed, noting first that risk to others was only an example of a qualification standard. But in addition, the Court found that risk to others and risk to self were not commonly paired items, so that the omission of one would not necessarily suggest a positive intent to exclude it as a permissible qualification standard. Since the disqualification of employees whose disability posed risks to themselves was otherwise "job related and consistent with business necessity," which was the broader test for a permissible qualification standard, the Court upheld the practice.

Nevertheless, the drafter should draft with the rule in mind. If a list is intended to be exclusive, then the drafter should state that expressly. If the list is not intended to be exclusive, then that should be expressed by appropriate language as well. To accomplish this, drafters frequently include the catch-all "and other" language. This, however, can also be extremely dangerous, as the next rule demonstrates.

5. THE RULE OF *EJUSDEM GENERIS*

When a sentence lists several specific items and concludes with a catch-all phrase like "and others," the rule of *ejusdem generis*—meaning "of the same kind"—provides that the general phrase is limited by the specific words that precede it. The rule is applied by identifying the common denominator of the specified items and then limiting "others" to entities also possessing that characteristic. The Federal Arbitration Act, for example, provides:

> *Nothing herein contained shall apply to contracts of seamen, railroad employees, or any other class of workers engaged in foreign or interstate commerce.*

As a matter of constitutional law, "foreign or interstate commerce" is an extremely broad concept, covering even the farmer who grows grain for consumption by his own cattle. But for the purposes of this act, the courts have construed the phrase as applying only to workers who share a salient characteristic of those listed—namely, being literally engaged in the interstate transportation industry, like seamen and railway employees. A farmer's contract with a laborer to harvest wheat for local consumption would thus not be included in the exclusion from coverage.

The problem with the technique of finding the common denominator is that a collection of items may have several common denominators. For example, "automobiles, trucks, and buses" have all the following common characteristics: (1) they are generally driven by an internal combustion engine; (2) they operate primarily on public streets and highways; (3) they operate on land; and (4) they have rubber wheels. So what would the phrase "and similar vehicles" cover? It depends on what the operative common denominator is. If it is (1), then a horse drawn carriage is excluded, although it would not be excluded under the others. If the common denominator is (2), then a golf cart or dune buggy is excluded, but again not under the others. If it is (3), then boats and airplanes are excluded, as they would also be under (2); a boat would be excluded under (4) but an airplane would not. If it is (4), then a vintage World War II tank is excluded, although it would not be excluded under (1), (2), or (3).

To determine what is included or excluded by the phrase "and similar vehicles," a court would be required to determine the intended common denominator. But this is a power the drafter should not casually surrender to a court. It is the drafter's function, not the courts', to identify the common denominator and make its identity express. The application of the rule of *ejusdem generis* is, thus, evidence of bad drafting.

Some drafters make the situation worse by adding a phrase like *or other vehicles [or whatever], without limitation or restriction to the generality of the foregoing*. This gives courts a wild card in determining what is or is not included in the provision.

6. THE RULE OF *NOSCITUR A SOCIIS*

This means that a word is known by its associates. Put differently, courts will construe words by reference to the context in which they appear. This is how the ambiguity that is associated with homonyms (words that are spelled the same but have more than one meaning) is frequently resolved. For example, a court rule might provide for the admission of the scientific testimony of competent witnesses. Here, "competent" is clearly being used in the sense of being an expert rather than in the sense of being sane.

The rule is also used to limit what would otherwise appear to be unqualified language. A workplace safety statute might provide:

> *In work areas, floors shall be painted with non-skid paint, yellow safety lines shall be drawn around all machinery, and all ceiling lights shall be 500 watts or greater.*

If the plant manager's office in a work area is carpeted, lacks a yellow line around the computer, and has a low intensity ceiling light, does this violate the statute? Probably not. The subject matter and context suggests that the requirements refer to production areas, not offices. The prudent drafter, however, should not intentionally rely on the rule as an excuse for sloppy drafting. If a word or phrase would be unclear except for the context, then clarify it. In this instance, for example, the drafter could have defined "work areas" to exclude the plant manager's office.

7. THE RULE OF *REDDENDO SINGULA SINGULIS*

This means that the court will refer each item in a series to its corresponding item in a matched series.

> *Seller will begin the manufacture, assembly, and shipment of the goods on June 1, July 1, and August 1.*

This would probably be construed as meaning that the seller will begin the manufacture on June 1, the assembly on July 1, and the shipment on August 1, rather than the Seller would begin the entire process of manufacture, assembly, and shipment three times, on the dates indicated. The meaning of that provision would be clearer, however, if it were presented in list or chart form, thus obviating the need to rely on the rule of interpretation.

8. THE RULE OF LAST MODIFICATION

Under this rule, also known as the "rule of the last antecedent," a qualifying phrase modifies only the immediately preceding word or phrase and not words or phrases more remote. *Lockhart v. United States*, 136 S. Ct. 958, 962–63 (2016). Thus, "This section applies to cars, trucks, and vans that are red" imposes a color limit only on vans. The rule is intended to resolve an ambiguity of modification that the drafter should not be guilty of in the first instance. Even if that is the interpretation the drafter intended, this should have been made express by the techniques of enumeration or tabbing discussed in Chapter 16.

9. THE RULE THAT HANDWRITTEN WORDS PREVAIL OVER TYPED OR PRINTED WORDS

Although all of the provisions of a contract should be consistent, the drafter should be especially cautious when some of the terms of an otherwise printed contract are added at the last minute in handwriting. If any ambiguity or inconsistency results, this rule gives the handwritten version priority. The theory is that the handwritten version reflects the conscious intent of the parties, who may have not read the printed portion thoroughly.

However, sometimes the inconsistency merely reflects last-minute carelessness. In any event, the drafter should carefully monitor the handwritten completion of a typed, printed, or word-processed contract to avoid any inconsistencies.

10. THE RULE THAT WRITTEN AMOUNTS PREVAIL OVER ARABIC NUMBER AMOUNTS

Under this rule, if a contract states the price is "two thousand, five hundred and fifty-six dollars and eighty-nine cents ($20,556.89)," the lower written price might prevail. Yet, if this would be grossly unfair or clearly inconsistent with the intent of the parties, modern courts would probably ignore the rule. But if the difference were limited to the " . . . fifty-six" versus "$. . . 57" portion of the price, the rule would probably be strictly followed. This rule is somewhat backwards, because studies have shown that, when confronted with both the written and the Arabic version of an amount, most people read only the Arabic version. The numerals, therefore, more likely reflect the mutual understanding of the parties.

The drafter can avoid the implication of this rule by simply presenting all dollar numbers in the Arabic form, and making sure that all the zeros and commas are correct. Numbers that do not reflect dollar amounts should be in either the written or Arabic form—but not both.

11. THE RULE THAT SPECIFIC LANGUAGE PREVAILS OVER GENERAL LANGUAGE OR PROVISIONS

This rule means that if one statute or private law document, or a provision within those documents, deals with a subject in general terms and another document or provision deals with the subject in a specific and detailed way, the more specific document or provision controls. Thus, the drafter should be aware of any statute or private law document between the same parties that deals with the same subject matter and should make the relationship between the two statutes or documents express, rather than relying on the court's invocation of this rule.

12. THE BORROWED LANGUAGE RULE

Drafters in one state often borrow specific language, particular provisions, and indeed entire statutes from the laws of other states. Under the borrowed language rule of interpretation, a court will give great weight to how the courts of the sister state have construed their statute. This is true not only of constructions existing at the time of the borrowing, but also of later decisions. The legislative drafter should make the legislative client aware of this possibility. If the client wants to avoid having the statute saddled with an untenable interpretation of a court in another state, then the drafter should provide for this. A statement in the preamble, for example, could identify the source of the statute but indicate that the decisions of the courts in that state are not controlling or perhaps even relevant.

13. THE RULE FAVORING AGENCY INTERPRETATION

Courts generally give considerable deference to the interpretation of a statute adopted by the agency charged with administering or enforcing that statute. For example, the *Interpretative Guidelines* of the Equal Employment Opportunity Commission sometimes have been treated almost as if they were formal regulations with independent legal effect. On the other hand courts have been known to disregard these *Guidelines* if they have adopted an approach courts disagree with.

In any event, if a statute will be enforced or administered by an administrative agency, the drafter should take the agency's general viewpoint into account when drafting the statute or amendments to an existing statute. If, in the past, an agency has been casual in the application of certain procedural requirements and the legislature wants to give it jurisdiction over another matter, but also wants the procedural requirements to be strictly construed, then the drafter should take that into account. The procedural requirements should be stated in positive, mandatory, and perhaps even jurisdictional terms.

14. THE RULE THAT A DOCUMENT MUST BE READ AS A WHOLE

Under this rule, a court is governed not by the apparent meaning of words in one clause, sentence, or part of the document standing in isolation, but rather by the meaning of the document as a whole. The drafter must keep this rule in mind when reviewing a document for internal consistency. The drafter may have used a vague term in one section of the document, not realizing that when the term is juxtaposed against what is contained in a later section, the vagueness resolves itself in one particular and not necessarily intended fashion.

15. THE RULE OF CONSTRUING STATUTES *IN PARI MATERIA*

This rule means that statutes dealing with the same subject and with the same general purpose must be construed with reference to each other. Whether statues truly are *in pari materia* is the critical question. A statute dealing with hospitals from a tax perspective might not be *in pari materia* with a statute dealing with hospitals from a licensing perspective, even though they both deal with hospitals. Indeed, the term "hospital" might even have different meanings under the two statutes.

If the rule applies, it has several consequences. First, it requires the courts to construe two statutes in a way that renders them consistent. This variation is simply an expanded version of the rule that a single document should be read as a whole. Thus, if a statute could be construed as prohibiting certain conduct or not, a court would normally construe it as "not" if another statute affirmatively authorizes the conduct. If the two statutes cannot be reconciled, then the courts normally fall back on the rule that specific statutes prevail over general statutes.

In addition, if two statutes are *in pari materia*, then the courts will generally construe them in the same way. For example, after the courts clarified the nature and allocation of the "because of" burden of proof in a race discrimination case under the Civil Rights Act of 1964, the courts took the same approach to the "because of" proof of age discrimination under the Age Discrimination in Employment Act, because the two statutes were said to be *in pari materia*. Similarly, if one statute defines a term and an *in pari materia* statute does not, the definition in the first statute will be imported into the second.

The drafter must be acutely aware of the *in pari materia* rule during the research stage of legislative drafting. If an existing statute deals with the same general subject matter or uses terminology that the drafter intends to use in the new legislation, then the drafter should regard that other statute as being potentially *in pari materia* and deal with it accordingly. For example, because the Civil Rights Act of 1964 and the Americans with Disabilities Act both deal with employment discrimination, they have been construed *in pari materia* on several points. The drafters apparently anticipated this when they drafted the Disability Act. Thus, in one instance they chose to draft around the rule. Both statutes require "reasonable accommodation"—Title VII of religious practices and the Disability Act of persons with disabilities—if the employer can do it without "undue hardship." The Supreme Court has construed "undue hardship" under Title VII as meaning anything more than a *de minimis* cost. Since Congress intended the disability accommodation duty to be broader than that, the statute expressly defines "undue hardship" as an action requiring significant difficulty or expense. And the legislative history expressly states that the Title VII approach is not to be followed in construing this portion of the ADA.

16. THE RULE DISFAVORING REPEALS BY IMPLICATION

If a provision in one statute is arguably inconsistent with a provision in a later statute, an advocate seeking to avoid the application of the first provision might argue that it had been implicitly repealed—and, indeed, that may have been the inadequately expressed legislative intent. The other side, however, would invoke the rule disfavoring repeals by implication. If the court accepts it, then the court will do whatever is possible to accommodate the two provisions, even if this results in a strained interpretation of both.

The message for the drafter is: Do not draft a statutory provision that is inconsistent with another statutory provision. If the intent is to repeal the earlier provision, do that expressly.

17. THE RULE OF *LEX POSTERIOR DEROGAT PRIORI*

This means that a later statute takes away the effect of a prior one. Under this rule, if a 1995 statute prohibits conduct that a 2020 statute affirmatively authorizes, the 2020 statute will prevail—which is inconsistent with the rule that repeals by implication are not favored.

In its most extreme form, the rule also posits that the order of occurrence within a document controls, with a provision at the end of a statute prevailing over an inconsistent prior provision. This is also contrary to the rule that a document must be read as a whole.

18. THE RULE OF CONSTRUING A DOCUMENT AGAINST THE DRAFTER

The party drafting the document usually has the advantage, in both choosing the terms to include and in wording them. Although the other party may have preferred other terms or that they be expressed differently, negotiating the changes sometimes does not seem to be worth the effort—except in retrospect. However, the other party can still exploit any ambiguity or vagueness by invoking this rule of interpretation. If successful, this turns the drafter's advantage into a disadvantage.

To avoid disagreements over who the drafter really was, the parties may want to include a provision stating that the document was drafted jointly and that this rule of interpretation has no application.

19. THE RULE OF ADOPTING A CONSTRUCTION THAT FAVORS VALIDITY

If a particular interpretation of a contract would render it invalid or if the interpretation of a statute would make it unconstitutional, the court is unlikely to adopt that construction. For example, if a party is attempting to void a contract on the ground that its principal provision, as construed by this party, is inconsistent with the controlling statute, but the other party contends that this construction is erroneous and that the contract provision actually means something else, the court is likely to agree and uphold the validity of the contract. Similarly, if the attack upon the constitutionality of a statute is predicated only on a tenuous construction of the terms of that statute, a court is likely to reject that construction and adopt one that would be constitutional.

Draft in a way that is both unambiguous and substantively valid.

20. THE RULE FAVORING THE CONSTRUCTION OF CONTRACTS IN A MANNER CONSISTENT WITH PUBLIC POLICY

Even if a relatively clear contract provision is not unconscionable or inconsistent with a common law or statutory requirement, a court, on public policy grounds, may refuse to enforce it or may construe it broadly or narrowly. This demonstrates that in some jurisdictions the philosophy of contract interpretation and enforcement has moved toward increased judicial scrutiny over both the process of contract formation and the substantive content of the resulting contract.

There is probably no sure way to draft around this judicial proclivity. Rather, the drafter must simply attempt to anticipate what some court is later going to decide is consistent with public policy and draft with that possibility in mind.

C. TOOLS FOR ANALYZING AND INTERPRETING STATUTES

1. USING TABULATION TO EXPLODE A STATUTE

Be alert in analyzing statutes. Statutes that are properly drafted constitute a checklist of sorts. When reading a statute, use a pen, pencil, or your keyboard to explicitly divide the statute into elements (requirements) and factors (things to be considered), insert numbers and letters to tabulate these features, and pay close attention to words like "and" and "or" to determine how many requirements, options, and considerations there are under the statute. Reformatting a statute in tabular form on a word processor or on paper, focusing on these factor and elements, rather than looking at the large block of text, is often useful. This is your first tool of statutory interpretation.

By exploding the statute or statement of law into its constituent parts, you can identify each element or factor, and then analyze each of them in light of a given set of facts. This is much like the way engineering diagrams explode a product for which a patent is sought in order to explain the product:

This is the heart of legal analysis: (1) spotting the issues, (2) finding the applicable laws, (3) breaking those laws down into their constituent parts, (4) applying the parts to a set of facts to reach a conclusion.

For example, take Restatement (Second) of Contracts section 24, which operates like a statute and defines what constitutes an "offer":

> An offer is the manifestation of willingness to enter into a bargain, so made as to justify another person in understanding that his assent to that bargain is invited and will conclude it.

Even this relatively simple block of text will benefit by being reformatted in tabular form so that it resembles a checklist:

> An offer is:
>
> (a) a manifestation of
>
> (b) willingness to enter into a bargain,
>
> (c) so made as to justify another person in understanding that:
>
> > (i) his assent to that bargain is invited and

(ii) will conclude it.

Exploding the statute enables you to easily see each of the elements and sub-elements and allows you to then examine any particular set of facts under the standard, checklist style, to determine if each of the required elements is present.

2. USING THE STRUCTURE AND OTHER SECTIONS OF THE SAME STATUTE

Do not read a statute in a vacuum. After you explode a statute and create a comprehensible checklist, be sure to look at the entire body of related statutes to understand the structure of the whole. Often complex statutes or bodies of statutes will have logical divisions, perhaps first stating the scope of the enactment, then providing definitions of key terms, then containing positive provisions, standards, and rules; then exceptions and exemptions. All of these features can be used to understand the context of the specific statute at issue and to construe it appropriately under the circumstances. In electronic research the sections of a statute are usually displayed in isolation. Thus it is difficult not only to know how that section relates to your issue. In other words, you may not be able to tell if there is a "better," more applicable section because you have not compared the section on the screen with others in the statutory scheme.

Moreover, there may be a section of the statute that sets out the legislative intent or policy reasons for enacting the statute or statutory scheme.

3. USING CASE LAW INTERPRETING A STATUTE

Often the section of the statute applicable to your matter has been interpreted by the courts. Case law interpreting a statute is your third tool of statutory construction. After you have exploded the statute and reviewed it in the context of its statutory scheme, you are ready to research and review case law dealing with the statute. Resist the urge to skip the first two steps and go directly to reading cases. Without a solid understanding of what the statute means, it will be much more difficult for you to grasp individual cases as well as synthesize them, that is, put them together in logical order.

In dealing with statutes, courts may:

1. Determine if they are *valid*. Do they conflict with a higher authority? Does a state statute conflict with the state or federal constitution? Does a regulation or ordinance conflict with a higher-ranked statute? Do rules from an appellate court case conflict with a rule or rules articulated in a Supreme Court case?

2. Determine *whether* a statute applies or *which* statute applies.

3. *Interpret* a statute—determine what its terms mean, what is required, permitted or forbidden under what circumstances.

4. *Apply* the statute to the facts before them and determine the outcome.

CHAPTER 5

DRAFTING ETHICS

Legal drafters are subject to the same ethical rules that govern the conduct of all lawyers. The discussion below is based generally on the ABA Model Rules of Professional Conduct, which in one version or another has been adopted in most jurisdictions. There are many local variations on the rules and differences of opinion about their meaning. This chapter will focus on identifying the ethical problems facing legal drafters.

Concrete answers to these issues would be difficult to ascertain. Most of the ethical standards address dilemmas from the perspective of the lawyer as a litigator. The profession has not paid special attention to the ethical problems associated with drafting. Consequently, the legal drafter is comforted by less formal guidance in the form of ethics opinions and court decisions than other lawyers and must rely more on an internal ethical compass.

The principle is: "A lawyer shall not materially misstate facts." In some formulations, this may or may not include both affirmative statements and omissions. Some things, like statements of value, are traditionally treated as opinions rather than facts. Distinguish between primary facts (like those contained in accurate financial statements) with factual conclusions (like the value of a business); the former is within the prohibition, but the latter may not be.

A. SOLICITATION

Drafters need to be concerned about several aspects of the general ethical limitations on solicitation.

1. ADVERTISING SPECIALIZATION OR CONCENTRATION

Subject to the rules against false and misleading statements, a lawyer may generally communicate that the lawyer concentrates on a particular area of the law. However, many states explicitly forbid the use of the word "specialize" and its variants, unless the lawyer has completed a certification or other process approved by that state's bar association. Thus, drafters who primarily do estate work or real estate transactions can represent themselves as such. But, a lawyer may not represent that he or she has been "certified as a specialist" unless such certification has been granted by a state agency or other organization.

2. MASS MAILINGS

Although advertising is generally allowed and personal solicitation is not, the line between the two is not always distinct. For example, mass mailings to strangers are generally permitted in most jurisdictions. Of particular interest to drafters is the question of mass mailings by real estate lawyers to real estate agents and homeowners. Attorneys should research their jurisdiction's professional conduct rules on solicitation to determine any language that must be included in the communication and the applicability of any "blackout" or waiting-period on follow-up contact with prospective clients.

3. SOLICITATION OF FORMER CLIENTS, FAMILY, AND FRIENDS

A lawyer is generally permitted to suggest the need for legal services to former clients, family, and close friends. For example, the drafter of a will or other document may later communicate with the client and suggest the need for an update because of changes in the law or the client's circumstances. The communication with former clients must, however, be related to the former employment. A lawyer may also suggest to a family member the need for a will and then accept employment as the drafter of that will, subject to the conflict-of-interest problems discussed below.

B. COMPETENCE AND DILIGENCE

Some of the highest legal and ethical duties of the lawyer are to be competent and diligent. The two are closely related. Mistakes often occur because the lawyer did not know any better and was too lazy to become better informed. Whenever a drafted document fails to produce the results the client expected, the client is likely to call the competence and diligence of the drafter into question. If incompetence or a lack of diligence exists, not only has the drafter violated professional conduct rules but also may face liability for malpractice. Examples of drafting incompetence and lack of diligence, drawn from cases and ethical opinions, include:

- Giving a client a set of standard forms and instructions on how to fill them out, when the forms did not actually meet the needs of the client.
- Ignorance of the requirements of a spendthrift trust, thus creating a trust that deprived the client of the desired creditor-protection benefits.
- Failure to include the agreed one-year non-competition-upon-termination term in an employment contract, thus allowing the client-employee to open a competing business before a year expired.
- Failure to provide properly for the intended beneficiaries of a will, thus creating liability to a third party.
- Drafting a contract containing an ambiguity that was later resolved against the client in litigation.
- Failure to obtain, in a timely fashion, a necessary signature on a mortgage, thus allowing the buyers to sell free and clear of the client's interests in the property.

C. SCOPE OF REPRESENTATION

A lawyer is bound by the client's decisions concerning the objectives of the representation unless they are criminal or fraudulent, and generally should consult with the client regarding the means for achieving them.

1. OBJECTIVES AND MEANS

The critical first step in the drafting process is to determine the client's objectives. The ethical corollary is that once those objectives are known, the drafter must generally honor them. If the drafter thinks these objectives are not in the client's own best interests or are of questionable legality, the drafter should discuss the matter with the client. This may be particularly troublesome when the drafter is representing an organization. In some instances, the drafter may be obliged to go over the head of the designated organizational representative and present the drafter's concerns to higher authority.

Depending on the nature of the relationship, the drafter may also want to discuss with the client the broader moral, economic, social, and political implications of a given objective. Clients may fail to realize that self-interest is often best served through decency and social responsibility; it is the lawyer's responsibility to make that point.

If the client is dedicated to achieving an objective that is deeply and morally offensive to the drafter, then withdrawal is the appropriate response. But under no circumstances may the drafter surreptitiously subvert the client's objectives or substitute the drafter's objectives for those of the client. The temptation to do this is particularly strong for the legislative drafter. These are generally career professionals, often with more tenure and experience in dealing with policy issues than those for whom they draft—whether the client is a specific legislator, a committee, or an administrative official. Indeed, the drafter is often asked to contribute to the formulation of agency or legislative policy. Ultimately, however, the drafter must defer to the wishes of the client. If the drafter disagrees with the proposed legislation, the drafter must still function as a competent lawyer, remain totally objective, and not allow his or her opinions about the wisdom of the legislation to subvert the client's objectives. If the drafter's social, political, and economic views are seriously at odds with those of the legislative client, then the drafter should seek employment elsewhere.

As in other lawyering contexts, the drafter has more discretion and responsibility in selecting the most effective means of achieving the client's objective. Indeed, many clients leave that up to the drafter entirely. If, however, the client wants a transaction structured in a particular way and the drafter thinks that is not the best way to achieve the ultimate objective, then the drafter should discuss the matter with the client rather than ignoring the client's wishes.

2. CRIMINAL, FRAUDULENT, AND OTHERWISE PROHIBITED TRANSACTIONS

The drafter who correctly advises a client that a particular transaction violates the criminal law and who later drafts the necessary papers is liable as an accomplice or coconspirator. For example, a drafter could not draft a contract of sale for goods known to be stolen. The "mere scrivener" defense was rejected centuries ago. Similarly, drafter participation in fraud may render the drafter liable in damages to the injured parties. The lawyer that advises against entering into a fraudulent transaction is protecting the client from liability by advising against that course of action and the lawyer has an ethical obligation to withdraw from the representation rather than participate.

Bottom line: Illegal fraud is an issue the transactional attorney must make a judgment about—and it is not that complicated. Ask yourself, "Am I helping the client misrepresent information in an effort to take someone's money or property?" If so, the attorney and her client face liability, and a competent lawyer is doing a client a disservice if she is not explaining the prospect of liability.

A more unsettled area of the law relates to drafter involvement with transaction documents that are not criminal or fraudulent, but that are otherwise unlawful, unenforceable, or a misrepresentation. For example, a business client might ask a lawyer to draft a covenant-not-to-compete that is geographically overbroad, hoping that the employee will not realize its unenforceability and will unwittingly comply with its limitations.

A drafter, however, may not always know whether a particular provision is criminal, fraudulent, or otherwise illegal for some reason. The law is rife with uncertainty. Good faith predictions are often wrong and the lawyer who makes them, and who drafts documents on the basis of those predictions, is generally not regarded as being unethical. But between the two extremes of a good faith prediction that is wrong and conduct that is clearly illegal lies a very large gray area. For example, would it be unethical for a drafter to state, "I honestly think this provision violates the criminal law, but I can certainly make arguments to the contrary if the issue is litigated," and then proceed to draft the document on that basis? The legal ethical community is not of one mind on the matter, but it is the considered opinion of many that what it takes to provide good advice in these gray areas is to be willing to make judgments and, ultimately, to advise against conduct in the gray area.

Fraud can be a particularly slippery concept. For example, an attorney might be asked to draft a contract containing a term that is so indefinite it probably will cause the contract to fail. The client intends to use this as an escape valve if performance under the contract later becomes unprofitable. Does that constitute fraud against the other party?

Similarly, in the legislative context, an administrative agency may want a particular substantive requirement but also privately acknowledge that Congress would never consciously impose it. Is it unethical for an agency drafter to write the statute in such an obscure way that Congress will not realize the implications, thus allowing the agency to later interpret the statute to suit its fancy? Whether an actual ethical violation or not, most drafters would view this as a violation of the public trust and refuse to participate in such machinations.

Disclosure situations are also troublesome, from both a legal and an ethical perspective. The classic example is the purchaser who contracts to buy a piece of land, knowing it contains buried treasure and that the current owner does not realize this. Compare that with the seller of property who contracts to sell without disclosing a latent defect to the buyer. Can the lawyer act as a drafter-participant in the transaction without insisting that the client disclose the information to the other party?

The drafter's duty of disclosure is fairly clear when mistakes find their way into the final written and signed version of a contract. If the parties have reached agreement and the lawyer for one of them is responsible for reducing the agreement to writing, that lawyer cannot intentionally and surreptitiously change the terms knowing that the other party is not going to catch it before signing. Moreover, if the later-discovered change or omission that favors the drafter's client was inadvertent, then the drafter should bring the matter to the attention of the other party after informing the drafter's client. Conversely, if an inadvertent clerical or mathematical error favors the non-drafting party, under the law of unilateral mistake the courts generally will not allow that party to snatch up the advantage and a lawyer should not advise that party to attempt to do so.

D. COMMUNICATION

A lawyer has the general duty to keep the client reasonably informed about the progress of the representation and to provide sufficient explanations to enable the client to make informed decisions. These client communication obligations affect the drafter in two ways.

First, if the drafter is also functioning as the negotiator of a contract, the drafter should keep the client apprised of the status of the negotiations, the nature of the counter-proposals, and the concessions that the drafter thinks are appropriate.

Second, if a lawyer has drafted a legally complex document for a client, the drafter should carefully explain to the client what the document contains and what its legal significance is. This is where a document summary plays an important role.

E. FEES

Ethical rules generally require that the lawyer's fee be reasonable. This, in turn, is dependent on such factors as the time and labor required, the novelty and difficulty of the representation, and the degree of skill that is required. But ethical rules also generally allow the fee amount to reflect the experience and reputation of the lawyer.

Sometimes, these two criteria may work against each other. Consider the lawyer who specializes in wills and estates. Over the years, through "from scratch" drafting of many estate planning documents, the lawyer has crafted provisions dealing with every possible contingency. These provisions are now incorporated into a computerized document assembly program. Basically, all the lawyer does now is obtain the necessary information from new clients, choose the appropriate previously drafted provisions, and merge the two. The time and labor involved in producing that specific document is minimal; but it reflects an enormous amount of experience, reputation, and ability on the part of the lawyer. Clearly, the drafter cannot bill for fictitious hours. The drafter may, however, adopt a value billing (set fee) approach as an alternative.

A similar problem drafters face involves the use of essentially the same document for multiple clients. For example, a lawyer may draft a document for a client from scratch, at $150 per hour for ten hours, or $1,500. A few weeks later, another client needs an almost identical document. Now it takes the lawyer only an hour to produce it. Must the drafter charge only $150? Can the drafter charge another $1,500? Or is the correct fee somewhere in between? Again, the lawyer cannot bill the second client at a fictitious hourly rate; the drafter may, however, charge a flat fee for the document that is in excess of the normal hourly rate, as long as this is agreed-to in advance with the client.

F. CONFIDENTIALITY

Professional ethics require confidentiality. Client communications are also protected by the attorney-client privilege.

1. ETHICAL REQUIREMENTS

The ethical rules all impose a duty of protecting the information learned in the representation of the client, subject to exceptions that vary widely by jurisdiction. This impacts the drafter in several particulars.

For example, when drafting private documents, the drafter often obtains personal information about individual clients and their families and commercially sensitive and trade secret information from business clients. A breach of the duty of confidentiality might be committed by the lawyer directly, for whatever reason, or it could be done by someone else privy to the information. Confidential information about prominent clients may be leaked outside the firm. A separation agreement between two movie stars, for example, might well contain many newsworthy tidbits of information. Confidential business information may also be leaked in this fashion, sometimes to the financial benefit of the person possessing the information, but often for no benefit at all other than to participate in a chain of gossip. The drafter has an affirmative obligation to educate all involved in the matter, even couriers, about the duty of confidentiality. Drafts of documents containing sensitive or confidential information should be shredded, not merely put in a trash can. Beyond ethical rules, breach of confidentiality also breaches a legal duty to the client and can result in liability for professional malpractice and breach of fiduciary duty.

Not disclosing client information to third parties is only part of the ethical duty. The drafter's own use of the information is also limited. The drafter of corporate documents may not use the information when buying or selling stock in the company. Such insider trading is not only a breach of the ethics rules, it may also violate state and federal securities law. Confidential client information is sometimes used for other forms of lawyer self-dealing. This is discussed further in the section dealing with conflicts of interest.

2. ATTORNEY-CLIENT PRIVILEGE

The duty of confidentiality also manifests itself in the form of an evidentiary privilege. In essence, a person who seeks legal advice or assistance from a lawyer may invoke an unqualified privilege not to testify about the contents of confidential communications with the lawyer. If asked to testify, the lawyer must also invoke the privilege on behalf of the client. Privileged documents may also be withheld from discovery.

The privilege probably attaches to most of the information that an attorney would obtain when preparing to draft a document. Oddly enough, however, unless it contains information that would be privileged, the drafted document itself is not generally privileged. In other words, the communication to the lawyer is privileged but not necessarily the facts that are communicated.

The work-product privilege would also arise only in the unlikely circumstance of the document being prepared in anticipation of litigation. Many transactional attorneys think everything is ultimately prepared in anticipation of litigation, but the scope of the work-product doctrine is usually construed narrowly to mean relating to particular litigation and not just the general possibility of future litigation.

The attorney-client privilege is subject to several exceptions of relevance to the drafter. First, the privilege does not arise when the lawyer is dealing with drafted documents in a non-attorney capacity, for example as a corporate officer, a business advisor, or a friend.

Second, lawyers drafting routine documents like deeds, who are acting on the instructions of a client and who are not giving any legal advice in connection with the drafting, have sometimes been referred to as "mere scriveners," meaning in this context that the privilege does not attach. The scope of this exception is unclear, however, since drafting even routine documents requires some degree of expertise, even if it is nothing more than knowing that a routine document will indeed suffice. The courts recognize the exception most often when the document is now unavailable and the purpose of the testimony is to establish that the document existed and what it contained.

Third, to be privileged, the information the drafter uses must come from the client, not third parties. This exception comes up most often in the corporate context, where the precise identity of the client is subject to considerable debate.

Fourth, the privilege does not apply to otherwise unprivileged client papers, even if they are given to the drafter for use in drafting a document that will cure whatever legal difficulty the papers present.

Fifth, when a lawyer is drafting a document for co-clients, information received from one client is generally not privileged from the other clients. This is another reason for declining to draft contracts on behalf of all the contracting parties.

Sixth, the privilege does not attach to information indicating a client's intent to engage in illegal or fraudulent conduct. This exception would apply if the drafter has been given information in connection with a request to draft a document to be used in a fraudulent transaction.

G. CONFLICT OF INTEREST

Ironically, the attorney-client relationship involves a conflict of interest at its very threshold: the conflict between the attorney who drafts the retainer contract and the client who is asked to agree to it. This is why attorney-client contracts are subject to fairly heavy regulation and scrutiny, especially with respect to fees. Moreover, any ambiguity in an attorney-client contract will nearly always be construed against the lawyer-drafter.

The other common conflict situations the lawyer-drafter faces are (1) representation against a current client; (2) representation against a former client; (3) imputed disqualification; and (4) former government lawyer-drafters who go into private practice.

1. REPRESENTATION AGAINST A CURRENT CLIENT

Lawyers are frequently asked to draft a contract for both parties, who say that they have agreed in principle and just want the lawyer to write it up in legal form. The representation of each may be representation against the other. This is because the parties' interests are almost always hostile to some extent, although they may not truly appreciate that fact. The question usually is whether the representation of one party will be materially limited by the lawyer's responsibility to the other party.

Many commentators believe that such a limitation is inherent in the drafting process. A skillful and conscientious drafter can nearly always draft in subtle ways that inure to the benefit of the client, and to the corresponding disadvantage of the other party, however minor. For example, if a lawyer is representing a buyer in a residential real estate transaction, that lawyer's ability to exercise drafting expertise will be materially limited by that lawyer's simultaneous representation of the seller in the same transaction. There are too many provisions that could be drafted in a number of ways. For example, a provision dealing with a termite certification letter could be worded as a mere condition (favoring the seller) or as a promise (favoring the buyer). This would seem to qualify as a situation where the interests of multiple parties are fundamentally antagonistic to each other, which should preclude representation even if both parties consent.

On the other hand, other commentators think it is inefficient and unnecessary to turn every simple transaction into a complicated matter by requiring each side to retain separate counsel. Many ethics opinions allow lawyers to act on behalf of both parties in drafting relatively simple contracts where the parties have agreed to the basic terms.

Conflict questions also arise when a lawyer is asked to draft wills or other estate planning documents for members of the same family, such as a husband and wife. This particular conflict is illustrated by the following, oft-debated hypothetical. Meeting together, a husband and wife tell the lawyer how they want their individual property to be distributed—to each other. Later, meeting alone with the lawyer, the wife indicates that she really wants her property distributed in a different way, but that she also does not want her husband to know about it because it would only make him angry. Can the drafter honor the wife's wishes and deceive the husband? Or should the drafter inform the husband and breach the wife's confidence and also precipitate marital discord? Or must the drafter decline to draft a will for either one of them? No easy answers exist to these questions unless they are addressed on the front end of the representation, preferably in the retention letter memorializing the terms of the attorney's engagement. That letter might, for example, discuss the lawyer's obligations of confidentiality and that, if either joint client asks the lawyer to withhold information from the other, the lawyer has the right to or will withdraw from the representation.

Business lawyers frequently encounter drafting-related conflicts in the context of simultaneous representation of the corporation and that corporation's officers, directors, or stockholders. The lawyer's primary duty as counsel to the corporation is *always* to the corporate entity. A corporate lawyer, thus, cannot draft documents or otherwise assist stockholders in setting up a competing enterprise or draft a separation agreement on behalf of a departing officer.

Corporate takeovers are full of conflict possibilities. Each member of the corporation may have a different interest and may be giving different and conflicting instructions to the lawyer who is negotiating or drafting takeover documents. Ultimately, the drafter must defer to the wishes of the board of directors.

As a general rule, courts are more tolerant of simultaneous representation in the context of a small, closely held corporation than in a large, publicly held corporation. Even in this context, however, if the venture sours and the interests diverge in fact, the lawyer can no longer represent anyone. If this occurs in the middle of drafting a complex document, the lawyer may be unable to collect a fee for the work begun but not completed.

The ethical rule of avoiding conflicts applies not only to direct conflicts of interest, but also to broader conflicts of loyalty. A lawyer cannot engage in active representation against a current client even in unrelated matters if it would adversely affect the relationship. However, the clients can both waive this conflict or potential conflict if the lawyer thinks she can represent both clients and obtains informed consent from each of them.

A lawyer who is drafting a complex construction contract for Client A cannot represent Client B who is suing Client A in an unrelated tort action. Since loyalty is an essential element in the lawyer's relationship with a client, it would be a rare case indeed where these clients would consent to the conflict of interest.

Some transactions between an attorney and a client are subject to an almost total prohibition. Several are of particular importance to the drafter.

- A lawyer cannot enter into a business transaction with a client unless the terms are fair, the client has the opportunity to retain other counsel, and the client consents in writing. A lawyer's business contract with a client is subject to intense scrutiny for overreaching. As an aside, it is not unusual for clients to suggest entering into a mutual business transaction with a lawyer, perhaps in exchange for a discount or in lieu of paying legal fees for associated work. This proposal may seem like a good idea at the outset but will almost certainly result in an ethics complaint and litigation if the client later becomes dissatisfied with the relationship, which happens all too often.

- A lawyer cannot use information relating to the representation of a client to the disadvantage of that client. A lawyer who has drafted a purchase offer cannot use that information to submit a better offer on the drafter's or someone else's behalf.

- A lawyer cannot draft a document, such as a will, giving herself (or a relative) a substantial gift from the client, except where the client is related to the donee. Although it is not expressly prohibited, naming the will drafter the executor or administrator of the estate is filled with conflict.
- Prior to the conclusion of representation, a lawyer cannot negotiate or draft an agreement giving the lawyer literary or media rights to matters relating to the representation.
- A lawyer that negotiates or drafts an agreement prospectively limiting the lawyer's liability for malpractice should be aware (and probably presume) that the agreement may not be enforceable, and certainly not unless the client is represented by another attorney with regard to the limitation of liability agreement.

2. REPRESENTATION AGAINST A FORMER CLIENT

Ethical rules generally prohibit a lawyer who has previously represented a client from later representing another person in the same or a substantially related matter if the new client's interests are materially adverse to the interests of the former client, unless both the current and former clients consent to this. The application of this ethical duty to the drafter is fairly straightforward. If a lawyer has represented a client in drafting a document, such as a contract or will, that lawyer cannot later represent another person in challenging the legality or efficacy of the document or in contesting the former client's conduct under that document.

3. IMPUTED DISQUALIFICATION

Lawyers generally practice in firms. This raises several difficult questions. For example, if one member, or former member, of the firm would be disqualified, is everyone in the firm similarly disqualified? At one time, the rules seemed to impose a virtually absolute disqualification. If Partner Abbott was disqualified from some form of representation in connection with a drafted document, then Partner Baker was as well—unless the original client or clients consented. The current view is more permissive, but also more complicated.

First, with limited exceptions, when lawyers are associated in a firm, if one has a conflict based upon a prior representation, it is imputed to the rest of the lawyers in the firm.

Second, when the disqualified lawyer has left the firm, the remainder of the firm is disqualified from representing a party with an interest that is materially adverse to that of the former client only if the matter is the same or substantially related to the prior representation *and* any lawyer remaining in the firm has confidential information relating to the matter. Thus, if departing Partner Abbott drafted a document for the client, Partner Charles could not represent a client in a matter challenging the meaning or efficacy of that document if any lawyer remaining at the firm knows or possesses confidential information about the prior representation. But, if no remaining lawyer has confidential information, the conflict is resolved.

An imputed disqualification generally does not follow a lawyer departing from a firm unless that lawyer actually acquired confidential information about the client. If Partner Abbott has drafted a will, Associate Darby probably could not, while still working at the firm, represent another client challenging the will. But when Darby goes to work for another law firm, Darby is disqualified from such representation only if Darby acquired confidential information relating to the will. And even if Darby is disqualified, Partner Ethyl in the new firm may arguably still undertake the representation if Darby is sufficiently isolated from the representation. There is, however, some disagreement over this last point.

4. FORMER GOVERNMENT LAWYER-DRAFTERS

Lawyers who work for the government and then go into private practice face special conflict of interest problems. The general rule is that a lawyer cannot represent a private client in connection with a matter in which the lawyer participated personally and substantially as a public employee, without the consent of the appropriate government agency.

Insofar as the lawyer-drafter is concerned, the principal question is whether a government lawyer could draft a regulation and then, after leaving government service, advise clients about the regulation, file cases based on it, or even challenge its validity. This is a question that has not yet been finally resolved.

H. DEALINGS WITH THIRD PARTIES

Lawyers are often called upon not only to draft contracts, but also to negotiate the terms with the other contracting party. It is unethical for a lawyer to make a false statement of material fact or law. Unfortunately, the line between a misrepresentation of fact and the expression of opinion about value—mere "puffing"—is not always clear.

On the other hand, a lawyer normally has no ethical obligation to disclose a material fact unless nondisclosure would assist the client in doing a criminal or fraudulent act or breach a duty owed by the client to that third party. The dimensions of this exception are unclear, however. In addition, drafters inclined to take advantage of that privilege should be aware that it is subject to two legal limits. First, in some situations, nondisclosure of a material fact might make a contract unconscionable and thus unenforceable. Second, the common law rules of unilateral or mutual mistake could apply in some situations, thus making the contract voidable.

Another ethical concern of the lawyer-drafter involves dealing with another contracting party who is also represented by counsel. The rule is that direct contact with this party is impermissible unless the other lawyer has consented to it. Thus, a drafter could not submit a contract counter-proposal or suggested revision directly to the other party.

Conversely, if the lawyer-drafter is dealing with a party who is not represented by counsel, the ethical obligation is to ensure that this person fully understands that the lawyer is not disinterested and that the lawyer is representing only the interests of the client. The lawyer should take particular care not to give legal advice to an unrepresented person. Although the lawyer can explain the meaning of various contract provisions, the better practice is to advise third parties to retain their own lawyers for that purpose.

I. LITIGATION ETHICS

Drafted documents are often involved in litigation—a breach of contract case, for example. Clients frequently retain in their files documents containing information relating to the contract and, indeed, prior drafts of the contract itself. Sometimes, these documents are relevant to the litigation, and sometimes they contain information that is adverse to the interests of the party who has retained them.

It is widely considered unethical and illegal for a lawyer to destroy or conceal documents that have existing evidentiary value. The simplest case arises when the opposing party has served a discovery request on the client for all documents relating to the contract. Clearly, the lawyer cannot advise the client to destroy incriminating documents, such as one indicating that the client had knowledge of a condition it was under a duty to disclose under a contract of sale.

Lawyers should counsel their clients (and their own firms) to adopt a document retention-destruction policy that is based on some objective standard, length of time based upon statutes of limitation, etc. These document retention policies should be consistently honored and, should a "litigation hold" letter or other demand be received, no documents or other records should be destroyed or otherwise compromised.

J. AIDING THE UNAUTHORIZED PRACTICE OF LAW

Lawyers cannot abet the unauthorized practice of law, which is often a grey area. In this area, the attorney must make an informed judgment about whether the conduct involved is the unauthorized practice of law so that the attorney can decide to avoid ethical and legal liability and advise the client regarding the risks involved.

A legal drafter is likely to become involved in the unauthorized practice of law in two situations. Do-it-yourself books and computer programs that enable lay persons to create their own legal documents generally do not constitute unauthorized practice, and entrepreneur lawyer-drafters may participate in the preparation of these materials. Courts, however, generally draw the line at giving advice that is personalized or directed at the specific problem of a designated or readily identifiable person. Also, inclusion of a telephone number or e-mail address that the consumer could contact for another lay person's assistance in completing the forms would be a form of unauthorized practice and a lawyer could not be involved in such an enterprise.

The second situation involves the age-old dispute over the role of real estate agents in preparing contracts and other documents involving the sale of land. A jurisdiction may hold that simply filling in the blanks on a form contract constitutes the practice of law. Presumably, lawyers in those jurisdictions cannot draft form documents that would be used in this manner. In the majority of states, however, realtors may fill out purchase contracts and other forms, provided they do not impose a separate charge for the service or give legal advice. Thus, in these states the lawyer could assist in the drafting of a form contract. Indeed, the real estate community would benefit from some competent drafting in that regard.

K. PROVIDING FREE DRAFTING SERVICES

The practice of law is a business, and it is not unethical for lawyers to treat it exclusively as such. The practice of law, however, is also a profession dedicated to the public good. Most lawyers aspire to provide a certain amount of free work. The drafter who is so inclined has two principal opportunities.

First, local bar associations frequently sponsor legal clinics where community members can get legal advice on various matters. In addition, these clinics often provide simple contract and will drafting services. Second, churches and charities frequently urge their members and contributors to include a bequest to the institution in wills or to establish a trust on behalf of the institution. In both instances, the skilled drafter can provide an invaluable service, by drafting the necessary documents without cost.

CHAPTER 6

LEGAL DRAFTING OVERVIEW

Some think of legal drafting principally in terms of writing the document. Although this is an important part of drafting, it is merely an intermediate part of a larger, more complex endeavor.

Although the process can be broken down into a number of discrete steps, that characterization is somewhat misleading since it suggests a rigid, linear progress. Drafting is more circular than linear. A step once taken may have to be repeated as the drafted document evolves. This chapter will identify and briefly describe these steps, which will then be discussed in more detail in subsequent chapters.

A. DETERMINE THE CLIENT'S OBJECTIVES

Determining the client's objectives is the most important part of the drafting process. It will affect everything that follows. The objective of all drafted documents is to achieve some good or avoid some harm. But it is the client's specific good to be achieved or harm to be avoided that counts, not some good or harm in an abstract sense. Until the drafter knows why the client wants the document, what purpose it is supposed to serve, and what problems it is expected to resolve or prevent, the drafter cannot begin to serve the client's needs.

Sometimes, the client's objectives are obvious and relatively simple: to sell a house, to form a partnership, or to empower someone to act on the client's behalf. The drafter can usually accomplish these objectives without much probing into motives. Other times, the drafter must look beneath the veneer of a stated objective and discover what impels the client to want this. A client may want to establish a trust for her son. If the client desires this because the son is a spendthrift, the drafter might set up the trust in one way. But if the son is mentally disabled, a different kind of document might be appropriate. Whatever the objective, it will affect the structure and substance of the trust agreement.

Discovering the legislative client's underlying purpose is even more important—and sometimes more difficult. Legislators tend to think in terms of specific instances and will assume that a prohibition or requirement is always the most appropriate solution. Legislation drafted from that perspective is usually ineffective in the long run. The drafter's function is to help the legislator think more broadly in terms of the harm to be prevented or the good to be achieved and also to consider approaches other than prohibition or requirement. A statute banning minors from driving personal watercraft or jet boats might be an appropriate response to a constituent's specific problem involving the annoying teenager across the lake. But if the underlying concern of the legislative client is really boating safety, then the drafter should suggest a more comprehensive statute. The stated objective might also be better met with mandatory training and licensing. The drafter must know what the ultimate objective is before the drafter can intelligently address the problem.

Exploring objectives with the client is discussed in more detail in Chapter 7, section A.

B. IDENTIFY THE AUDIENCE

The primary audience of a document is always the client. First and foremost, the drafter's responsibility is to that client. This is the bedrock on which drafting ethics is based. If the document must be drafted with careful attention to many technical details, then the drafter must have the knowledge and skill to do that. But the drafter must also have the ability to explain what all of it means to a client who may lack any experience in this type of transaction.

The drafter must also recognize that other people will use the document, in a variety of different ways. Unless the drafter knows this audience, anticipates their sometimes conflicting uses, and protects the client as necessary, the drafting venture will be a failure. For example, a simple contract for the sale of a house may well satisfy the desires of the seller-client and also those of the buyer. Yet, the closing attorney, who essentially represents the mortgage company, may find some of its provisions unacceptable. Audience identification is discussed further in Chapter 7, section B.

C. EXPLORE THE BROADER LEGAL AND FACTUAL CONTEXT OF THE DOCUMENT

Drafters cannot be myopic. They must have a bird's-eye view of the entire legal and factual landscape that will surround the document to be drafted. This vision influences both the form and the content of the document and will also prevent the document from having unintended consequences.

For example, the legal context of a heavily regulated industry, such as a public utility, is radically different from that of the sale of a house. A long-term supply contract that might be perfectly adequate for one could prove disastrous for the other. The drafter need not be an expert in every area of the law. But the drafter should have a wide exposure to as much substantive law as possible—enough to recognize potential problems and pitfalls, as well as the ability to master whatever substantive details are necessary to integrate the drafted document into that legal landscape without creating conflicts and unintended consequences.

Legal context is also important to the legislative drafter. The drafter of a new criminal provision must understand how the prohibition fits into the broader scheme of criminal law and procedure within both that jurisdiction and similar jurisdictions. Statutory drafters must also know the existing law on the subject being legislated and draft within that context. If legislation on the same subject already exists, the drafter must determine if it needs to be repealed, amended, or reconciled with the legislation being drafted. Consider the example of a state legislator, who, upon receiving many complaints about the number of defamation suits brought against employers as a result of unfavorable employment references, drafted legislation creating a limited immunity for this. The immunity was broader in some respects and narrower in others than the immunity already available at common law. The legislation, however, did not indicate whether it replaced or merely supplemented the common law. The legislator reportedly admitted later that he had forgotten the common law already recognized an immunity. This unfamiliarity with the existing law created a totally confusing body of employment-related defamation law in that state.

Similarly, the drafter must discover and fully understand the factual context of the transaction. One cannot draft a construction contract without knowing something about the construction business, accepted practices within that industry, and the tacit assumptions that guide the enterprise. Certain areas of the law have become specialty areas, with lawyers often limiting their practice to that area, not only because the law is extremely complex, but also because practice in that area requires an extra-legal knowledge of the factual context within which these laws operate. Only the specialist can hope to master both the substantive law and become sufficiently familiar with the facts to practice in this area effectively.

Legislative drafters must also fully understand the totality of the complex web of behavior the statute is going to regulate. Without that understanding, the statute is apt to have unforeseen and sometimes unintended consequences. A securities regulation drafted by someone who does not fully understand the securities market, the specialized vocabulary of securities brokers, and the history and reasons for a practice that is now being subjected to regulation will probably be inadequate to the task at hand and either fail to promote the good or prevent the harm intended. Determining the legal and factual context of a document is discussed further in Chapter 7, section C.

Similarly, a drafter should be sure to give readers enough context or background information to easily understand the various details you supply—including how those details fit and why they are important. By the time you are ready to draft a document you will have analyzed all of the facts and issues and become thoroughly familiar with them. Remember that your reader is not as familiar with these facts and issues. Thus, recitals can be used in contracts and instruments to provide context for the specific detailed, operative provisions that follow. The same is true of legislation.

D. RESEARCH THE LAW

Eventually, the drafter's focus must shift from the general legal landscape to the law that is going to bear directly on the document being drafted. Private documents like employment contracts, corporate charters, and wills are heavily impacted by substantive law. A particular provision may be required, prohibited, or merely authorized. Or, the law may require that a particular provision appear in a particular format. The law also determines the meaning of the words that are used and the legal consequences of the substantive provisions. The drafter must know all of this and draft accordingly.

Technique and style count for nothing if the content is substantively deficient.

The rules that apply to legislative drafting, are more limited, and usually consist of constitutional provisions that dictate both the form and the substantive contents of legislation. It is not uncommon, for example, for state constitutions to require that titles contain particular information, to prescribe the exact wording of enacting clauses, and to limit each bill to a single topic. The legislative drafter must know these things. At the local level, state law may affirmatively prohibit certain kinds of ordinances. Drafters of state and local law must also be aware of the federal law of preemption.

At the substantive level, both the federal and state constitutions are full of limits on what the legislature may do. Thus, the legislative drafter needs to be familiar with the prohibition against ex post facto laws and bills of attainder, with the requirements of due process, with the equal protection notions of over- and under-inclusion in the creation of regulated classes or categories, with the ever changing scope of the First Amendment, and with a host of other constitutional provisions. How the law impacts directly on the drafting process is discussed in Chapter 8.

E. DETERMINE SUBSTANCE

What does a drafter need to include in a contract for the sale of a house or an ordinance establishing a teenage curfew? The answer to that question lies in a blend of the drafter's legal knowledge and experience, plus the client's desires. The contract drafter will know that some provisions are essential for the document to be valid, while others are extremely important in protecting the client's interests. Conversely, some provisions may be affirmatively illegal. Beyond that, substance is determined mainly by what the client wants. The client, however, may be unaware of the possibilities, thus shifting the responsibility back onto the drafter to educate the client. Checklists, both commercial and drafter-prepared, play an invaluable role here.

Similarly, in drafting legislation, the drafter will know that some provisions would be unconstitutional or inconsistent with a law emanating from a higher authority. The drafter's experience may also suggest that a particular provision would be unenforceable or ineffective for some other reason. Beyond that, however, substance is again something for the client to determine.

General principles regarding the substance of both private-and public-law documents are discussed in Chapter 9.

F. GET THE FACTS

Once the drafter and the client agree generally on what will go into the document, the drafter must then get down to the specifics. In a contract of sale, the identity of the goods and the price are easy to determine. But providing the specifics of a plant manager's duties under an employment contract may be something else altogether.

Similarly, the legislative drafter must address all the troublesome details of the statute. Who will be subject to the statute? Who will enforce it? What are the penalties? Where does a person file the application for an exception? These matters are important but sometimes hard to elicit from legislative clients, who are often content to let the drafter decide.

G. IDENTIFY THE PROPER LEGAL AND FACTUAL CONCEPTS

The drafting process has thus far moved from the general to the specific. The process has been one of analysis—breaking the whole down into its component parts, both legally and factually. The conceptualization stage reverses that process. It involves a process of synthesis—building the components back up in a different form. This synthesis is accomplished principally through the use of concepts.

First, in moving toward the realization of the client's objectives, the drafter must choose from potentially competing legal concepts. Will the client's purposes be better served if the other contracting party is conceptualized as an independent contractor or an employee? Should the conduct that legislation is going to prohibit be conceptualized as a crime or merely a civil wrong? Those legal concepts have different legal consequences.

Second, the drafter must conceptualize the facts in a manner consistent with the client's objectives. Here, the drafter has three sets of choices:

- **General versus specific.** Will the document address a broad category, "domesticated animals," or something more specific, "dogs"?
- **Vague versus precise.** Will the document require that something be done within a "reasonable time," or within "10 days"?
- **Abstract versus concrete.** Will the document focus on an abstract result, "the inducement of fear of physical injury," or something more concrete, "a threat to hit another with a club"?

These conceptual alternatives are discussed in Chapter 10.

H. DEVELOP AN ORGANIZATION

Most well-drafted contracts follow a standard organizational format. The same is true of statutes. Other documents—like wills, corporate charters, and partnership agreements—also have fairly standard formats. Within these broad parameters, the drafter still has considerable discretion over how to organize the substance of the contract or statute. Making the correct organizational choice involves the process of division, classification, and sequence.

Division involves splitting the subject matter of the document up into subcategories. A rational division follows three rules: (1) the subcategories must be mutually exclusive; (2) when combined, the subcategories must equal the whole; and (3) the division must be based on one consistently applied principle. Dividing the student body of a law school into 1st year, 2nd year, and 3rd year is a rational division. Dividing it into 1st year students, women, and people over 5′7″ tall violates all three rules.

Classification involves putting each provision in its proper subcategory. This sometimes involves a difficult choice. A provision dealing with the return of the security deposit could go in the section dealing with rent or in the section dealing with the termination of the lease. The key is to group similar provisions together and to put specific provisions where a reader would most likely expect to find them.

Sequence involves the order in which the subcategories are presented. This can range from an essentially chronological sequence to one based on the relative importance of the subcategory.

It is essential to a well organized document that the drafter place familiar information before new information. Placing familiar information before new information is similar in purpose to providing context before details—ensuring easy comprehension by the reader. The first step is to first make sure you familiarize your reader with important information you will use and build on later in the document.

Principles of organization are discussed in Chapter 11.

I. WRITE THE DOCUMENT

This is probably the easiest part of the drafting process. From a linguistic perspective, the drafter is concerned with these matters: (1) avoiding ambiguities, (2) rules or style and usage, (3) definitions, (4) terms creating legal consequences, and (5) format.

1. AMBIGUITIES

Ambiguity is the cardinal sin of legal drafting. Ambiguity exists when a provision is capable of two or more mutually inconsistent meanings. Unlike vagueness, which merely involves some uncertainty at the margin and can be employed purposely to great advantage, ambiguity is always bad. Drafters who deliberately uses ambiguity to deceive or mislead the other contracting party are engaging in suspect (if not outright unethical) conduct that may ultimately harm rather than help the client, since courts generally construe ambiguities against the party that created them.

Ambiguity comes in three forms. Contextual ambiguity exists when one provision says one thing and another provision says the contrary. Semantic ambiguity arises out of the use of words with multiple meanings. Syntactic ambiguity arises out of the order in which the words are used and how they are punctuated. These three forms of ambiguity are discussed in Chapter 12.

2. RULES OF STYLE AND USAGE

The drafter's rules of style and usage are designed not only to avoid ambiguity, but also to promote consistency, brevity, clarity, simplicity, and professional tone. Although all legal writing shares those objectives, they are the essentials of good drafting. These rules are discussed in Chapter 13.

In some areas of the law, a document must use a specific term of art to accomplish the intended result. This is true, for example, with respect to will drafting and conveyances of real property. Also, particular language is, or should be, used for creating definitions and specific legal consequences. Apart from that, however, there are very few magic words that must always be used in drafted documents.

3. DEFINITIONS

Definitions are powerful tools, capable of making the drafter the master of the language rather than being constrained by it. Definitions also promote both clarity and brevity. The drafter, however, must construct definitions with care. The linguistic difference between "means," "includes," and "does not include" is enormous, and the choice of one term over another can radically alter the substance of a document. Definitions are discussed in Chapter 14.

4. TERMS CREATING LEGAL CONSEQUENCES

Drafted documents create rights, duties, privileges, immunities, conditions, authority to act, and other legal relationships. Different words are used to create each of these legal relationships. They include "shall," "shall not," "will," "may," "must," "is entitled to," "is," "represent," "warrants," and others. The difficulty is not in matching the right word with the intended consequence. Rather, the difficulty is in deciding which legal consequence to create. Would it be better to make something a "right" or a "privilege"? The two are significantly different. Or should something be made a mere condition rather than a duty? Again, each has very different legal consequences. These terms are discussed in Chapter 15.

5. FORMAT

The physical arrangement and appearance of a drafted document is more important than one might think. Look into a United States Statutes-at-Large volume from the late 1800s or resurrect from a firm's client files a contract drafted in the 1920s. What you may see is a gray mass of page after page of sparsely paragraphed, dense prose without any bolded headings or subheadings. These documents are a nightmare to read. They should not be. A drafted document should be easy to read, easy to use as a reference, and easy to understand. Ample white space, numbered lists and enumerations, leader dots, tabbing and indentation, and numbered and captioned headings and subheadings all promote these objectives. These and other formatting techniques are discussed in Chapter 16.

J. REVIEW THE DOCUMENT FOR SUBSTANCE AND STYLE

Following the drafting process just discussed will produce a document that is still perhaps only 90% of what it should be. At this point, it will certainly look final and complete, but that appearance is deceptive. The document must still endure a top-to-bottom, left-to-right review and revision. The drafter must ensure that the document includes everything the client wants, in addition to anything that the law requires. The document must be tested to determine if it will meet the client's objectives. Deficiencies of structure and style must be identified and cured. Typographical errors must be eliminated and the revised version proofread yet another time. Then, perhaps, the document is ready to be submitted to the client. The process of document review is discussed in Chapter 17.

K. POST-EXECUTION MONITORING

As long as a drafted document has operative effect, the drafter is responsible for it to some extent. Changes in the law and in the client's situation often require changes in the document. The drafter should monitor the document during its lifetime and, within the limits of professional ethics discussed in Chapter 5, advise the client if changes are necessary.

L. 25 CONTRACT DRAFTING CONSIDERATIONS THAT COMPRISE A PHILOSOPHY

1. A person of reasonable intelligence who knows nothing about the transactions should be able to understand the transaction after one reading of the contract. This is the standard that we should strive to attain in drafting contracts.

2. Attorneys often function as sales people. We are advocates for our clients, whether we are practicing in the courtroom or not. When drafting a contract, we are persuading the other party to sign

now and to perform voluntarily later. When drafting, we plan ahead to persuade a court to enforce the contract if the other party does not comply.

3. Think like an attorney, but try not to sound like an attorney.

4. It is easier to resolve problems before they happen than after they happen. In drafting contracts, we need to anticipate problems and provide solutions.

5. There is no such thing as a perfect document. There are bad documents, good documents, and better documents. Every document can be improved.

6. Our goals are precision and clarity.

7. Concepts should be arranged in a logical order.

8. The answer to most questions about whether a provision is needed is: "It depends." It depends upon the facts and the client's needs for this particular transaction.

9. Easy reading is the result of hard drafting. Easy drafting is the result of hard thinking.

10. Every paragraph, sentence, and phrase should have a unique purpose.

11. We should constantly ask, "why?"

12. The person who drafts the contract has a significant advantage over the person who reviews the contract. Subtle refinements can be included by the drafter that are easily overlooked by the reviewer.

13. Never change your language unless you wish to change your meaning. And always change your language if you wish to change your meaning.

14. The use of definitions or defined terms enables us to simplify and clarify and can even prevent inadvertent changes of language. Defined terms also help the contract to be gender-neutral.

15. Defined terms carry the extra baggage of the generic meaning of the words used. Careful selection of defined terms can help clarify the contract and persuade the reader.

16. When using a form or a prior document, never leave in a provision because you do not understand its purpose. Never take out a provision because you do not understand its purpose. First, figure out its purpose. Then, determine whether it should be retained, deleted, or modified.

17. Technology enables us to dramatically improve the quality of our documents and the efficiency with which we produce them. Technology also enables us to make mistakes faster than we have ever been able to make them before and memorialize them forever.

18. The appearance of a document affects its credibility. Neatness counts.

19. Use:

(a) "will" to state a future fact,

(b) "shall" to state an obligation,

(c) "may" to state an option or a right, and

(d) "must" to state a condition precedent.

20. Use the present tense when stating continuing obligations.

21. Use the active voice because it more clearly identifies the actor.

22. Use gender-neutral language.

23. Say it once. Say it clearly. Save it.

24. Your work needs to be cost effective for your client.

25. Your client usually cannot make money unless you find a way to make the deal work. Be a deal maker, not a deal breaker, and you will add value to the transaction for your client. Identify your client's business goals and then choose the correct structure for the transaction, which may be one that your client has not thought of or used before.

PART II

PREPARATION AND PLANNING

CHAPTER 7
GETTING STARTED

The first three steps of the drafting process involve understanding the client's objectives, knowing the audience, and appreciating the legal and factual context in which the document will operate. These three steps are closely related, as they provide the foundation on which everything else is built.

A. DETERMINE CLIENT OBJECTIVES

A drafted document is not an end unto itself; it is merely a means to an end. Documents of the same general type—wills, for example—may have radically different objectives, depending on the client. The cookie-cutter drafter who does not appreciate this potential for difference among clients is not likely to produce a document that fully meets the client's needs.

Contracts—good contracts—are not solely the product of legal knowledge and skill. They are also the product of business and practical knowledge—*do not leave your common sense at the door to the law school or law firm.* This business and practical knowledge will be used to interpret the contracts, especially in jurisdictions where a weak form of the parol evidence rule is in force. As a result, this knowledge is needed in order to initially draft a good contract. Hence, it is critical that counsel understand the client's business, its goals, and the forces that drive the enterprise. This will enable the drafter to produce practical, precise documentation that will properly allocate risk between the parties, provide a legal mechanism for exchange and redress for shortfalls in performance, and stand up to interpretation and enforcement in litigation when everything has broken down.

1. THE BASIC QUESTIONS

The questions the drafter needs to ask of every client can be expressed in several different ways. All of them relate to the client's objectives, motivations, and purposes.

- **Why** do you want to give your son a general power of attorney? **Why** do you want to make it illegal for a person to keep or own more than three dogs within the city limits?
- What **purpose** is this exclusive dealership agreement supposed to serve? What is the **purpose** of requiring residents to remove their trash cans from the street within six hours after pick-up?
- By establishing a trust for your granddaughter, what **good** are you trying to provide for her and what **harm** do you want to protect her from? By making it illegal to operate car washes on Sunday, what **good** do you intend to promote and what **harm** do you intend to prevent?
- What **experiences** have you had with this particular type of transaction? Did it go smoothly? What made it work? What went wrong? What **experiences** have you had with

this particular problem? What are the desirable aspects of the activity that the legislation should either encourage or leave alone? What exactly were the undesirable aspects that should be corrected or prohibited?

2. HOW THE INFORMATION IS USED

The information these questions elicit will dictate both the form and content of the drafted document. Knowing the client's objectives, the drafter can move toward them in the most direct and efficient manner and not clutter the document with provisions irrelevant to those objectives.

Suppose a member of a county council says to the part-time county attorney, "A strip club has opened up out on Highway 647 and I want you to draft an ordinance dealing with this problem." Wait. What exactly is *the problem*? What is the ultimate objective? Consider the possible alternatives and how they affect the drafter's response to the request.

- **Suppression of purportedly immoral conduct.** If this is the objective, then the drafter's job is to define the prohibited conduct in a constitutionally sufficient manner and prohibit it.
- **Impact on neighboring residential property values.** If the location of this type of establishment (rather than the intrinsic nature of the enterprise is the problem), then

the drafter should probably approach it from a zoning perspective.

- **Connection with alcohol.** The county council member may feel that "adult" entertainment and alcohol are a bad combination. If so, the drafter would want to address the problem from a liquor-licensing perspective.
- **Noise, lights, traffic, and parking concerns.** If this is the problem, the drafter may want to avoid the constitutional problems entirely by broadening the regulation to include establishments other than strip clubs.
- **Competitive or economic pressure.** The county council member may be under pressure from less controversial drinking establishments to eliminate this form of competition. If so, the drafting would want to approach the problem from an economic perspective.

Sometimes the specific document the client requests is not the document the client needs at all. A client may ask a lawyer to draft a living will when what this person really needs is durable power of attorney. The drafter cannot know that without making the basic inquiries. Likewise, a legislator's objectives may already be the focus of another statute, with the problem being one of inadequate enforcement rather than the lack of a basic prohibition. If so, the drafter needs to suggest an appropriate solution, such as increased funding for enforcement.

3. OBJECTIVES FROM A VARIETY OF PERSPECTIVES

In addition to asking these questions directly, the drafter can also address the client objective inquiry from a variety of other perspectives.

a. Other Parties to the Transaction

Although the drafter typically drafts on behalf of one of the parties to a contract, with that client's objectives being preeminent, the drafter must also keep the other party's objectives in mind. After all, the client's threshold objective is to obtain this other party's assent to the contract or legislation. The client's ultimate objectives are often limited accordingly. Put differently, the client's relevant objectives are the attainable objectives. The drafter must make the client understand that.

In counseling the client in this regard, the drafter may discover that the client really has no desire to contract at all. The proposed contract, rather, will serve some ulterior purpose. For example, a person who is under a duty to bargain with another person but who has absolutely no desire to contract with that person may propose a contract whose terms are patently unacceptable. Or a legislator may want to propose legislation, not in anticipation of it being passed, but rather to serve as political window dressing. The preparation of such documents is game-playing, not drafting in the true sense of the word.

b. Scope of Anticipated Use

The client's intended use of the document is also important. If the document will be used between two named parties and the objective is limited to regulating the transaction between them, then the focus can be limited accordingly. But if the client's objective is to use the document in many transactions, with different parties, each having slightly different circumstances, then the focus must be broader to cover all the possibilities. The drafter of a standard lease agreement that will be used in a large apartment complex must anticipate and deal with all the rental issues that might arise from renting to a wide variety of tenants (differing in occupation, age, marital status, children, pets, and the like). The garage apartment lease agreement between Aunt Maude and her nephew Calvin will have a more limited and focused objective.

Similarly, legislation that is intended to affect a limited and discrete class of persons or transactions will be drafted with a different set of considerations in mind than legislation with a wider anticipated impact.

c. Multiple-Client Objectives

Determining client objectives is more complicated when the client consists of more than one person or entity. A three-person partnership may decide that it wants to subcontract some of its operations. Partner

A may want to save on production costs, Partner B believes a subcontractor can do the work better, and Partner C is looking at the tax advantages. Before the drafter can hope to produce a suitable contract, the drafter must tell the partners that their objectives differ and may even conflict. If the drafter can accommodate all three objectives, and everyone understands why the document might contain provisions totally irrelevant to their particular interest, fine. But if a conflict develops—for example, the higher quality that Partner B seeks is going to conflict with the lower cost objective of Partner A—then the drafter must simply tell the client to work it out.

A similar problem exists when drafting on behalf of a corporation. Accounting may have one objective, Sales may have another, and Research & Development a third objective. For some purposes, a married couple is treated as a single legal entity. Again, however, the individual components of these collective entities may have differing objectives. But until the client becomes of one mind about its objectives, by either consensus or resort to higher authority, the drafter cannot proceed any further.

Finally, the most difficult multiple-client problem arises when two persons purport to share a common objective, but actually have conflicting interests they do not fully realize. Between buyer and seller, the common objective might relate to the sale of a car at a certain price. Between a tortfeasor and an injured person, it is an amicable settlement. But beyond a generally shared objective, the specific interests of the parties are apt to differ appreciably.

Legislative drafters face equally difficult multiple-client problems. The drafter who works for a legislative drafting service usually drafts statutes at the request of an individual legislator, who is the client. But the legislative drafter may also be on the staff of a committee, with each member having a slightly different agenda. A consensus may exist over the need for a statute creating liability for sales of alcohol to already intoxicated patrons, but the legislator who is an active member of Mothers Against Drunk Driving may have one objective in mind, while another who is beholden to the Tavern Keepers Association may have another. Whose objective does the drafter attempt to serve? An attorney in private practice drafting proposed legislation on behalf of a consortium of business interests may face similar dilemmas.

4. EVALUATING CLIENT OBJECTIVES

The drafter's role in evaluating the client's objectives is limited. The general rule is that the client's objectives are the client's business; the drafter's business is to accomplish them. This rule is subject to three exceptions.

First, if the client's objective is illegal or fraudulent, then the drafter cannot produce a document accomplishing that result. However, this rule is easier to state than it is to apply. A contract for murder is one thing; the merger of two companies, possibly resulting in the creation of an illegal monopoly, is quite another.

Second, the drafter has an obligation to point out the other legal ramifications that achieving a particular objective might have. For example, the client's immediate objective might be to obtain total operational control over a particular business entity. Even if that particular transaction is not itself illegal, on a cumulative basis it may pose an antitrust problem for the client in the future.

Third, depending on the nature of the relationship, the drafter should be sensitive to and warn the client of objectives that, when achieved, would frustrate other, more important client objectives. A stringently drafted company policy on taking sick leave might serve the narrow objective of correcting sick leave abuse, but it might be inconsistent with a broader objective of creating good employer-employee relationships. If appropriate, the drafter should advise the client of this. Similarly, it is not unheard of in legislative politics for opposing factions to reach a truce of sorts, under which both sides tacitly agree not to introduce legislation on a particular matter. If the drafter prepares and the legislator introduces legislation in violation of this truce, the result may be retaliatory legislation that is definitely not consistent with the legislator's objectives. The savvy legislative drafter will advise the legislator of this.

In sum, the drafter is more than a thorough planner, investigator, and writer. The drafter is also a counselor to the client, in the highest sense of the word.

B. KNOW THE AUDIENCE

The client is the primary user of the drafted document. But drafted documents are nearly always read and used by a wide variety of people, often for different purposes. This is the audience of a document. The drafter should identify each member of this audience and draft with their varying uses in mind.

1. IDENTITY OF THE AUDIENCE

Assume, for example, that the owner of a piece of commercial property wants to have an office building constructed on the site. The owner asks a lawyer to draft a construction contract. The client's purposes and those of the other potential users of this document can be summarized as follows:

- The **owner** will first use the contract, with attached plans and specifications, to solicit bids from contractors. Later, the owner will use it to monitor the contractor's performance and determine the owner's duty of payment.
- The **mortgage company** will use the contract in evaluating whether to make a construction loan.
- The **zoning or building commissioner** will use it in determining whether to grant a building permit.
- The **potential contractors** will use it in formulating their bids.

- The **winning contractor** will also use it to determine exactly what must be done—when, where, and how.
- Potential and actual **subcontractors** will also use it in making bids and performing their portion of the work.
- **Assignees of rights** and **delegatees of duties** will use it to determine the scope of their rights and duties.
- The **bank** will use it to determine when and whether to issue progress payments.
- The **architect** will use it to determine whether to issue a certificate of completion.
- If litigation ensues, **opposing counsel** will use it to prove or disprove breach.
- The **judge** or **jury** hearing the case will use it to determine liability and damages.

2. CHARACTERISTICS OF THE AUDIENCE

The drafter must not only consider the identity and purposes of each potential user of the document, the drafter must also consider the personal characteristics, dispositions, and attitude of each user. The tone, style, terminology, and layout of a document may radically differ, depending on whether its users will be unsophisticated consumers lacking an opportunity to bargain over the terms or lawyers and officers of two large corporations.

The drafter must also take into account whether the various users are going to be friendly or hostile to the interests of the client. For example, although the beneficiary of a will is usually friendly, the disinherited son certainly will not be. Thus, the disinheritance provision should be drafted with special care. Drafters also need to keep the "reader in bad faith" in mind. A contract might be perfectly adequate for regulating the relationship between two parties who are dealing with each other on a good faith basis. But if the drafter suspects that the other party might later discover a strong economic incentive for getting out of the contract, then the drafter should go over the document with a fine-toothed comb—looking for vagueness, anything that is even remotely ambiguous, substantive terms that are left to implication, and other possible loopholes.

The drafter must also recognize that courts are users of legal documents that may be hostile to some kinds of contracts and contracting parties. Contracts of adhesion may not be enforced at all; contracts are construed against the party who drafted them; insurance companies, banks, large corporations, merchants, and employers may also be targets of hostile contract interpretation. Courts also scrutinize some types of statutes very closely, such as those purporting to deprive the court of jurisdiction.

3. ACCOMMODATING THE VARIOUS AUDIENCES

Accommodating multiple audiences and purposes is often a difficult task for the drafter. What the lawyer-audience wants and needs in the way of precise legal language, the lay-user audience finds stuffy and incomprehensible. A subject matter that must be quite detailed to satisfy the needs of one audience may need to be more general to satisfy the needs of another. The dilemma is not easily resolved. All the drafter can do is exercise sound discretion, always keeping the client's interest foremost in mind.

Occasionally, a drafter may conclude the document is intended to have too many people within its audience, each with divergent characteristics and inclinations that cannot be accommodated. Thus, rather than a tri-partite contract between Able, Baker, and Carol, the drafter may decide to create two bilateral contracts—one between Able and Baker, efficiently using terms of art and working from a prior history of business dealings; and another contract between Baker and Carol, but one that avoids trade jargon and the existence of a shared set of assumptions about what each party is going to do.

C. DETERMINE THE CONTEXT OF THE DOCUMENT

Drafted documents do not exist in a legal vacuum. The drafter cannot simply research only the law that impacts directly on the drafted document or obtain from the client only the specific facts that will be incorporated into the terms of the document. The drafter must fully appreciate the broader legal and factual environment in which the document is going to function.

1. LEGAL CONTEXT

Basic contract law aside, the broader legal context will vary appreciably from contract to contract. For example, a contract in the heavily regulated securities industry may be perfectly legal and effective when viewed in isolation; however, when it is put in the context of other legal requirements and constraints on the conduct of the parties, it may not accomplish the desired objective. Also, contracts involving performance in a foreign jurisdiction often fail their purpose simply because the drafter did not fully understand the broader legal context in which the document was to operate.

Similarly, if the case law evidences a growing hostility toward a particular type of governmental action, for example, regulatory takings under the Fifth and Fourteenth Amendments, and the legislative drafter does not appreciate this legal environment, then the legislation may ultimately fail, even though at the time of its enactment it apparently met all the controlling tests. A drafter more sensitive to the trend might have drafted the legislation, accomplishing essentially the same objective, in a slightly different manner.

Another kind of legal context that the drafter must accommodate relates to the other contracts the client may have with either the other contracting party or third parties. The new contract must mesh with the existing framework, or the existing framework may need to be revised.

For example, an employer should not enter into an employment contract with an individual who is subject to a covenant-not-to-compete with their former employer. Doing so may subject the new employer to a suit for inducement of breach of contract. It may never occur to the employer-client to inquire about this, but the drafter should. And if the prospective employee is not forthcoming with the information or seems duplicitous, particularly in an industry where such covenants are standard, then the drafter should inquire of the former employer (with the client's consent). And if this employer is not cooperative in providing that information, then the drafter should consider including a warranty and indemnity clause in the contract, where the employee warrants no existing legal impediments to the contract and agrees to compensate the employer for any losses as a result of a breach of the warranty.

Similarly, a drafter preparing an exclusive dealing contract for a client should make sure that this client does not have an exclusive dealing clause buried in a contract with another party. Clients can be totally ignorant of what they have agreed to in various contracts.

One of the problems with American legislation is that it usually does not follow the code format of civil law countries. The codes of federal and state law are often more like individual statutes that legislative councils and codifiers have attempted to put together into a coherent form. Thus, in American law one may find several different statutes, enacted at different times by different legislatures, dealing with the same broad topic. For example, there are over 50 separate federal statutes that deal with some aspect of the employer-employee relationship. Many of these statutes were apparently enacted in total disregard of the existing fabric of federal employment law. The result is an enormously complex and litigation-ridden set of statutes. The Equal Pay Act and the Civil Rights Act of 1964 suffer from this deficiency, because they both prohibit wage discrimination on the basis of sex.

To avoid this, the legislative drafter should first attain a bird's eye view of the entire corpus of relevant law—the statutes themselves and the cases construing them—dealing directly or tangentially with the subject matter at hand. This will then provide the legal backdrop against which the new statute can be drafted. First, an understanding of the full legal context will enable the drafter to avoid duplicate legislation. Second, new legislation should mesh with existing legislation like the gears in a car's transmission. This is possible only if the drafter is aware of what the existing gears look like and how they function.

2. FACTUAL CONTEXT

Documents regulating business, commercial, and significant social transactions are predicated on a number of often unstated assumptions and usages of trade. For example, in the field of commercial real estate, rents are quoted in annual rent per square foot of space. Thus, "$120/ft" is really $10/ft per month. Someone outside the industry with experience only in residential leases as a tenant may not know the convention, which the parties assume everyone knows, and could mistakenly draft the lease with rent twelve times higher than the parties intend. The drafter must be familiar with the prior practices between the parties, the usages of the trade in general, and the whole factual context in which the regulated activity is going to occur. This enables the drafter to know generally what should be included in the document.

It would be difficult, for example, to draft a contract between a movie producer and director based solely on information elicited directly from either or both the parties. At the minimum, such an undertaking would require knowledge of how movies are made, the traditions of the producer-director relationship, the tacit assumptions of producers and directors about their duties and responsibilities, and the expectations of each. Similarly, the lawyer who does not understand the complex traditions of the construction business is ill-equipped to draft a document regulating that process. The standard practice of incorporating various trade-association-approved provisions, which are notoriously ill-drafted, is itself enough to drive the neophyte drafter to distraction—because they are based on factual assumptions about trade practices that the drafter is unfamiliar with.

Drafters inexperienced in a particular field are at a distinct disadvantage. This is not the kind of information that can be acquired from a book. However, the beginning drafter can do one of three things. First, the drafter may have to decline the representation, on grounds of lack of competency to draft the requested document. Second, the drafter may choose to associate with a more experienced attorney and count it as a learning experience. Third, if the factual context is not too arcane, the drafter may be able to learn enough by asking the client to provide a tour of the plant or business, to explain what is happening and why, and perhaps to discuss the business in general. Most clients are flattered by this interest in their affairs and attention to detail, provided the lawyer does not bill excessively for it.

Legislative drafters are usually more aware of the need to become immersed in factual details than are drafters of private law documents. This, ostensibly, is the purpose of the extensive hearings that Congress and the state legislatures hold on pending legislation. Legislation at the city and county level, however, often suffers from a lack of factual understanding by both the drafter and the public officials. This may be due to a lack of resources, political pressure to do something quickly, or an ignorance of the need for such information. The conscientious local legislative drafter should, however, do whatever is practicable to find out exactly what the facts are before drafting ordinances involving them.

CHAPTER 8
DRAFTING WITHIN THE LAW

The law has an enormous effect on both the form and substance of drafted documents. Constitutions, treaties, executive orders, statutes, court rules, ordinances, administrative regulations, common law rules, and case law form a maze through which the drafter must pass to reach the desired client objective. Some paths lead to a dead end. Some paths are shorter than others. Some paths are blocked by gates that can be opened only with the right key. The drafter should not try to get through the maze by trial and error, but should see the maze from above, plot the path in advance, and obtain the necessary keys. In other words, the drafter must know the law.

A. FORM

Back in 1977, the New York General Assembly passed a law requiring that certain consumer contracts be "written in a clear and coherent manner using words with common everyday meanings" and that the document also be "appropriately divided and captioned by its various sections." This marked the beginning of what became known as "Plain English" legislation. Other states followed, as did Congress. Today, a plethora of statutes and regulations require, in a variety of ways, that consumer contracts be readily understandable by the average person. The requirements of the law in this area are complex, overlapping, and sometimes contradictory. However, many of them mandate satisfaction with a numerical readability index. One of the more common readability indexes is discussed and illustrated in Chapter 17.

Plain English requirements are not limited to consumer contracts. President Carter once issued an ironically obtuse Executive Order requiring that federal regulations be written in understandable form. Department of the Defense regulations also require that equipment manuals written by government contractors satisfy a certain readability formula.

Other laws affect the form of drafted documents in more specific ways. For example, UCC § 2–316 requires that a disclaimer of the warranty of merchantability be conspicuous. To determine what this means, however, the drafter must consult the case law. Some state statutes prescribe the exact wording and typeface for living wills; the slightest deviation may result in the document being declared void. The Federal Trade Commission's "Holder in Due Course Rule" mandates that a specific notice appear on all consumer credit contracts.

Compliance with these statutes can be tricky. For example, the Uniform Arbitration Act requires that "[n]otice that a contract is subject to arbitration pursuant to this chapter shall be typed in underlined capital letters, or rubber-stamped prominently, on the first page of the contract. . . ." That seems straight-forward enough. However, one state court of appeals held that the requirement was satisfied by a notice that was typed in all-capital, boldface letters, in a font somewhat larger than that used for the text of the contract, but not underlined. The court held that the purpose of the requirement was to make the notice prominent and that this notice satisfied that purpose. The court rejected a bright-line, literal interpretation of the statute, noting that the following notice would not satisfy the statute if it were construed in that fashion:

> **This Contract Is Subject To Arbitration Pursuant to § 15–48–10 of the South Carolina Code of Laws (1976).**

This notice would fail because it has no line drawn under it and is not in all-capital letters. On the other hand, the court suggested that while the following would satisfy the literal requirements of the statute, it would not serve the intended purpose and might, thus, also be ineffective because of the size of the type.

> THIS CONTRACT IS SUBJECT TO ARBITRATION PURSUANT TO § 15–48–10 OF THE SOUTH CAROLINA CODE OF LAWS (1976).

The court rejected a literal interpretation that would disallow the first notice but allow the second one. Although the court's approach is reasonable, it flies in the face of express statutory language—which is what a drafter should be entitled to rely on, but in this instance could not.

B. MEANING

Bridging the gap between form and substance are the words that the law requires a drafter to use to achieve a particular legal result. Some of these are true terms of art. A word can qualify as a legal term of art in three ways:

First, some specific words must be used to accomplish a particular result; no synonym will do. For example, to be negotiable under UCC § 3–104, a note must be payable to "order" or "bearer." "Merchantability" is also a term of art since that specific word must be used when disclaiming it under UCC § 2–316.

Second, some words are terms of art in the sense that they serve as an abbreviation for a complex legal concept that would take many words to describe fully. In estate law, "*per stirpes*" is such a term. Similarly, the term "Rule of 78" refers to a formula for computing the portion of a finance charge that has been earned at different times during the life of a bank loan. One statutory version of this rule is a confusing 185 words long. But people in the industry know exactly what it means and it can even be used in consumer documents.

Third, some words are terms of art in the sense that the legal meaning is materially different from the conventional meaning. For example, "insane" has a legal meaning that is considerably narrower than its colloquial meaning.

The drafter must be aware of all three forms of terms of art and use them appropriately.

The drafter must also be aware of the legal meaning of other words, even though they are not terms of art. For example, a drafter in a particular jurisdiction might discover that the courts have construed the word "street" as not including alleys, but that "public way" covers both. The drafter would then choose the word that matches the intent of the client.

Occasionally, a statute will impose a meaning on words that are used in certain types of documents. A New York statute, for example, dictates the meaning of a real estate mortgage acceleration clause that is worded in a certain way.

C. SUBSTANCE

The law also affects the substance of drafted documents.

1. PROHIBITION

Laws frequently prohibit certain contract provisions. Some prohibitions are express. For example, the UCC prohibits a contract provision that limits consequential damages for personal injuries resulting from defective consumer goods. Other prohibitions are implied. For example, a person cannot effectively contract away statutory rights if the statute serves a broader public good or if the purpose was to limit this exercise of freedom of contract. An employee cannot contract away the minimum wage and maximum hour protections of the federal Fair Labor Standards Act.

Similarly, the law may prohibit certain agreements by rendering them unenforceable. For example, the law makes employment termination agreements releasing the employer from possible violations of the Age Discrimination in Employment Act unenforceable unless the agreement contains certain specific provisions. Contracts that are unconscionable or contrary to public policy are similarly prohibited, in the sense that the courts will not enforce them.

In some cases, however, a violation of the prohibition may result in civil or criminal liability. The Uniform Residential Landlord and Tenant Act prohibits certain provisions and imposes a penalty of three months' rent on landlords who knowingly include these provisions in lease agreements. Wage Payment statutes frequently provide treble damages for violations.

Private law documents can also operate by way of prohibition on other private law documents. For example, a contract may effectively prohibit the delegation of duties or assignment of rights under that contract. The drafter needs to know this before attempting to draft a document purporting to do either.

2. REQUIREMENT

Some laws affirmatively require that certain things be done or that they be done in a certain manner. The Statute of Frauds requires several types of contracts to be evidenced by a signed writing. State laws frequently require that wills be witnessed by a designated number of persons. UCC § 6–107 requires that bulk transfer notices contain certain specified terms.

Usually, the failure to satisfy these requirements only makes the document unenforceable. A drafter's failure to adhere to some legal requirements, however, will also result in civil or criminal liability for the client. For example, under some state laws, the failure to include a notice of latent defects in a contract for the sale of a house will subject the seller to liability.

3. PERMISSION AND AUTHORIZATION

Some laws merely permit or authorize things to be done or allow them to be done in a certain manner. The National Labor Relations Act allows employers and unions to include in collective bargaining agreements a provision that requires employees to become union members as a condition of employment—a requirement that would otherwise be illegal. Another provision of the statute, however, also authorizes states to outlaw these provisions—a power they would not otherwise have.

Often, the permission is subject to a condition. Living will statutes create the authority for a person to order the cessation of life support systems, but only if specific conditions are satisfied.

4. DENIAL OF PERMISSION OR AUTHORIZATION

Some laws limit the power or authority of certain persons or entities. For example, a not-for-profit corporation lacks the authority to engage in certain activities. The drafter of a not-for-profit corporate charter needs to have those limits well in mind.

Similarly, the law generally limits the power or authority of minors to contract.

5. OTHER CONSEQUENCES

The law may establish other consequences the drafter must be aware of. For example, conflicts law determines which state's substantive law controls the interpretation and enforcement of a contract made between individuals living in different states. The drafter needs to know which state's law will control under these conflicts rules and what that law provides, in contrast to the law of the other state. The drafter may then want to alter the result through a choice-of-law provision in the contract. Drafting estate documents is also heavily influenced by the tax consequences of distributing the assets of the estate one way rather than another.

6. IMPLIED TERMS

The drafter needs to know what terms the law will imply if a document is silent on a particular point. Statutes frequently contain "unless otherwise agreed" provisions that supply omitted terms for certain types of contracts. UCC Article 2, chapter 3 contains innumerable gap fillers—terms that will be read into a contract for the sale of goods if the contract is silent. Even in the absence of a statute, if a court determines that the parties intended to create a contract, the court may imply a term to keep the transaction from failing. For example, if a contract is silent on the time for performance, the courts will often hold that performance must be within a reasonable time rather than find an absence of assent over what is usually regarded as a critical contract term. Likewise, under both the common law and the UCC, custom and usage are implied terms of many contracts. The courts will also imply a covenant of good faith and fair dealing in certain types of contracts.

A drafter should never deliberately rely on implied terms to fill gaps in a document. Although the drafter may know that these terms will be implied, the parties may not. This may come as an unpleasant surprise later, when the client angrily tells the drafter that this is not what was intended. And even if the implied term is consistent with the client's desires, the better practice is to make it express.

D. CREATING LEGAL CHECKLISTS

A drafter cannot count on remembering everything that the law prohibits, requires, permits, denies authority for, attaches meaning to, or implies. Thus, the drafter's knowledge must be systematized. A legal checklist is an indispensable drafting tool.

Unlike the factual checklist that draws information primarily from the client, a legal checklist draws from the drafter's knowledge of the law. Often, the legal checklist and the factual checklist will be consolidated, for the drafter's benefit, into a single document. The legal aspect of the checklist, however, should cover all the categories of substantive law discussed above. The drafter should create this checklist during the research step of the drafting process. If the drafter anticipates doing this type of document on a recurring basis, then the checklist should be retained in an active file and kept current as the statutory and case law changes.

E. DRAFTING WITH STATUTORY LANGUAGE IN MIND

Tracking specific statutory language is sometimes necessary to achieve a desired result. For example, a merger or "integration" clause is designed to trigger the operation of the parol evidence rule, by stating that what is written represents the final and exclusive terms of the agreement between the parties. An effective merger clause can be drafted in a variety of ways. However, in a contract for the sale of goods, a drafter should follow the language of UCC § 2–202, which is a statutory form of the parol evidence rule:

> § 2–202. Final Written Expression: Parol or Extrinsic Evidence (emphasis added)
>
> Terms with respect to which the confirmatory memoranda of the parties agree or which are otherwise set forth in a writing **intended** by the parties as a **final expression of their agreement** with respect to such terms as are included therein may not be contradicted by evidence of any prior agreement or of a contemporaneous oral agreement but may be explained or supplemented
>
> (a) by course of dealing or usage of trade (Section 1–205) or by course of performance (Section 2–208); and

> (b) by evidence of consistent additional terms unless the court finds the writing to have been intended also as a **complete and exclusive statement of the terms of the agreement**.

The purpose of a contractual merger clause is to make the parties' intent express. The parties may intend to do one or all of three things: (1) to indicate that the writing is the final expression of the terms stated, thus achieving a partial integration; (2) to also indicate that these are the only terms the parties have agreed to, thus achieving a full integration; and (3) to indicate that no other agreements of any kind exist with respect to the subject matter of this transaction or, alternatively, to indicate that they do.

The merger clause below incorporates the critical language of the statute (in bold print above) with commentary enclosed in square brackets:

> The parties **intend** for the terms contained in this written contract to be the **final expression of their agreement** with respect to these terms [achieving *partial integration*]. The parties also **intend** for this written contract to be the **complete and exclusive statement of the terms of this agreement** [achieving *full integration*]. No other agreements of any kind exist between the parties [excluding even contracts that might otherwise be deemed *collateral* and thus not subject to the parol evidence rule].

Alternatively, if the parties do not intend to deny the existence of other contracts, then the drafter would replace the last sentence with the following:

> This contract is not **intended** to supersede or negate the existence of a separate contract of this date giving Buyer an option to purchase additional Widgets on the terms and conditions stated in that contract.

Sometimes, however, precisely tracking the statutory language in this manner will get the drafter into trouble. For example, federal law permits employers and unions to include in collective bargaining agreements provisions that "require as a condition of employment **membership** [in the union] on or after the thirtieth day following the beginning of such employment or the effective date of such agreement, whichever is the later. . . ." A contract provision worded in just that fashion would, however, be illegal. This is because the courts have construed the term "membership" as meaning nothing more than the payment of a pro rata share of the union's expenses as the bargaining representative—a meaning that is vastly at odds with the literal and colloquial meaning of the term. The courts have also held that a union commits an unfair labor practice if it fails to inform employees about the limited nature of their obligation to the union. A union security provision that merely tracks the statutory language would not provide the necessary information, since an employee would normally construe the term "membership" as requiring actual membership.

F. VALIDATION CONCERNS

Historically, a written signature was needed to prove that a party had unequivocally manifested his or her assent to a contract. But what is adequate to satisfy this requirement when a contract is assented to via electronic means? The answer to this question is not always straightforward. Accordingly, federal legislation was enacted in an attempt to provide some clarification as to what satisfied the traditional authentication requirement when contracting via electronic channels.

In 2000, the Electronic Signatures in Global and National Commerce Act, 15 U.S.C. §§ 7001 to 7006, 7021, and 7031, validated the practice of recognizing either a clicked "I accept" button on an Internet site or a faxed or e-mailed signature for contract law purposes. The E-Signature Act provides that:

> Notwithstanding any statute, regulation, or other rule of law . . . , with respect to any transaction in or affecting interstate or foreign commerce: (1) a signature, contract, or other record relating to such transaction may not be denied legal effect, validity, or enforceability solely because it is in electronic form; and (2) a contract relating to such transaction may not be denied legal effect, validity, or enforceability solely because an electronic signature or electronic record was used in its formation.

15 U.S.C. § 7001(a).

An electronic signature is defined by the Act as "an electronic sound, symbol, or process, attached to or logically associated with a contract or other record and executed or adopted by a person with the intent to sign the record." 15 U.S.C. § 7006(5). Examples include clickwrap (but not browsewrap) licenses, signing a name or the letter "x" to an e-mail, using passwords or credit card numbers to establish the intent to conclude a transaction, biometric authentication such as fingerprints or handprints, and digital signatures.

Complying with E-Sign will negate a statute of frauds defense based on federal law and state law statute of frauds defenses if the state in question has not enacted The Uniform Electronic Transaction Act ("UETA"). E-Sign thus gives electronic contracts validity equal to that of paper contracts.

CHAPTER 9

DETERMINING SUBSTANCE

The substantive content of a drafted document is subject-matter specific. A residential lease, a contract for the sale of an airplane, and a statute prohibiting extortion would probably contain few, if any, identical substantive provisions. Yet, the content of all drafted documents is similar at a very high level of generality. Content derives from two sources: the law and the exigencies of the transaction. The types of provisions that are discussed below all derive from one or both of those sources.

A. TYPES OF PROVISIONS

The substantive provisions in both private law and legislative documents are of four types: (1) required by law; (2) going to the essence of the transaction; (3) extremely important; and (4) optional.

1. REQUIRED BY LAW

Statutes frequently require that certain provisions be included in documents relating to a particular regulated transaction. The absence of a necessary provision will often deprive the document of its legal efficacy. For example, a waiver of possible age discrimination claims must inform the employee of the right to consult with an attorney before signing. The waiver is otherwise legally ineffective. State constitutions often require that certain prefatory language be included in all statutes. Without that language, the attempted legislation has no legal status. The purpose of legal checklists is to ensure that all the required provisions are included in the document.

2. GOING TO THE ESSENCE OF THE TRANSACTION

Although not affirmatively required by law, some provisions are inherently necessary to the legal efficacy of the document. A criminal statute that contains no sanction, express or implied, is a nullity. Similarly, an alleged contract for the sale of unidentified and unidentifiable goods suffers from a fatal indefiniteness that makes it unenforceable. Unless the parties have expressly agreed to what the courts regard as all the essential terms of that type of contract, a court is likely to conclude that no enforceable agreement yet exists. Courts disagree over what is truly an essential term and modern courts will go out of their way to supply them by implication. For example, under UCC Article 2, the only essential elements to a contract for the sale of goods are the identity of the parties, the identity of the goods, and the quantity. Everything else can be supplied by the Code's gap fillers—including price, delivery terms, payment terms, warranties, and other seemingly fundamental provisions.

The drafter, however, needs to know what the essential provisions are and ensure that the document contains them.

3. EXTREMELY IMPORTANT

Beyond knowing what is mandatory or intrinsically essential, the drafter must also rely heavily on prior experience and judgment in assessing what else should be included in a drafted document. For example, one drafter might believe that a buyer's interests are better protected by a termite clause in the form of a warranty by the seller, rather than a clause that merely makes a satisfactory inspection report a condition of the duty to buy. Another drafter might believe otherwise. Similarly, one experienced legislative drafter might feel strongly that administrative enforcement of a particular type of statute will be more effective than enforcement through civil or criminal litigation, while another equally experienced drafter might think that private-party enforcement is best.

The extremely important provisions of a document will usually become readily apparent if the drafter uses the process described in Chapter 7—Getting Started. Major contingencies that must be dealt with will surface with the proper "what if?" questions. In addition, the drafter must be alert to the friction points of the transaction—a borrower's required representations and warranties, for example—and deal with them clearly and concisely, thereby eliminating them as sources of controversy later on. This information can then be put into the form of a substantive term checklist, discussed below.

4. OPTIONAL

Beyond what is required, essential, or strongly recommended, the substantive content of the document is mostly up to the client. The drafter's function is to make the client aware of all the possibilities. An employer desiring to have an employment contract drafted may have never considered whether, in addition to the usual terms, the contract should contain a prohibition against releasing confidential information to competitors. The legislative drafter should likewise review similar legislation in other states for ideas about what might be included in a statute of the type being drafted.

In either case, the drafter's responsibility is to cover all the possibilities, to determine the client's wishes, and to incorporate those desires into the drafted document.

B. SUBSTANTIVE TERM CHECKLISTS

Even the most inexperienced drafter can research the law to determine what terms are mandatory or essential—and reduce this information to a legal checklist. New drafters, however, frequently feel inept at identifying the extremely important provisions or covering the full range of optional provisions. Substantive term checklists provide the necessary help.

1. COMMERCIALLY PREPARED

Formbooks frequently contain annotated drafting checklists that not only identify possible substantive provisions, but also discuss the legal and practical significance of these provisions. With respect to each possible provision, a good checklist will also indicate the specific facts the drafter should elicit from the client. These checklists are often the most valuable aspect of these books. The model forms themselves may be poorly drafted.

The legislative drafter can obtain similar checklist-type assistance by looking at legislation in other jurisdictions and model acts, such as those prepared by the National Conference of Commissioners on Uniform State Laws, the American Law Institute, and the Council of State Governments.

2. DRAFTER PREPARED

The conscientious drafter will use a formbook checklist only as a point of departure and will add to and refine this base as experience dictates. Although the specific content of a checklist will depend on the nature of the document, all checklists focus on the same general categories of information. In developing a base or generic checklist covering these areas, the drafter should begin with the "who," "what," "when," "where," and "how" questions that journalists are instructed to ask when investigating a story. From the answers to these questions, the drafter can then determine what provisions should be in the document and what specific information the drafter needs from the client.

The most commonly drafted documents fall into several categories: contracts, legislation, estate planning, and business organization. Since contracts and legislation are the broadest of the four categories, covering a multitude of substantive matters, examples of the journalistic technique for creating checklists will be drawn from those areas rather than from the other two more specialized, substance-specific areas. The same basic principles, however, apply there as well.

Who. The primary "whos" to a contract are the parties. Ensure that names and addresses are correct. If one of the parties is a business entity, use the full legal name, "Wateree Properties, A Limited Partnership," rather than the name the business usually goes by, "Wateree Lake Properties." In addition, determine the legal status of the parties.

- Is either party a minor? If so, it may be better to select an adult, say a parent or guardian, to contract on behalf of the minor. In some states, court approval of contracts for non-necessaries is a prerequisite to enforcement. In some states, the minor's representation that he or she has attained the age of majority will estop them from later seeking to avoid the contract due to minority.

- Do both parties have the mental capacity to contract? This can be a sensitive matter, but if one of the parties is hospitalized or in a nursing home, then the issue needs to be resolved clearly. If in doubt, obtain a doctor's certificate or use witnesses—even if the document does not otherwise require them.

- Is either party operating as an agent? If so, identify the principal and ensure that the agent is acting within the scope of the delegated authority.
- If one of the parties is a business entity, ensure that it is properly formed and has the capacity to sue and be sued in its own name.
- Ensure that the person negotiating or signing on behalf of the business entity has the authority to do so. Indeed, this information should be obtained even before negotiations begin. It is pointless to negotiate an agreement with a person who lacks the capacity to bind the entity. Drafters should also be particularly careful when the client is a domestic corporation that is negotiating a contract on behalf of a foreign subsidiary; the subsidiary may be immune from suit in this country. This is, at least, something the drafter needs to determine in advance.

A collateral "who" relates to the persons the other contracting party may have contracted with in the past. A lawyer drafting a contract between a movie-producer client and the author of a book should inquire about the author's contract with the publisher, to determine if the movie rights have already been contracted away.

The "whos" of legislative drafting are also important. Here, the basic question relates to the appropriate level of generality. Should the protected class be limited to persons classified as "employees"?

Or, should it include anyone with a contractual relationship, which would cover "independent contractors"? Should the subject of a prohibition against odometer tampering be universal? Or, should it be limited to persons who are in the business of selling automobiles?

Sometimes, the intended "who" of a statute has no known prior referents. Through the processes of conceptualization and definition, the drafter creates a new category of "whos." Some stalking statutes, for example, carve out a definition of an offender that has no precedent.

What. This goes to the essence of the document. In drafting a contract, the critical "whats" are as follows:

- Determine the subject matter of the contract. If it is a contract of sale, obtain a description of the goods or realty. If it is a contract for services, find out exactly what is to be done.
- Because most contracts involve an exchange of money, determine the amount and method of payment. In some contracts, the payment provisions are complicated. Find out exactly who is going to pay for what.
- Inquire about possession and delivery.
- Identify exactly what else each party will be obligated to do under the contract. Walk through the transaction with the client, identifying every occurrence or non-occurrence that is necessary to bring the transaction to a successful conclusion.

- Inquire about external events the client assumes will or will not happen. If necessary, protect the client by making the occurrence or nonoccurrence of the assumed events conditions precedent or subsequent. This is where the drafter must play a relentless game of "what if?" What if that brand of pipe is unavailable? What if the builder inadvertently uses a different brand? The drafter needs to resolve these "what if" questions and incorporate the client's desires into the document. The client may want to designate an alternative brand or declare that the contract is voided. Or, the client may want a provision declaring that even an inadvertent use of a different brand a material breach, thus justifying termination of the contract.
- Find out what the client would like to do in the event of breach. This will affect the remedies section of the contract.

The "what" of legislative drafting requires a thorough, probing examination of the harm that is to be corrected or the good that is to be promoted. In 1935, Congress believed that certain forms of employer opposition to unionization were causing strikes which were detrimental to the economy. But figuring out exactly what to prohibit or require involved a closer examination of the problem. Eventually, in the National Labor Relations Act, Congress decided to prohibit employer interference with union activities, company-sponsored unions, discrimination against union members, and a refusal to recognize and bargain with a majority union. Those are the "what's" of that legislation, designed to prevent a particular harm. In 1948, Congress determined that certain union conduct also contributed to the harm the NLRA was trying to prevent, so the statute was amended accordingly. The point is that the relevant harm or good is always the progenitor of the more specific "what" provisions of a statute.

The legislative drafter with experience in a particular field can be an enormous asset to the legislator who perceives a harm to be corrected or a good to be achieved, but who is either indifferent to or ignorant of the various ways of accomplishing that objective.

When. All contracts, expressly or implicitly, contain a time element.

- Find out how important time is to the client. If it is very important, include a "time is of the essence" clause or word the time requirement so that it is both a promise—the breach of which results in damages, and an express condition—the failure of which excuses further performance by your client. If time is important but not critical, find out what the client will accept as excusable delay and consider the possibility of reasonable liquidated damages for other delay.

- Generally, the law is that time is *not* of the essence, and delayed performance will be found to constitute substantial performance rather than material breach unless the parties make time for performance an express condition. Thus, the inclusion of the venerable "time is of the essence" clause is often buried in the boilerplate section of the contract. Those "magic words" seem to fix the problem, right? No. Cases are legion in which courts have found that they are "mere boilerplate" and are contradicted by other words in the contract or the party's actions. The solution lies in making it clear that the parties agreed that time of performance was material to their deal. To this end, reference to the time of performance, and perhaps the reason for its importance belong in the recitals of the contract. A covenant of timely performance also belongs in the consideration section along with all the important economic terms. Finally, an argued consequence of untimely performance such as notice, an opportunity to cure (or not), and a remedy should be provided. A drafter cannot handcuff a determined judge or jury, but can make it harder for them to dismiss a boilerplate five-word statement of such an important condition.

- Even if the contract involves only a one-time exchange, find out when performance is to occur. Do not rely on the "reasonable time" gap-filler. Some contracts (like construction contracts and complicated real estate transactions) will contain many time periods within which certain things must be done.

Review the duties of each party and determine if performance should be subject to a specific time limit.

- Time-of-payment should be dealt with expressly. Often a contract will identify the goods and the sale price but will leave the timing of the exchange unclear. It then becomes a question of who must make the first move and whether a formal tender is necessary. Resolve all these uncertainties.
- Duration is an important term in transactional and long-term contracts. It could be measured by a date certain, the occurrence of an event, or notice by one or either party.

Time periods are also important in statutes. Perhaps the most critical time relates to when the statute goes into effect. Indicating the effective date of the legislation is not enough. This only tells the courts when they must consider the effect of the legislation; it does not tell them what the effect is intended to be. The effect can vary.

For example, substantive legislation that prohibits, allows, or requires certain conduct could apply either to pre-or post-effective date conduct. Whether such retroactive legislation is constitutional is another matter. Similarly, legislation that changes procedures or available remedies could apply to all causes of action, whether a lawsuit has yet been filed or not; only to cases filed as of the effective date or later; only to cases filed after the effective date; or only to causes of action arising after the effective date. Other permutations of effective date, operative events, and procedural posture are also possible. Courts are notoriously inconsistent in how they deal with these reference points when trying to resolve effective date issues. The legislative drafter should think about these matters and provide for them expressly rather than leaving them up to time-consuming and expensive judicial determination.

Another important "when" involves the limitations period under a statute. The omission of limitations periods in statutes has caused an enormous amount of unnecessary litigation. The courts are forced to imply one. For example, a federal law without a statute of limitations is said to borrow the appropriate state-law statute of limitations, raising the question of which statute of limitations that might be.

Statutes that require a person to do something within a specific time period should indicate whether compliance is jurisdictional or whether it is subject to waiver, estoppel, or tolling.

Where. In drafting contracts, find out where the agreed performance will occur. Is delivery to be at the seller's or the buyer's place of business? Location is extremely important in construction, service, and employment contracts. It will often affect the scope and nature of the duties to be performed. For example, a contractor who agrees to provide service and maintenance on "all Acme Company trucks" would be dismayed to discover later that some of them are at a facility 3,000 miles away. Incorrectly identifying the geographic coverage of an exclusive dealership agreement could result in liability to the dealer already awarded that territory.

Most statutes cover the entire geographical jurisdiction of the enacting entity. But some statutes are location-specific. State hunting regulations may vary from county to county, depending on the nature and size of the game population.

How. Many clients think only in terms of the end result. The client wants an office building built. The drafter, however, must force the client to think about how the client wants to accomplish this. Does the client intend to be its own general contractor and hire subcontractors? Or will the client hire a general contractor? What construction methods will be used?

The drafter should play an active role in helping the client resolve the "how" questions. This is where the drafter's experience, knowledge of the law, imagination, and ingenuity come into play. For example, the client may be planning to get into the business of acquiring, developing, and managing mobile home parks. The drafter needs to consider, and discuss with the client, all the various ways the business entity might be set up. Would it be better to do this under the umbrella of a single corporation? Or, for tax and liability purposes, should the land acquisition and ownership be done by one corporation and the management by another? Or would some other form of business organization serve the client's needs best, such as a limited partnership?

The "how" of legislative drafting is chiefly a matter of policy, and this is one type of policy where the drafter's input and active involvement is appropriate. The legislative client may know what harm needs to be addressed or what good should be promoted. But, prohibiting or requiring the relevant conduct is not the only or even necessarily the best option. Doing it by prohibition might not work, since that could drive the activity underground. A requirement might be unenforceable. Rather, the more appropriate "how" might consist of the creation of alternatives, incentives, or collateral disadvantages. Discovering and exploiting these possibilities is the drafter's responsibility.

The drafter can create either a generic or a document-specific checklist by focusing on who the document covers, what the regulated conduct is, when various things will happen, where they will happen, and how the ultimate objective is to be achieved. If the document contains substantive provisions dealing with all these matters, then it is likely to be complete.

C. THE ELEMENTS OF A LEGAL RULE

Drafted documents, whether of the private or public law variety, can be conceptualized as a collection of rules. An effective rule has five critical elements that can be used to ensure that the drafted documents cover everything that it should, at least in a broad sense. The five elements of a rule are: (1) the person; (2) the conduct; (3) the object of the action; (4) the circumstances; and (5) the consequences.

1. THE PERSON

A rule must identify the person to whom the rule applies. The subject may be universal (everyone) or nearly so (everyone within a broad class).

- No person [universal] shall park within 15 feet of a fire hydrant.
- All subcontractors [universal within the class] are subject to the arbitration-of-disputes provision, ¶ 56(a).

Or a rule may be selective with respect to whom it applies.

- Only the Vice-President of Finance may authorize payments in excess of $10,000.

2. THE CONDUCT

A rule must identify the conduct that is being prohibited, required, or permitted. In the above examples, parking and using the arbitration-of-disputes provision are the relevant conduct.

3. THE OBJECT OF THE ACTION

A rule usually identifies an object of the action. This may be universal, in which case no further identification is necessary, or it may be limited.

- A person shall not destroy or damage the property of another [universal].
- The Fire Marshall shall investigate all reports of arson of a house of worship [limited] within 24 hours.

4. THE CIRCUMSTANCES

A rule often identifies the circumstances of the action. This may consist of when or where the command is operative.

- In Class II cities, the mayor may appoint the city attorney.
- After 10 days, Buyer may terminate the contract and recover fees paid.

Those rules limit the operative place or time. Or the circumstances may consist of a condition that must be satisfied before the command is operative.

- If the Joint Appendix is more than 300 pages, it must be printed on both sides of the page.
- If Landlord provides 24-hour notice, Landlord may enter the premises for the purpose of showing it to prospective tenants.

Circumstances may also consist of an exception to the rule.

- Retail stores shall not sell alcohol on Sunday, except in counties that have approved these sales through a referendum.

5. THE CONSEQUENCES

A legislative rule prohibiting or requiring conduct must identify the consequences of noncompliance. This is sometimes called the "sanction." The consequences may be criminal liability, civil liability, forfeiture of goods, invalidity of a document, or ineligibility to obtain something.

- A person violating this section is guilty of a misdemeanor and shall be fined $100.
- Documents not bearing the notarized signature of two witnesses are void.

If the consequences of satisfying a requirement are eligibility for benefits, then the rule must identify specifically what they are.

- A person who is 65 years of age or older is entitled to enroll in Medical Plan C.

Legal consequences in private law documents are usually implicit in the terms used to create the consequence. If something is intended to create a right, then the legal consequence is that the right-holder may use the coercive power of the state to compel the person with the correlative duty to perform or to pay for the damages caused by non-performance. Sometimes, however, the drafter may want to make a legal consequence express.

- Because the vintage automobile that is the subject of this contract of sale is unique and no substitute is available on the market, if Seller fails to deliver or otherwise breaches, Buyer is entitled to a decree of specific performance.
- Contractor shall use only Reading brand pipe. Contractor's use of any other brand of pipe is a material breach. Owner may immediately terminate the contract and Contractor forfeits his or her right to payment.

In sum, if the rules in a drafted document identify the persons to whom the rule applies; the permitted, required, or prohibited acts; the object of those acts; the circumstances of the action; and the consequences of action or non-action, then the document will usually be substantively complete.

D. SUBSTANTIVE GAPS

A document that does not adequately deal with the who, what, when, where, and how of the transaction, or that does not contain all the necessary elements of a rule will nearly always contain substantive gaps. But substantive gaps can also emerge as a result of bad writing.

For example, "if [condition], then [consequence]" provisions can contain substantive gaps, (1) if the drafter does not make clear whether the condition is a necessary condition for the consequence to follow—"if and only if", or (2) if the drafter does not address what happens if the condition is *not* satisfied.

Another kind of substantive gap can arise when a contract or statute contains a list of ranges of time, price, or some other numerical element. Consider, for example, this statute:

> A person violating the speed limits established by this section is guilty of a misdemeanor and, upon conviction for a first offense, shall be fined or imprisoned as follows:
>
> (1) in excess of the above posted limit but less than 10 miles an hour by a fine of not less than $15 nor more than $25;

(2) in excess of 10 miles an hour but less than 15 miles an hour above the posted limit by a fine of not less than $25 nor more than $50 dollars;

(3) in excess of 15 miles an hour but less than 25 miles an hour above the posted limit by a fine of not less than $50 nor more than $75; and

(4) in excess of 25 miles an hour above the posted limit by a fine of not less than $75 nor more than $200 or imprisoned for not more than 30 days.

This statute covers speeds at 1–9, 11–14, 16–24, and 26+ over the posted limit. Although the statute prohibits driving at any speed over the posted limit, it does not provide sanctions when the driver is going exactly 10, 15, or 25 miles over the posted limit. That is the equivalent of not prohibiting driving at those speeds altogether. That is, in other words, a substantive gap.

One technique for discovering substantive gaps is through the creation of a flow chart of the document once it is in the initial draft stage. Creating a flow chart is discussed in Chapter 17.

CHAPTER 10

CHOOSING THE RIGHT CONCEPT

At this point, the drafter has some idea of what the client desires the drafted document to accomplish, understands what the law requires or prohibits in this regard, and has determined the substantive content. Translating all of this into written form requires the drafter to engage in conceptualization.

A. DEFINITION

A concept is the idea of something formed by mentally combining all its characteristics or particulars. Concepts exist only in the mind. They may be so narrowly conceived that they encompass only one known referent, something that can also be perceived by the senses, as in "the object upon which I am sitting at this moment." On the other hand, the broader concept of a chair encompasses something with four legs supporting a flat surface, with a back and often with arms, which people sit on. This concept thus encompasses an infinite number of referents, many of which may differ radically in their particulars. A chair designed by Salvador Dali, for example, would differ significantly from one fashioned by an Amish carpenter. Any individual chair is capable of being perceived by the senses, but the concept of "chair" is not.

B. THE IMPORTANCE OF CONCEPTS IN DRAFTING

Satisfying client objectives is the fundamental goal of drafting. The drafter's ability to think conceptually and to choose and express the correct concept determines how well that goal is met. Assume that the owner of a small, sophisticated, performing arts theater wants a contract for the purchase of seating. The drafter words the contract in such a way that the supplier can, without breach, supply the seating in the form of a mixture of beanbag chairs, benches, and bar stools. That drafter either failed to match the appropriate concept with the client's objectives or lacked the ability to express that concept in appropriate words. However impeccable the contract might be in form, organization, and style, the result is a total failure.

C. TYPES OF CONCEPTS

Concepts come in two types, legal and factual.

1. LEGAL CONCEPTS

The drafter can draw from many well-established legal concepts. "Just cause for termination," "negligence," "*per stirpes*," "consideration," "goods," "employee," "fraudulently," "agent," "corporation," and others all have established meanings. These concepts are often complex. Sometimes they are vague. But once the drafter fully understands the client's objectives, the drafter may be able to match those objectives with one of these legal concepts. The client, for example, may want to retain the services of someone to perform a specific task; this person will supply his or her own tools and will work without the need for client supervision. Here, the client's objectives match up with the legal concept of "independent contractor" rather than the concept of "employee."

Serving the client's objectives may sometimes require the drafter to consolidate several existing legal concepts into a new one. Thus, a legislative drafter addressing the phenomenon known as "stalking" may decide to define it in terms of a combination of the existing legal concepts of "threat," "invasion of privacy," and "assault." The resulting amalgam will eventually take on a conceptual identity of its own. But in the meantime, because it draws upon three well fleshed-out and understood doctrines, it should avoid constitutional vagueness problems.

Sometimes, however, the operative legal concept has no prior name or definition and one cannot be cobbled together out of existing concepts. For example, federal disability law defines a "handicapped individual" as a person who "has a physical or mental impairment *which substantially limits one or more of such person's major life activities*." That represented the creation of a new legal concept, the meaning of which continues to evolve.

Some new legal concepts are defined with a fair degree of precision—either by the legislature or, as is increasingly the case, by the administrative agency charged with enforcing the statute. Other times a legislature may choose to characterize a new legal concept in deliberately vague or open-ended terms, leaving it to the courts to work out the details. The Sherman Antitrust Act of 1890, for example, simply prohibits "unreasonable restraints on trade," and the courts have spent over 125 years giving meaning to the concept.

Private law documents may similarly require the use of old legal concepts in new ways or the creation of new legal concepts. A condominium developer, for example, may want to structure the relationship between the various owners in a way that is unconventional. The drafter will thus carefully define that relationship and give it a name.

2. FACTUAL CONCEPTS

The difference between the concept "objects that can be sat upon" and the concept "theater-style seating" is a critical one. Drafted documents deal with four kinds of facts: people, things, conduct, and events. In choosing or creating the factual concept that will best effectuate the client's intent, the drafter is faced with three sets of decisions with respect to those three types of facts: (1) determining the proper degree of generality/specificity; (2) determining the proper degree of vagueness/precision; and (3) determining the proper degree of abstraction/concreteness. In all three instances, what is proper depends on the client's objectives.

a. General Versus Specific

Words or word combinations are like boxes into which any number of specific referents can be fit. "Dakota, a Great Pyrenees-Labrador mix owned by Donna Looper" is a very small box into which only one referent will fit. "Dogs owned by Donna Looper" is a larger box into which Dakota, J.D., and many others would also fit. "Dogs" is a larger category yet, as are "domesticated animals" and "animals." Put differently, going from Dakota to animals involves moving from the specific to increasing levels of factual generality.

Determining what level of specificity/generality to use requires a keen and thorough understanding of the good to be achieved or the harm to be avoided. If the good or harm consists of more than one referent, then the drafter must know what all of them are. If all of these referents will fit into a recognized category or box, and if nothing else will fit into that box, then this is the level of generality at which the document should be drafted.

For example, the drafter of an animal control ordinance must decide what category of animals to include in the regulation. Although the county council member who requested the ordinance may be acting in response to a constituent's complaint about a particular dog, Dakota, getting into her trash, an ordinance drafted at that level of specificity/generality would probably be inadequate. Dakota is probably only one of many referents causing the type of harm the council member wants to prevent; and that harm may not even be limited to the trashing of trash cans. So, the category of "dogs" might not be the proper level of generality and the offensive conduct might also need to be expanded. For example, what about cats who spray and make smelly deposits in a neighbor's flower bed? Or pet rabbits who get into Mr. McGregor's carrot patch? If the activities of these animals are also part of the harm to be prevented, then the drafter will want to try to move to a higher level of generality. However, "domesticated animals" is too broad because it encompasses horses, cows, pigs, and many other animals that do not cause the kind of harm the statute is expected to prevent. And, unless the ordinance is intended to be a leash law, "running loose" might be too broad as the prohibited conduct.

Sometimes the specific referents the client has in mind have no previously recognized conceptual label such as dogs, cats, and rabbits in the prior example. Here, the drafter is required to create a new factual concept and give it a name. This is usually accomplished with a definition, a drafting technique discussed in Chapter 14.

Finding the proper level of generality is usually more of an issue in legislative drafting than in private-law document drafting. Legislation, by definition, deals with broad classes of persons and things. The matter also has constitutional significance. Unless the legislated category is a fairly close match with the harm to be avoided or the good to be achieved, the statute may be over- or under-inclusive, and would thus violate the Equal Protection Clause.

Private law documents, on the other hand, are usually more specific in their focus. A particular car is being sold or a specific individual is being hired. This is not always so, however. The contract duties of an individual, rather than being specifically listed, might fit nicely into a recognized category or higher level of generality, like "prepare and package the goods for shipment"—which, under the customs of the industry, means doing it in a particular way. Likewise, an employment policy that is intended to provide a particular benefit may specifically identify the individuals who are eligible for the benefit or, as more likely will be the case, it may identify them in increasing broad categories or levels of generality—managers and supervisors, first shift employees, or all employees.

Instead of drafting in terms of the appropriate generality, some drafters instead try to draft in terms of all the specifics that encompass the generality. This is bad drafting for two reasons.

First, the drafter may overlook something. In Dick Francis' novel *Banker*, the owner of a breeding stallion had, in a long list of specifics, insured the horse against almost every conceivable contingency capable of diminishing the horse's value as a stud. No one imagined that the horse might produce deformed foals, but it apparently did. No one was willing to use it for breeding and it was not insured against this total loss in value. As the owner aptly put it, "The policy had been too specific. They should have been content with something like 'any factor resulting in the horse not being considered fit for stud purposes.' "

Some drafters who are prone toward listing specifics try to avoid this kind of unintentional exclusion by adding a catch-phrase at the end, such as "and other similar . . . ," counting on the *ejusdem generis* rule of interpretation to take up the slack. This, however, only adds one bad drafting technique to another. It gives the courts, rather than the client, the power to determine inclusion or exclusion.

Second, drafting in terms of the appropriate generality is more efficient. Referring to "elected city officials" is shorter than listing them all, even if the list is complete. The following National Park Service regulation is a classic example of wordy over-specificity:

> § 50.10 Trees, shrubs, plants, grass, and other vegetation.
>
> (a) General injury. No person shall prune, cut, carry away, pull up, dig, fell, bore, chop, saw, chip, pick, move, sever, climb, molest, take, break, deface, destroy, set fire to, burn, scorch, carve, paint, mark, or in any manner interfere with, tamper, mutilate, misuse, disturb or damage any tree, shrub, plant, grass, flower, or part thereof, nor shall any person permit any chemical, whether solid, fluid, or gaseous, to seep, drip, drain or be emptied, sprayed, dusted or injected upon, about or into any tree, shrub, plant, grass, flower, or part thereof, except when specifically authorized by competent authority; nor shall any person build fires, or station, or use any tar kettle, heater, road roller or other engine within an area covered by this part in such a

manner that the vapor, fumes, or heat therefrom may injury any tree or other vegetation.

In other words, "Do not harm the plants."

b. Vague Versus Precise

A term is vague when its definitional lines are uncertain. Thus, it may be difficult to determine whether a specific referent is within the category in question. As any painting contractor can tell you, the term "red" is extremely vague. A particular color may seem red to one person, orange to another, and maroon to yet a third. The term "reasonable" is commonly used in commercial contracts, such as where one party is required to do something within a "reasonable time". The term, however, is also vague. Whether a specific unit of time is reasonable depends on the nature of the transaction, the context, the prevailing commercial practice, the past practice of the parties, and many other variables. A precise term, on the other hand, has fixed and easily identified definitional boundaries. "Red #567"—from the printing industry's standardized color chart, describes the color with precision, as does "twenty-four hours" with respect to a unit of time.

Vagueness should not be confused with generality. "Dangerous pit bullterriers kept within city limits" is vague (because of the terms "dangerous" and "kept"), but it is fairly narrow or specific with respect to the size of the class it covers (excluding non-dangerous dogs of this breed, other breeds, and dogs outside of the city limits). Conversely, "persons with a Texas driver's license" covers a large number of persons and is a high level generality, but it is also very precise. A term can be both vague and general. A standing-to-sue provision covering anyone "adversely affected" by an administrative regulation is both vague and general. Once the vagueness is resolved and some meaning is given to the term by the courts, this will also serve to delimit the size of the class or the generality of the term.

Vagueness should also not be confused with ambiguity, which refers to a term with mutually inconsistent or contradictory meanings. As discussed in Chapter 12, ambiguity is an unmitigated evil in drafting. Vagueness, on the other hand, may have certain advantages when employed deliberately.

First, using a vague term is sometimes the only alternative. If a right, duty, or condition is dependent on particular circumstances that are infinite in number, variety, and combination, no human drafter possesses the prescience to anticipate all of them. For example, a drafter would be guilty of over-precision by attempting to define a term like material misrepresentation with the same degree of specificity that one might use in defining a term like "regulated industry."

Second, even if further particularization were possible, a vague term may still be the preferred approach. Using vague terms cuts down on transaction costs. It would take a lot of thought, and thus drafting time and cost, to reduce the vague term, "the reasonable value of the goods and services provided," to a precise list of prices, particularly if the identity of the goods and services that are going to be provided is itself somewhat open-ended and the market value of these goods and services will vary over the term of the contract. Thus, it may be more efficient to assume that the parties in good faith will be able to agree on this later, as the need arises. Alternatively, the parties may want to agree in advance to a mechanism for resolving the vagueness, such as a neutral third party or a price index.

Indeed, at some point, the transaction cost of drafting with precision may be so high that the transaction does not occur. At the contract negotiation stage, the parties have a semi-adversarial relationship and are apt to bargain hard to achieve even the most minute of advantages. The greater the number of specific details the parties must bargain over, the more likely it is that they will be unable to reach an agreement. Stubborn disagreement over the precise content of some relatively inconsequential term or over how to resolve a contingency that may never even arise may become a deal breaker. The greater economic advantage of the transaction, to both parties, is thus lost.

The third advantage of vagueness is that in private law documents it provides the flexibility that is necessary to make the transaction work. A "reasonable time for performance" provision recognizes that different situations may call for different time periods. But once the hard bargaining is over and the contract is agreed to, a subtle shift often occurs in the relationship between the parties. It goes from being semi-adversarial to being collaborative. Consummating the transaction is now the objective of both parties, and they are not likely to let it be frustrated by minor disagreements over vague terms. Good faith and a little give-and-take by both parties can avoid that.

Fourth, in the statutory context, vagueness is often used deliberately to produce an evolving, almost experimental approach to the resolution of a problem. The legislature is content to paint with a broad brush, using intentionally vague terms and leaving it to the courts to determine on a case-by-case basis whether the facts fit within the coverage of the statute or not. This is unremarkable because the meaning of similarly vague common law rules is determined in an identical fashion. Perhaps the most fundamental of all deliberately vague documents is the United States Constitution, whose drafters deliberately avoided many specifics so as to achieve agreement and ratification, leaving many specifics within its vague provisions to be worked out over time through Constitutional litigation.

However, vagueness does have shortcomings as a drafting technique. Most of the disadvantages are simply the downside of the advantages. First, there is greater possibility for disagreement over the meaning of vague terms than precise terms. Despite the professed flexibility and good faith of the parties, sometimes these disagreements cannot be resolved short of litigation. Similarly, a legislature would be ill-advised to use vague terms when drafting legislation that is likely to be vigorously resisted by a significant segment of the population. Labor legislation, for example, is frequently drafted in vague terms. But the question of what is or is not within the scope of the legislation can have a profound financial impact on a business enterprise, which provides a great incentive to litigation. Hence, employment-related litigation has occupied both state and federal courts for many years, much of it relating to the fundamental meaning of the vague terms used in the statute.

Second, the legal drafter has a responsibility to protect and advance the interests of the client, whether that client is a single individual who desires a contract or legislator acting on behalf of the public. This responsibility carries with it the concomitant power to control the content and meaning of the document. This is not a responsibility and power that should be casually regarded. Whatever affirmative justification the drafter has for drafting with vague terms, this comes at the cost of surrendering the responsibility and power to determine document content and meaning.

In contracts, this is fine as long as the parties are willing to engage in on-going good faith negotiations over the administration of the contract. But if they are unable to do that, the drafter's ability to protect the client's interests turns on litigation rather than drafting skills. Similarly, the legislative drafter who insists upon vaguely worded statutes must be made to understand that these words will be construed by judges who may be hostile to the objectives of the legislation. Conversely, an overly zealous administrative agency may be impervious to the implicit compromises and tacit agreements as to the intended meaning of the legislation among groups with an interest in the legislation. In either event, the drafter and the drafter's client have lost control over the document and what they created may be a far cry from what they intended to create.

What emerges from this consideration of the pros and cons is that vagueness should be used only with conscious deliberation. The drafter should be sure that the advantages of using a vague term outweigh the dangers. Thoughtless or inadvertent vagueness, on the other hand, is inexcusable sloppiness in drafting.

Although a high percentage of English words possess some degree of vagueness, those most often used in drafting are:

adequate	available
approximately	best efforts
comparable	convenient
discretion	due care or diligence
excessive	good faith
immediately	material
necessaries	neighborhood
practicable	prejudicial
promptly	proper
reasonable	regular
remote	safe

satisfactory	serious
substantial	sufficient
suitable	temporary
undue	valuable

c. Abstract Versus Concrete

An abstract term is one that deals with a quality or result, while a concrete term relates to something that causes or manifests that quality or result. "Hard" is abstract; "steel" is a concrete counterpart.

A drafter should use abstractions cautiously, because they are more difficult for people to grasp. When encountering a word, people try to form a visual image of a tangible reality. "Washington Monument" evokes a mental picture of that specific structure. "Car" likewise easily evokes a mental picture of one of those tangible realities, although that image may vary from individual to individual. But the mind fuzzes over when it encounters "an object capable of being held in the hand that is often used to drive something that is straight, thin, and inflexible through or into two other hard objects for the purpose of holding them together." Eventually, the mind will figure out that this refers to a "framing hammer." Second, because abstractions are often fairly high level generalities, they are subject to the danger of over- and under-inclusion. In addition, since abstractions are also often vague, they are subject to all the drawbacks associated with that drafting approach as well.

However, factual abstractions are sometimes the best way to conceptualize and present the substance of a document. Two situations come to mind.

First, an abstraction can be used when this is the only way the client has identified the object of the document or provision—the good to be accomplished or the harm to be prevented. For example, a buyer's only concern might be that the seller package and ship the goods in a manner that ensures their safe and prompt delivery. The buyer does not care if they are packed in stout cardboard boxes, cushioned with foam pellets, and sent UPS; or wrapped in plastic bubbles, put in barrels, and shipped air freight. Rather, the buyer will be content to have the seller's duty stated abstractly: "Seller shall pack and ship the goods in such a manner as to ensure that they arrive at the place of delivery promptly and undamaged."

Second, an abstraction can be used when the specific, concrete referents are numerous, infinite in variety, and thus incapable of being listed with precision or completeness. For example, courts have taken the abstract approach to the problem of "hostile environment sexual harassment." Roughly speaking, they define it as any kind of conduct that a reasonable person of the plaintiff's sex would find offensive because of that person's sex. In other words, the offense is defined in terms of the abstract effect of the conduct rather than in terms of the conduct itself. A drafter attempting to codify this form of discrimination would likely adopt a similar approach.

D. CHOOSING THE RIGHT WORD TO REFLECT THE CONCEPT

Once the drafter has the concept in mind, the next task is to choose the right word to communicate this concept to the reader. This aspect of the drafting process is fraught with difficulty. The English language is notoriously slippery, and words often have multiple meanings. For example, the operative concept may be that of a small child or baby, so the drafter uses the term "infant." A court, however, may construe the term as referring to any minor. Similarly, to someone brought up on a ranch, a "large animal" would probably mean something like a horse or cow; but to a resident of Manhattan, it might include a Great Pyrenees-Labrador mix.

To ensure that the word matches the concept, the drafter should consult an English dictionary as well as a legal dictionary. However, in addition to the lexical and legal meaning of words, the drafter must also consider their conventional meanings. The Supreme Court once determined what it means to "use" a firearm in connection with a drug offense by relying on a linguistic study of how people actually use the word.

CHAPTER 11

ORGANIZATION

The drafter has determined the client's objectives, identified the full audience, mastered the legal and factual context in which the document will operate, decided with the client what to include in the document, and chosen or created the appropriate legal and factual concepts. The drafter now has a mass of data and insights that must be assembled into some kind of order. Organization consists of division, classification, and sequence.

A. DIVISION

Division involves creating the hierarchical categories into which the data is to be placed. In the document, they will appear as numbered and headed sections. Rational division is based on three rules: (1) mutual exclusivity, (2) total coverage, and (3) singularity of the principle of division. To illustrate these rules, assume a division that separates the class of "motor vehicles" into two subclasses, "Ford cars" and "red cars." Consider how that division violates all three rules.

Rule One—Mutual Exclusivity. The categories must be mutually exclusive, meaning no datum can fall into two or more categories. If the categories are mutually exclusive, then a particular provision can go in only one place. Where, then, would one put a red Ford Mustang?

Rule Two—Total Coverage. The categories together must equal the entire class; there must be nothing left over. Everything that the drafter wants to put into the document must have a place. But where in the motor vehicles classification scheme suggested above would one place a green Toyota Tundra? The drafter who cannot find a place in the divisional scheme for a particular provision often creates a new category, "miscellaneous," that ends up being full of minor, unrelated, substantive provisions. This is the sign of a bad divisional scheme.

Rule Three—Singularity of the Principle of Division. The division should be based on one consistently applied principle. Red cars and Fords are divisions based on two principles—color and make. This division would confuse a user of the document.

Within each category, the drafter should create as many levels of sub-categories as is needed—moving from the general down to each specific provision. Each sub-category should also follow the rules of division. For example, within the "cars" category, a drafter might create the following sub-category levels in descending order:

III. Cars

  A. Manufacturer

    1. Model

      a. Year

      b. Color

      c. Vehicle Identification Number

Alternatively, a numbers-only sequence of hierarchical headings can be used:

1. Primary Category
    1.1 Secondary Category
    1.2 Secondary Category
        1.2.1 Tertiary Category
        1.2.2 Tertiary Category
    1.3 Secondary Category
2. Primary Category
    2.1 Secondary Category
    2.2 Secondary Category

As in that example, the primary category and every sub-category should have an appropriate letter or number designation for easy identification and a descriptive heading—although that is sometimes omitted at the lowest level of division. For statutes and ordinances, the drafter must follow the rules or conventions of the jurisdiction in this regard. But the private law drafter has total discretion and should exercise it in the direction of more rather than fewer sub-categories.

If a category is going to have sub-categories, it must have at least two. Although often violated, this is not just an arbitrary rule. Its logical justification derives from the fact that a category is the sum of its parts. The category heading is simply a more generalized way of expressing what the various parts add up to. A well-organized outline provides information and insight about both (1) the individual components, indicating what they represent as a whole, and (2) the whole, indicating what it consists of. On the other hand, the following is a meaningless distinction or division:

I. Compensation

A. Salary

If the compensation under the contract is a salary of $80,000 a year and that is the whole of it, simultaneously giving it a broad designation, "compensation," and a more specific designation, "salary," is pointless. Call it one thing or the other and make a single category of it.

Headings should be carefully worded. The designation must accurately identify what is contained in that category. If each provision has been properly classified and put within a particular category, then these provisions will have a common denominator. Determine what it is and word the heading accordingly. The common denominator of base salary, commissions, incentive pay, and bonuses is that they are the compensation the employee will receive. Give the category the heading "Compensation", rather than something vague like "Employee Rights"—which also suffers from over-inclusion, since the employee will also have other non-compensation rights under the contract.

A correct description is important for two reasons. First, a reader looking for a particular provision in the contract will be able to scan the bolded headings and find the relevant provision quickly. If it is buried under a non-descriptive heading, finding it will be difficult and time consuming. Second, the wording of the heading may have legal significance. A court may refuse to enforce a disclaimer of warranties that is contained in a section entitled "SELLER'S WARRANTIES." And if a category is headed "Employee's Duties," this may make it difficult for the employer to later claim that the document created an independent contractor relationship rather than one of employer/employee.

Some state statutes that dictate the form and content of legislation contain a provision stating "headings are not part of the statute." This is designed to prevent the wording of a heading from having any legal significance regarding the interpretation of the statute. The legislative drafter, however, should not be indifferent to the wording of headings, since the average citizen may rely on them in trying to determine what the statute means, whether the courts do or not. Unfortunately, disclaimers of this kind also sometimes appear in private law documents. This should be regarded as an open admission that the drafter is either too lazy to find the proper words to describe a collection of provisions or lacks the linguistic competence to do so.

B. CLASSIFICATION

Classification involves putting each bit of information into its proper category and sub-category. If the drafter of a lease has created a category entitled "Limits on Occupancy," then a specific provision dealing with overnight guests should be included under that heading, not under one dealing with "Alteration of the Premises." Conversely, a provision prohibiting the replacement of ceiling fixtures should not be put in the "Limits" category.

The classification decision is more difficult if the drafter has fudged a bit in complying with the rules of division, especially the one requiring the sub-classes to be mutually exclusive. Indeed, no division can be completely airtight, and some items can usually fit into more than one category. For example, a prohibition against smoking at the worksite could go in an employment policy's Safety section or in its Employee Rules of Conduct section, depending perhaps on the purpose of the rule. In making classification decisions, the drafter must always keep the user in mind. If a user wanted to find a provision dealing with a specific topic, where would that person look first? That is where the provision should go.

In practice, division and classification are not two separate intellectual processes. Although a rough divisional scheme usually comes first, the process of classification will often reveal defects and may even suggest an entirely different scheme. Moreover, the division and classification rules reflect the ideal. Sometimes it is not practicable to follow them rigorously, especially when dealing with subsections. After all of the provisions of the document have been classified, the drafter may find an odd one that does not seem to fit anywhere. Rather than completely redo the division scheme and force it to a level of abstraction that is more confusing than useful, the drafter should include this provision in whatever section it is most relevant to. This is preferable to putting it in a "Miscellaneous" category.

C. SEQUENCE

The sequence of the major components of contracts is discussed in Chapter 2 and of statutes in Chapter 3. However, within the substantive components themselves—as distinguished from the definitions, recitals, preambles, housekeeping provisions, and formalities—several sequences are possible. The overall document may follow one general sequence, but the major sections may have their own internal logical sequence of a different variety. Whatever sequence the drafter adopts, the measure of its validity is the extent to which it helps readers use the document in the regulation of their affairs. The major sequential possibilities are as follows:

1. CHRONOLOGICAL

If the document will regulate a relationship extending over several phases, then the drafter can deal with the events in the order in which they are going to occur. The sequence of a construction contract, for example, could parallel the construction process itself. Similarly, the major divisions of a lease can be presented in roughly chronological order, as follows:

- **Pre-occupancy:** identity of the parties, identity of the premises, duration, rent, and other fundamentals.

- **Occupancy:** limits on use of the premises, landlord's right to enter for maintenance and repairs, noise abatement, and other matters relevant to when the tenant is in possession.
- **Termination:** condition of the premises, return of security, and other post-occupancy matters.

The headings of a chronologically-divided document should indicate what is happening in this order. Readers can better understand a complex document if it is organized by reference to the sequential actions of the various parties rather than to abstract legal classifications. Thus, rather than referring to "Revocation Rights," which is a legal concept, title it "Revoking the Contract," which puts the emphasis on the action.

2. IMPORTANCE

Within a category of related rules, a drafter might choose to present the most important ones first. For example, in an employment contract, salary is a very important term, while the employee's choice of make and color of company car probably is not. Unscrupulous drafters will sometimes put an extremely important provision that strongly favors their client at the end of a long document, following or included among a series of trivial provisions. In extreme cases of deception, usually involving consumer transactions, the courts have declined to enforce these provisions.

3. FREQUENCY OF OCCURRENCE

Provisions dealing with events that are likely to occur frequently during the transaction can precede those dealing with rare or episodic events. For example, in a construction contract change orders are a frequent occurrence; discovery of historical artifacts is not. That should dictate the order in which these matters are dealt with.

4. FAMILIAR BEFORE UNFAMILIAR

Some transactions are built around a familiar set of facts or events, with the rights and duties of the parties being fairly commonplace. A particular transaction, however, may move off into previously uncharted territory. To give the parties a shared point of departure, the drafter may choose to deal with the familiar provisions first and then move into the more novel aspects of the undertaking.

5. RULES BEFORE EXCEPTIONS

First state generally what a requirement or prohibition applies to. Then identify any exceptions. For example, a section of a harbor regulation might contain a long list of things that a vessel under way is required to do. This could then be followed with a list of situations where the general rules do not apply, such as in an emergency. Putting the exceptions before the general rule would only confuse the reader.

6. WHAT BEFORE HOW

A description of what the parties to a document must do should generally come before a description of how they are required to do it. For example, a contract for the sale of goods would normally indicate what is being sold, by and to whom, and for how much; it would then cover how delivery and payment are to be made.

7. SUBSTANCE BEFORE PROCEDURE

Regardless of the nature of the document, the substantive provisions should normally come before the procedural or enforcement provisions. For example, an employer's sexual harassment policy would first identify what is being prohibited; it would then describe the procedures that the employer will follow in enforcing the policy.

PART III

DRAFTING TECHNIQUES

CHAPTER 12

AVOIDING AMBIGUITIES

The *Oxford American Writer's Thesaurus* provides a number of synonyms for the word "ambiguous" reflecting how this word is often used colloquially. These include "open to debate/arguable," "abstruse," "dubious," and others. In drafting, however, the term is used in its formal, logical sense. That is what this chapter is about.

A. DEFINITION

"Ambiguity" means capable of having two or more distinct and inconsistent meanings. An ambiguous term can either mean one thing or it can mean another thing, but it cannot mean both.

Although the two terms are often used interchangeably, ambiguity is distinct from vagueness, which merely means that the term in question has indistinct borders. A "reasonable time" is vague, because the two points that bracket a "reasonable" time—"unreasonably" short on one side and "unreasonably" long on the other—are both uncertain and will have to be determined by the particular circumstances. But it unambiguously refers to times somewhere between the uncertain lower and upper limits of what is "reasonable" and does not refer to any times beyond them.

B. THE CONSEQUENCES OF AMBIGUITY

Ambiguity is the greatest cause of litigation over drafted documents and litigation is always expensive, whether one wins or loses. The results of ambiguity-based litigation are always bad for someone. An ambiguity could be fatal to the efficacy of the document, rendering a contract or statute void, frustrating the objectives of the contracting parties or a legislative body. Or, a court might construe the ambiguity against the drafter, causing the client serious disadvantage and opening the door to a malpractice action. If the ambiguity was a deliberate contrivance to deceive, the drafter may also be guilty of an ethical violation. Ambiguity is fundamentally inconsistent with the central mission of drafting, which is to avoid problems without the need for expensive and often unsuccessful litigation.

Consider two possible litigation scenarios involving an ambiguous term. The contract is for the sale of goods to arrive on the ship *Peerless* from Bombay. Each party has in mind one particular ship, but unbeknownst to either party, two ships named *Peerless* are scheduled to sail from Bombay at different times. The term *Peerless* has two mutually inconsistent meanings and is, thus, ambiguous. Moreover, the buyer, knows only of the October *Peerless*, and the seller knows only of the December *Peerless*. The ambiguity, combined with the different meanings that the parties attached to the term, would defeat the existence of a contract based upon the doctrines of mutual mistake or misunderstanding. The drafter's fault, although perhaps understandable, consists of a failure to investigate sufficiently the facts surrounding the transaction and to identify which ship *Peerless* was meant, perhaps by specifying its sailing date.

But suppose the buyer knows that two ships *Peerless* exist. The buyer still intends the October *Peerless* and knows or has reason to know that the seller thinks only one ship *Peerless* exists, the one sailing in December. The buyer's attorney, aware of all this, nevertheless drafts the contract in terms of the ship *Peerless*, without qualification. Although the ambiguity still exists, in this instance it will probably be resolved under the doctrine of unilateral mistake against the buyer, who will be bound to a contract for the goods arriving on the December *Peerless*.

C. TYPES OF AMBIGUITY

There are three types of ambiguity that may infect a document: contextual ambiguity, semantic ambiguity, and syntactic ambiguity.

1. CONTEXTUAL AMBIGUITY

Contextual ambiguity exists when one allegedly controlling provision is inconsistent with another allegedly controlling provision. An internal contextual ambiguity exists when the inconsistency is within the contract or statute itself. Consider the two following provisions in a lease:

> 3. **Security Deposit:** Within 30 days after the termination or expiration of the lease, landlord will return the security deposit, less any amount owed for damage to the premises caused by tenant.

> 28. **Unpaid Rent:** At the termination of the lease period, landlord may apply the security deposit to any rent then owed by tenant.

A reasonable interpretation of the security deposit provision would be that subject to the landlord being entitled to withhold only any amount that is due for damages to the premises, the entire amount must be returned. That interpretation, however, is negated by the unpaid rent provision, which allows the landlord to also use the security deposit to cover rent still owed.

Faulty definitions are another common source of internal contextual ambiguity. An insurance policy that defines both "building" and "business personal property" as including machinery and equipment is ambiguous if the two classifications have different and mutually inconsistent legal consequences, such as deductibles or limits of liability, with respect to the items that are included.

Some contextual inconsistencies, however, are more subtle and are often the result of poor conceptualization. The Civil Rights Act of 1964 contains the following definition:

> The terms "because of sex" or "on the basis of sex" include, but are not limited to, [1] because of or on the basis of pregnancy, childbirth, or related medical conditions, and [2] women affected by pregnancy, childbirth, or related medical conditions shall be treated the same for all employment-related purposes, including receipt of benefits under fringe benefit

programs, as other persons not so affected but similar in their ability or inability to work, ... (Bracketed numbers added).

Congress apparently did not have a clear idea of what it intended to prohibit. Phrase [1] imposes an unequivocal prohibition against discrimination because of pregnancy, but phrase [2] requires only equal treatment. Those are not equivalents and are potentially inconsistent. Suppose an employer has a policy of not hiring persons who will need significant leave time during the first year of their employment. Under this policy, the employer has declined to hire persons who anticipate having major surgery during the first year. When the employer declines to hire a pregnant woman under this policy, that decision is clearly because of her pregnancy, but it is also equal treatment. Which prevails? The Supreme Court ultimately resolved the ambiguity in favor of the second phrase. But that expensive litigation could have been avoided if the drafter had conceptualized the prohibited conduct better and characterized it in a single, unambiguous way.

References to other documents can also create a form of contextual ambiguity. A general contractor agrees to remedy "all the itemized defects per owner's punch list of 9/2/20." If two lists of that date exist, containing a materially different itemization of defects, this creates an ambiguity. To avoid this ambiguity, the referenced document should be physically attached to the agreement. Even if only one other document exists, physical attachment will prevent this other document from getting lost, creating not an ambiguity but a void.

Statutes that incorporate by reference portions of other statutes run a high risk of contextual ambiguity. First, since the incorporated material was probably not intended to focus on the specific problem now being legislated, a perfect fit between the incorporating and the incorporated materials is highly unlikely. Conflicting implications frequently arise. Second, when the material incorporated by reference is later repealed or amended, the effect of this on the incorporating legislation is unclear. A statute in the Virgin Islands poses a similar problem. In 1921, the legislature adopted as the common law "the restatements of the law prepared and approved by the American Law Institute." The reference in 1921 was implicitly to the first Restatement, with a contextual ambiguity arising when subsequent Restatements were published.

An external contextual ambiguity arises when the inconsistency is between what one contract or statute says and what another contract or statute says. For example, a client asks the drafter to prepare a contract for the purchase of a house and specifies the terms and conditions. The drafter fails to discover that the client already has a lease on the house and that it contains an option to buy, albeit on different terms. Which document controls? Similarly, the legislative drafter who does inadequate research may draft a statute that appears to require what another statute prohibits, creating an ambiguity.

2. SEMANTIC AMBIGUITY

Semantic ambiguity arises out of the use of specific words and phrases. The following categories of words are among the most troublesome.

a. Homonyms

Homonyms—words that are spelled the same but have different meanings, can sometimes cause confusion in drafted documents. The word "bar," for example, could mean to block or forbid, or refer to a place where drinks are served, a device to secure a door, something used to pry objects loose, something every lawyer must pass, what lawyers practice before, or a measure of music. Usually, the context will inform the reader of the intended meaning of a homonym, as in that example. But some words with multiple and mutually inconsistent meanings cannot be resolved by context. The drafter should be especially aware of these words and expressions:

- **Doctor.** This could refer to a Ph.D., an M.D., a D.M.D., a D.V.M., a D.O., a Psy.D., a D.N.P., an LL.D., etc. The difference could be important if the document is identifying the qualifications of persons eligible to hold a particular position.

- **Public.** When used in reference to a place, this may mean a facility that is governmentally owned, a place that is accessible without restriction, or a place that can be readily seen by other persons. A reference to a public parking lot or a prohibition against doing something in a public place may be ambiguous.

- **Residence.** This could refer to one's legal domicile (for voting or tax purposes) or one's place of abode at any given time.
- **Sanction.** This can mean either an approval or a penalty. To refer to "conduct sanctioned by the legislature" is thus ambiguous.
- **Since.** This word can be used both to express a causal relation and to indicate the passage of time. A recital in a contract might state, "Since the seller defaulted on the prior contract, buyer has begun manufacturing its own bolts." This could indicate when the buyer began to manufacture its own bolts or it could indicate why. To avoid this ambiguity, some drafters limit "since" to its temporal connotation and use "because" to indicate causation.
- **While.** Similarly, the word "while" can be used to express a time period or to mean although. Assume that a contract modification stipulates as follows: "While the delivery date of June 19, 2020, is suspended due to the Canadian embargo, buyer shall not attempt to obtain goods from another source." The "while" could either mean "during the time that" or "although." Because of this potential for ambiguity, the preferred usage of "while" is in its temporal sense. And the

drafter should also make sure that this is clear from the context.

b. "And"

This word can mean either jointly or severally. For example, if a contract says, "Executor shall distribute $1,000 to Bill and Mary," this could mean that they must share the $1,000 jointly. Or it could mean that each of them separately gets $1,000. The drafter should choose between the following, depending on the testator's intent:

> *Executor shall distribute $1,000 to Bill and Mary, to be shared jointly.*
>
> *Executor shall distribute $1,000 each to Bill and Mary.*

The use of "and" following a preposition can also cause significant problems. Suppose Bill and Mary were once married and had children; they have since divorced and remarried and both have children from their second marriages. What does "To the children of Bill and Mary mean?" It could refer only to the children of their union. Or it could also include the children of their second marriages.

Ambiguity may arise when the reader cannot determine from context whether the "and" is intended to identify several different entities or to identify the traits of a single entity. This is especially true when the "and" phrase includes modifiers. The classic example comes from a will litigated in 1799, where the testator bequeathed to a particular individual, "All my black and white horses." He died leaving six white horses, six black horses, and six horses with both black and white colors. Which horses should the beneficiary inherit?

Similarly, a document might refer to "charitable and educational institutions." Does this mean to institutions that are both charitable and educational? Or does it refer to two entities, charitable institutions and educational institutions? The drafter can avoid this ambiguity by referring to "institutions that are both charitable and educational," to "institutions that are either charitable or educational," or to "institutions that are charitable, educational, or both."

An ordinance might provide that "Every owner and operator of a taxicab shall report annually." Does the ordinance apply to a single entity, namely someone possessing both the trait of being an owner and the trait of being an operator? Or does it apply to two classes of entities, persons who are owners and persons who are operators? Depending on what is meant, the ambiguity could thus be resolved as follows:

> *A person who is* ***both the owner and operator*** *of a taxicab shall report annually.*

> *A person who is* ***either the owner or the operator*** *of a taxicab shall report annually.*

Similarly, sometimes drafters intend to use "and" in the disjunctive rather than the conjunctive sense, although this can only be determined from the context, which thus makes it ambiguous.

Bill and Mary are entitled to exercise the option to repurchase the land.

Bill and Mary cannot each separately exercise the option because the property cannot be sold twice. But the sentence could mean that they must do it jointly or it could mean, construing "and" to mean "or," that either one of them can do it—presumably, whoever acts first. Depending on what the client intends, the drafter could draft it in one of the two following ways:

Bill and Mary are entitled to exercise the option jointly.

Either Bill or Mary is entitled to exercise the option.

c. "Or"

The word "or" can have an exclusive connotation, meaning "A or B, but not both." It can also be used in an inclusive sense, meaning "A or B, or both." Suppose a criminal statute imposes a penalty of "a $1,000 fine or ten days in jail." Does this mean that the judge can impose the fine or the term in jail, but not both? Or can the judge impose both? Or suppose a will states, "The Executor is authorized to sell my jade collection in New York or Chicago." Does this mean that the executor must choose between the two cities? Or may the executor sell parts of the collection in both cities?

Although a simple "or" is usually construed in its inclusive sense, the drafter should make this clear. Say "$1,000 or ten days in jail, or both." If the disjunctive is intended, say "either $1,000 or ten days in jail, but not both."

Drafters sometimes intend to use "or" in its substitutionary sense, creating further uncertainties. If a will provides, "To Bill or his heirs," an executor or court would construe this as meaning that the bequest goes to Bill's heirs, but only if Bill is not alive, since Bill cannot have heirs until he is dead. Here, the substitutionary sense of "or" can be determined from the factual context. Still, to be clearer the drafter could state:

> *To Bill, or if Bill is not alive at the time of my death, to his children.*

Sometimes the substitutionary sense cannot be determined by context. For example, the will provides, "To a non-profit corporation devoted to the restoration of 18th Century homesteads, if one exists, or to the Texas Historical Foundation." Is this "or" being used substitutionally or alternatively? When "or" is used in its substitutionary rather than alternative sense, make this clear.

A related ambiguity exists when "or" is used to connect classes of entities from which a selection is to be made. For example, a contract might provide, "Seller shall ship 1,000 red or blue widgets." If it is important to the buyer that all the widgets come from the same color class, then the contract should make that express by requiring the seller to ship "either 1,000 red widgets or 1,000 blue widgets." Otherwise, the seller might feel free to ship 500 of each color.

d. "And/Or"

"And" is generally inclusive. To draw on tort language, it is joint and several. "And" can mean A and B, together (jointly), and each separate and apart (severally). But there are times when "and" needs to be restricted to its joint sense (when "A and B" means only both together). "Or" can be exclusive (A or B but not both) or inclusive. *See American Surety Co. v. Marotta*, 287 U.S. 513 (1933) (holding that "or" includes "and"); 11 U.S.C. § 102(5) (accord). Since both "and" and "or" are potentially ambiguous, combining them into one term only multiplies the ambiguity. Because of this, "and/or" has met with hostility from courts and commentators.

The hostility is warranted. Suppose a contract provides a sales commission for "transactions originating and/or consummated within the Chicago city limits." Construed inclusively, the "or" component suggests that the commission is due if the transaction originated in Chicago, was consummated in Chicago, or both originated and was consummated in Chicago. If the "and" is construed as referring to two entities with separate characteristics, that reaches almost the same result. On the other hand, if the "or" is construed in its disjunctive sense and the "and" is construed as referring to a single entity with two characteristics, then the result mandated by the "or" is inconsistent with the result mandated by the "and."

The same ambiguity exists in a statute that says, "Any person found guilty of operating a motor vehicle while in an intoxicated condition and/or who shall cause injury to person or property shall be guilty of a felony." The "and" component suggests that this is a single offense consisting of two elements, intoxication and causing injury. The "or" suggests that the statute defines two possible offenses, intoxication and causing an injury.

The few remaining drafters who defend the use of "and/or" contend that it is a concise way of saying "A or B or both." Certainly, that is one way it can be construed. But since there are also other ways it can be construed, the phrase remains ambiguous. Thus, if the drafter intends "A or B or both" he or she should say exactly that.

In addition, drafters may fail to indicate whether the items in an enumeration or list are cumulative or alternative.

> *An employee may be allowed up to 30 days unpaid personal leave each calendar year if—*
>
> > *(a) The employee requests the leave in writing at least 7 days in advance;*
> >
> > *(b) The reason for the leave could not have been anticipated at the time the employee took his or her regularly scheduled vacation.*

The provision implies "and/or," making it just as ambiguous as if the term was express. Does this impose two requirements? Or does (b) operate as an exception or alternative to (a)? The implied, or silent, "and/or" in an enumeration should be changed to "and" or "or," depending on what the client intends.

A partial solution may be the use of "and" only jointly, "or" only severally, and "and/or" to indicate joint and several relationships. This could be accomplished by use of a provision defining the terms. This would require one to carefully and consistently use the defined terms appropriately. Because 100% consistency is the exception rather than the rule, this may be unworkable in the rigors of actual practice. One can also use constructions such as "A or B or both," "A or B but not both," or "A and B together but not separately" and the like. In any event, confront this issue, adopt a workable solution, and apply it uniformly to your drafting.

e. Specific Dates

Drafters use a variety of expressions in reference to specific dates. Some are clear. But some have been construed in different ways. Others have a legal meaning that is inconsistent with the conventional meaning.

- "Between . . . and . . . "

  Buyer may exercise the option ***between*** *July 1, 2020,* ***and*** *July 29, 2020.*

Courts generally construe this literally. Thus, the option could not be exercised on either of those two dates, only in the period between them. However, that construction is inconsistent with how many lay persons would construe the language, namely including the two dates and the period between the dates.

- "By . . . "

  Buyer must exercise the option ***by*** *July 29, 2020.*

Most courts hold that the option may be exercised on or before July 29, 2016, but, the phase could be construed as requiring the option to be exercised before that date.

- "From . . . to . . . "

  Buyer may exercise the option ***from*** *July 1, 2020,* ***to*** *July 29, 2020.*

Some courts hold that the option can be exercised on neither date. Some courts hold that the "from" date is excluded but the "to" date is included. Some courts hold that both dates are included.

- "Until . . . "

  Buyer's option is open ***until*** *July 29, 2020.*

Most would hold that the option can be exercised on that date.

Because all of these date-related phrases have been variously construed and are thus ambiguous, the drafter should avoid them. Usually, they can be replaced with a set of terms that are generally regarded as not being ambiguous, whether they are used together or individually, as follows:

- "After . . . before . . . "

  Buyer may exercise the option ***after*** *July 1, 2020, and* ***before*** *July 29, 2020.*

Buyer must exercise the option ***after*** *July 1, 2020.*

Buyer must exercise the option ***before*** *July 29, 2020.*

Courts hold that the option may not be exercised on either date. Many, however, find it counter-intuitive to specify in a document a date that is not included in the allowed time period. To accommodate both legal and conventional understandings, many drafters use "on or after" and "on or before" terminology.

Buyer may exercise the option ***on or after*** *July 2, 2020, and* ***on or before*** *July 28, 2020.*

Because "on" is fairly consistently construed to include the full day referenced, many drafters are content to use it in lieu of any "after . . . before" expression.

Buyer's option begins ***on*** *July 1, 2020, and ends* ***on*** *July 29, 2020.*

Drafters exercising extreme caution would also include the times, at "12:01 a.m." and "at 11:59 p.m."—or some other times, if desired.

f. Time Spans

Drafted documents often refer to time spans rather than specific dates. Precisely measuring the beginning or end of the time span can sometimes be difficult.

- **"Within . . . "**

  If a document requires that something be done "within 30 days," an immediate question arises, "Within 30 days of what?" Often, the intent is that it be done within 30 days of the signing of the contract. But if the contract requires Able to do something and then Betty to do something "within 30 days," does the 30 days still refer to the date of the contract or does it refer to the date of Able's act?

- **"After . . . "**

  *The option lapses 7 days **after** the Landlord receives Tenant's notice of non-renewal.*

As is true with respect to specific dates, courts consistently hold that the day of the triggering event is not included and that the reference is to full days. Thus, if the landlord received the notice on July 5th, July 6th would be the first of the seven days and the option would lapse at the end of the day on July 12th. The careless use of the word "time" in this kind of provision can cause possibly unintended consequences, however.

> *The option lapses 7 days **after the time when** the Landlord receives Tenant's notice of non-renewal.*

If the landlord received the notice at 2:00 p.m. on July 5th, then the option is likely to lapse at 2:00 p.m. on July 12th, even though that might well not be the intent of the parties.

- **"Before . . . "**

Alternatively, the option provision could be expressed as follows:

Tenant must exercise this option ***before 11:59*** *p.m. of the seventh day after the day on which the Landlord receives Tenant's notice of non-renewal.*

Although "before" and "after" are fairly safe to use in identifying time spans, the drafter must be careful not to create unintended substantive gaps.

Penalties for late filing are as follows:

1. *10 days and before the 20th day—$45.*
2. *After 20 days and before the 30th day—$100.*
3. *After 30 days—$500.*

What is the penalty for the person who files on the 20th or the 30th day? Using "on or before" would cure that problem.

- **"Within . . . "**

A Tenant who files a notice of non-renewal must then exercise the option ***within*** *7 days.*

Most courts construe this as beginning on the first day after the filing of notice and ending at 11:59 p.m. on the seventh day. Alternatively, some drafters use "before the expiration of" or "before 11:59" of instead of "within." If the "within" is used in reference to a future date certain, as in "within 30 days of June 15," does this refer to the 30 days prior to June 15, the 30 days after June 15, or both?

g. Days, Weeks, Months, and Years

These terms are used in connection with time spans, which present one form of ambiguity, as discussed above. The terms, however, can also be ambiguous in their own right. A document is signed at 2:00 p.m. on Wednesday, July 28, 2020. It provides:

> *Buyer has two days to arrange financing, one week to secure insurance, three months to make the first payment, and five years to make the final payment.*

Does "day" mean calendar days, beginning on the midnight of July 28th, or consecutive 24-hour periods, beginning at 2:00 p.m. on July 28th? Do "days" include weekends and holidays? Or is the intended reference to business days? If the term "business days" is intended or used, does its meaning change depending upon when the parties operate their businesses? In this increasingly 24/7 world, arguably every day is a business day. Similarly, does a "week" mean seven consecutive calendar days? If so, does the week include that Wednesday and thus end on Tuesday? Or does it begin on Thursday and end on the next Wednesday? Or does "week" mean the next unit beginning on Sunday and ending on Saturday? If the document was signed on Monday, is it possible that the reference is to a five-day business week? Similarly, does "months" refer to full calendar months, beginning with August and ending on

October 31? Or do the three months run from the time and date of signing, with the three months ending at 2:00 p.m. on October 28? Or perhaps it means the lunar month of 28 days. Similar problems exist with respect to the exact length of and how to mark the beginning and end of a "year."

The usual construction is that "days" includes Saturdays, Sundays, and holidays; that a "week" refers to seven consecutive days; that a "month" covers the period between and including a date-certain in the starting month (July 4) and the day before that date in the next month (August 3); and a "year" covers the period between and including a date-certain in the starting month (July 4, 2020) and the day before that date in the next year (July 3, 2021). But if the context would suggest otherwise, or if the intent is otherwise, then the drafter should not leave matters to chance. If a specific date can be calculated, then reference it in the manner discussed above. Alternatively, express the length in words that leave no room for uncertainty.

> *Each party has 7 days to object to the report, beginning on the day and at the time the report is filed and ending at 5:00 p.m. on the seventh day (excluding weekends and federal holidays) following the day the report is filed.*

If the report was filed at 10:00 a.m. on Friday, October 5, 2020, objections would be due before 5:00 p.m. on Wednesday, October 14, 2020.

In statutes and complex private documents, if days, weeks, months, or years are referred to in several places, then a definition identifying when these periods begin and end would eliminate the awkwardness of the provision suggested above.

> *"Day" means the next full 24-hour period following the event referenced, beginning at **00:01** a.m., and each consecutively following full 24-hour period, exclusive of Saturdays, Sundays, and federal holidays.*

h. "Bimonthly," "Biannually," and "Biennially"

These terms are all ambiguous. Bryan Garner's *A Dictionary of Modern Legal Usage* says that "bimonthly" means every two months and "semimonthly" means twice a month. But he recognizes that "bi-" is also used to mean twice. The *New Oxford American Dictionary* says that bimonthly can mean either twice a month or every two months. Garner says that "biannually" and "semiannually" both mean twice each year, while "biennially" means every two years. No further proof of the ambiguity of these terms is needed. Drafters should avoid these terms altogether and instead, use "every two" or "twice a . . . ", depending on what the drafter intends.

i. Hours

A contract that requires something to be done "by no later than 2 o'clock" is probably intended to refer to 2 p.m., since few people are out and about during the early morning hours. But the context of the contract might suggest otherwise, thus creating an ambiguity. Drafters should always clarify their time references with "a.m." or "p.m."

Even these references can be ambiguous in one instance. Assume that a city ordinance prohibits parking in a certain area "between 8 a.m. and 12 p.m." A person is given a ticket for parking in the area at 1:30 p.m., assuming that the "12 p.m." reference was to noon. The city maintains that "12 p.m." refers to midnight. Although that is how "12 p.m." is normally construed, with "12 a.m." being construed as referring to noon, the term is at least potentially ambiguous. And technically, neither party is correct. According to the Naval Observatory Time Service Division, "p.m." refers to the time from when the sun is directly overhead to when it is directly overhead the directly opposite part of the earth and "a.m." refers to the time from then until the sun is back directly overhead. But neither term can be used to describe when the sun is directly overhead or in the converse position. The Observatory recommends using "noon" or "midnight."

"Noon" may be safe enough, but "midnight" is not. A reference to "midnight on October 23, 2020," could refer to the midnight joining the 23rd with the 24th, which is the generally accepted American usage, or it could refer to the midnight joining the 22nd with the 23rd, which is how it is used in some European countries. The clearer references would be either to "00:00:01 a.m. on October 23, 2020," or to "11:59:59 p.m. on October 23, 2020."

j. Relational Words

Do not use "now," "currently," or "presently." The danger is that this time reference will be construed literally, when that is not what is intended, thus creating potential for ambiguity. For example:

> *Seller shall not charge a price in excess of that **currently** charged in the Atlanta wholesale cotton seed market.*

What if the allowed price is $1,000 at the time of contracting but when the price is actually charged the Atlanta regulated price has dropped to $900? Which controls? If the contract price is intended to fluctuate, delete "currently" and add "in effect the time of delivery." If the reference is to the price allowed on the date of the contract, delete "currently" and add "as of the date of this contract." Alternatively, simply write in the existing price as of that date.

k. Ages

Contracts refer to the ages of the parties less often than do statutes and private law documents like wills. These references are often ambiguous

> *Nephew will not smoke or drink until he is over 21 years of age.*

Can the nephew start smoking and drinking after his 21st birthday? Or must he wait until after his 22nd birthday? Whichever interpretation is intended, it should be stated in just those terms.

Nephew will not smoke or drink until after his 21st birthday.

l. "Provided That"

The word "provided" is ambiguous because it can be used in so many senses. Its only proper use is as a verb.

Seller will provide transportation for the goods.

The phrase "provided that" traces its origin to the time when the Latin phrase *provistum est* was used to introduce each separate and independent section of a statute. The full English translation was used later. "It is provided that. . . ." This at least gave the sentence a grammatical subject. Eventually, the "it is" was dropped, however. What is left defies grammatical analysis. Moreover, provisos produce single sentences that are often hundreds of words long. Thus, knowledgeable drafters do not use them.

Apart from being a grammatically incorrect, "provided that" is ambiguous because it can be used variously to introduce exceptions, qualifications, conditions, and even new substantive provisions. For example:

> ***C. Cure.*** *Seller may attempt to cure any defects,* ***provided****, however,* ***that*** *notice of intent to cure is given within* ***10*** *days of the notification of the defect; and* ***provided that*** *buyer does not waive notice; and* ***provided*** *further* ***that*** *if the attempt at cure is unsuccessful, seller will replace the item and compensate buyer for any losses due to delay.*

The first proviso imposes a condition precedent. The second proviso states an exception. And the third proviso deals with an altogether new substantive provision. These should be dealt with directly, using the terms that create each of these legal consequences, as follows:

> ***C. Cure.*** *(a) Seller is entitled to attempt to cure any defects. (b) If seller elects to attempt to cure, seller must give notice of that intent within **10** days of notification of the defect, unless seller has waived notice. (c) If seller's attempt to cure is unsuccessful, seller will replace the item and compensate buyer for any losses due to delay.*

Implementing this suggested usage is an uphill battle, as the introduction of baskets and materiality thresholds in contracts with "provided, however, that" and "provided further, however, that" is widespread and accepted practice in, among other places, the majority of large transactional law firms.

m. Legalese

Apart from being archaic and unnecessarily wordy, some legalese is also ambiguous because these terms often have multiple referents. Suppose that a sentence in a regulation concludes, "and the benefits provided herein are available to all dependents who file within 30 days of termination of service." Does this apply only to whatever benefits are described in that sentence, to benefits described in that particular section, or to benefits described anywhere in the regulation?

"Hereunder" could also be construed as referring to any of those three possibilities, or it could be construed as referring only to things appearing in the agreement after the word is used. Similarly, a reference to "aforementioned benefits" is ambiguous if the document has earlier referenced several different sets of benefits. Are all of them included, or only the last grouping?

Replace these ambiguous terms with specific references, like "the benefits provided in subsection 304(a)(ii)."

If you are trying to say "in this document," say that—name the document (using a defined term—this Agreement, this Lease, etc.—can be helpful here). If you are trying to say "in this paragraph/section/etc.," just say it.

The same applies to all the here-, there-, and-said words like "hereby," "hereinafter," "therefore," "therein," "aforesaid." Similarly, "same" and "such" used as referents to other provisions, documents, or things should be avoided if possible. They are weak substitutes for proper pronouns and good defined terms. They can also create ambiguous references.

n. Shall, May, Will, and Must

The key problem here is that "shall" is commonly used for all four words, causing ambiguity. "May" is permissive—meaning the actor has an option of taking an action or receiving a benefit—it expresses a single right. "Shall," on the other hand, means that the actor has no choice; he has a duty. Differentiate between rights (permissive) and duties (mandatory). Rights are "may" phrases (tenants may landscape the area adjacent to the patio); duties are "shall" phrases (tenants shall clean and maintain the area around their front doors in good repair). It is best to use "shall" to refer to duties, which is the standard in United States practice. "Must" is appropriate for creating a condition precedent.

"Will" is predictive but is otherwise similar to "shall," as it may refer to a duty. When indicating a duty, it is best to stick to "shall" and eliminate "will" to avoid the implication of different meanings. "Will," however, being predictive, is appropriate when speaking of future events.

If the name of a party does not appear before the word "shall" in an apparent shall/duty clause, it is probably an incorrect use of the imperative tense. For example, agreements often state that they "shall" be governed by the law of a particular state. This is incorrect. Rather the agreement should stat the choice of law clause as a present tense actual circumstance, i.e., using "is," as in "This Agreement is governed by California law without reference to its choice of law principles."

And when drafting, include consequences of a failure to perform the duty, either by listing it as an event of default that may trigger a remedy or by specifying that failure to, for example, approve or disapprove performance by June 1, 2020, will not be deemed to be approval.

o. "Among" and "Between"

The Oxford English Dictionary says to use "between" to express the relation of a thing to other things individually.

The contest will be ***between*** *the various plant managers.*

But use "among" to express the relationship of a thing to other things collectively and vaguely.

Fund recipients must work ***among*** *the poor.*

The conventional wisdom, however, is that "between" refers to two things and "among" refers to more than two things.

This is just ***between*** *you and me, but I intend to distribute the reward evenly* ***among*** *Ann, Betty, Carol, and Diane.*

Still, number is not the operative distinction between "between" and "among." A contract is made *between* three parties, not *among* them. Essentially, "between" indicates a direct relationship from each party to each party. "Among" is less specific and may connote an arrangement where some parties are directly connected and some are not.

Suppose a will says:

*The Executor shall divide my estate [****among*** *or* ***between****] my son and the two children of my deceased daughter.*

If the choice is "between," then a court adhering to the conventional wisdom would divide the estate into two equal shares, one for the son and the other split into equal amounts for the two children. But if the choice is "among," then the same court would divide the estate into three equal shares. The drafter should not leave such an important matter to the whims of conventional wisdom.

3. SYNTACTIC AMBIGUITY

Syntactic ambiguities arise principally out of the order in which words appear and how they are punctuated, which affects what other words they modify or refer to.

The most common forms of syntactic ambiguity are:

a. Pronoun Reference

The general rule is that a pronoun refers back to the immediately preceding noun. When this construction is inconsistent with the reader's expectation of the provision, an ambiguity arises. Consider this classic example:

> *Holding up a cookie box for his sister to see, a boy says, "If you can guess what kind of cookie is in this box, I'll give* ***it*** *to you."*
>
> *"Chocolate chip," she replies.*
>
> *"Right," he says, as he removes the cookie, eats the cookie, and hands her the now empty box.*

Here, the antecedent "it" is ambiguous. The sister reasonably believed the prize was the cookie. The boy, however, can rely on the general rule and assert that the grammatical reference was to the box.

Or suppose a contract provides as follows:

> *Seller will load a dumpster onto a vehicle provided by Buyer.* ***It*** *will be capable of holding three tons.*

Common sense dictates that "it" does not refer to the buyer, although that is what the rules of grammatical construction would suggest. But does it refer to the dumpster or the vehicle?

In addition to being in bad style, using "such" as a demonstrative pronoun often creates ambiguity:

> *Employees shall not remove any die tap tools from the plant that are not checked out with the Tool Supervisor and each Shift Supervisor shall inventory* ***such*** *tools weekly.*

Does the Shift Supervisor have a duty to inventory all die tap tools weekly, to ensure that none are missing? Or does the duty extend only those that are checked out, to determine how many are checked out and where they are?

b. Modifiers

Modifiers are a ready source of ambiguity and come in a variety of forms.

Items in a Series. It is unclear in some phrases whether an adjective is intended to modify only the noun that immediately follows or all of the series of nouns that follow. Similarly, it is often unclear whether a trailing clause modifies only the last preceding noun or other parts of the sentence as well. Suppose that a will authorizes the executor to select and give a certain amount of money to "educational institutions and corporations working with the hearing impaired." This could mean at least four different things, depending on what is construed as modifying what. A technique known as tabbing allows the drafter to identify the possibilities inherent in this phrase, as follows:

- educational institutions

  and

  corporations working with the hearing impaired.

- educational

  institutions

  and

  corporations working with the hearing impaired.

- educational institutions

  and

  corporations

  working with the hearing impaired.

- educational

  institutions

  and

corporations

working with the hearing impaired.

Each option reflects a different intent. The ambiguity can be easily resolved through the technique of enumeration, discussed in Chapter 16. This simply involves putting those examples in sentence form, using numbers and letters in parentheses to identify the groupings, and perhaps also using the tabbing or indentation convention, as follows:

*I direct the Executor to distribute **$10,000** to one or more (a) educational institutions or (b) corporations, either of which works with the hearing impaired, with the selection of the recipients and amount given to each recipient to be within the discretion of the Executor.*

—or—

*I direct the Executor to distribute **$10,000** to one or more*

(a) educational institutions or

(b) corporations

who are working with the hearing impaired, with the selection. . . .

Quality Versus Identity. When an entity is modified by a chain of adjectives, it may be unclear whether the modifiers in combination describe the collective quality of the thing, or are suggesting that separate entities are involved—each possessing one of the qualities described.

> *Distributor shall supply red, white, and blue caps.*

Must each cap contain all three colors (quality)? Or may the distributor supply solid red, solid white, and solid blue caps (identity)?

Linkage Problems. Does "working dog owners" refer to persons who own a dog classified within the working breed category—linking "working" and "dog" together? Or does it refer to persons who work and also own dogs—linking "working" and "owners?"

Dangling Modifiers. Another form of ambiguous modifier is one that "dangles." A modifier, usually an introductory phrase, dangles if the reader cannot identify what the modifier refers to in the main clause of the sentence. Consider the following provision in a will:

> *If alive but incompetent at the time of my death, my son's guardian shall inherit half of my estate for his continued care and keeping.*

Suppose the son is dead and the guardian is alive but now incompetent. Does the guardian inherit? Grammatically, the introductory clause applies to the guardian, who should thus be entitled to inherit. This, however, is not the likely intent of the testator. This potentially legally significant dangling modifier can be corrected by making the subject of the introductory phrase express.

> *If my son is alive but incompetent at the time of my death, his guardian shall inherit half of my*

estate to provide for my son's continued care and keeping.

Squinting Modifiers. A modifier "squints" if the reader cannot determine whether it modifies the preceding or the following word or phrase.

If buyer determines the goods are defective ***within 20 days*** *seller shall replace them.*

Is the buyer's determination limited by the 20 days? Or does that relate to the seller's duty of replacement?

Passive Voice. The passive voice often contributes to the use of dangling modifiers—which is just another reason to avoid it. Consider this sentence:

To prove satisfaction of the notice requirement, a courier service approved by the Department of State under 34 U.S.C. § 89–667 must be used.

Upon first reading, it would appear that "a courier service" is the entity trying to satisfy the notice requirement. That obviously is not what is intended, as is finally indicated by the trailing passive voice phrase "must be used." The ambiguity can be resolved by stating the main clause in the active voice.

To prove satisfaction of the notice requirement, the parties must use a courier service approved by the Department of State under 34 U.S.C. § 89.667.

c. Participles

A passive past participle can produce ambiguities of status.

> *Each person who was admitted to the Club* ***on*** *January 1, 2020, is eligible.*

Does this include only persons who became members on that particular date? Or does it refer to persons who enjoyed the status of membership on that date? Even an active voice participle can be ambiguous if the noun it modifies is unclear.

> *No person shall accost another wearing a police uniform.*

Does this provide protection to persons wearing police uniforms? Or does it mean that you cannot don a police uniform and accost people?

d. Chain Prepositions

Chains of prepositions create ambiguity because it is unclear what they refer to.

> *Each stockholder* ***of*** *a Chapter 9 corporation* ***in*** *Georgia is entitled to. . . .*

Does this refer to each Chapter 9 stockholder who resides in Georgia? Or does it refer to each stockholder in a corporation that operates in Georgia?

e. Negative Pregnants

A negative pregnant is a sentence that denies something in particular, but that can also be construed as an implied admission of what is not denied. Because the implication may or may not be read into these sentences, they are necessarily ambiguous. Suppose, for example, the contract is for the sale of widgets, smidgets, and gidgets. A recital states:

> *The parties acknowledge that Seller is not a merchant of widgets.*

Later, an issue arises over seller's status as a merchant of smidgets or gidgets. Is the recital an implied admission that the seller is a merchant of these other items?

f. "If . . . Then" Sentences

Many drafters use the "if . . . then" construction when dealing with conditions. Usually, this causes no problems. But, as was discussed in Chapter 9, "if . . . then" sentences can present substantive gaps. If a gap can be filled in two plausible ways, as is often the case, then an ambiguity exists. Thus, although the "if . . . then" configuration is a useful one, it is fraught with potential ambiguities that the drafter should be aware of and avoid.

For example, suppose a contract provides:

> ***If*** *delivery is on or before June 30, 2020,* ***then*** *purchaser will tender cash.*

This pretty clearly imposes a duty on the purchaser to tender cash when the seller elects to make delivery on that date. But suppose on June 30th the purchaser tenders cash and demands immediate delivery? Is the seller under an affirmative duty to make delivery on that date? As a matter of formal logic, the answer is no. From "If A, then B; B," one cannot infer "A." That is known as the fallacy of affirming the consequent. But the context, circumstances, or prior conduct of the parties may suggest that the tender of cash activates a duty to make delivery on that date. The drafter should determine the intended relationship between the delivery date and the tender of cash and make that relationship express through appropriate language, thus avoiding the ambiguity.

g. "Because" Clauses

A sentence containing a "because" clause may be ambiguous if the reader is unsure if the clause modifies only the immediately preceding phrase or if it modifies the entire statement.

> *Owner may not deny requests for time extensions* ***because of*** *anticipated labor disputes.*

Does this refer to an unacceptable reason for denying a request for a time extension, namely because of an anticipated labor dispute? Or does it refer to a particular type of request for extension that cannot be denied, namely those based on an anticipated labor dispute?

h. "Unless" Clauses

"Unless" is a term used to state a condition and generally means except under particular circumstances.

Unless the ship Peerless *comes in on Wednesday, Acme will buy the cotton.*

An "unless" clause that relates to a clause that is itself already stated in negative terms can cause confusion.

Seller will not ship by rail ***unless*** *the Teamsters are still on strike on December* ***10, 2020.***

If the "unless" clause is satisfied and the Teamsters are still on strike, this negates the prior clause. Logically, this means, "It is not the case that Seller will not ship by rail." But what does that mean when translated into conventional English? Does it merely mean the duty to not use that mode of shipment is vacated, still leaving it open to the Seller to use it or other methods of delivery? Or does it mean that Seller now has an affirmative duty to ship by rail, with the two negatives canceling each other out? To avoid confusion, the clause should be drafted in the affirmative, and not use "unless."

Seller will ship by means other than rail ***if*** *the Teamsters are still on strike on December* ***10, 2020.***

i. "Only"

Technically, the word "only" modifies the word or phrase it immediately precedes. Under this rule of construction, the placement of "only" is very important. Note how the meaning of the sentence changes by the addition and location of "only."

Base Sentence: The buyer shall inspect the goods on the dock.

(1) ***Only*** *the buyer shall inspect the goods on the dock.* [This means that no one except the buyer shall inspect.]

(2) *The buyer* **only** *shall inspect the goods on the dock.* [This was probably intended to reflect the same idea as sentence (1). Technically, however, it modifies "shall inspect", which means that the activity is limited to inspection, perhaps in distinction to taking possession of them.]

(3) *The buyer shall* **only** *inspect the goods on the dock.* [Splitting the compound verb with "only" makes it even clearer that buyer's dock activity is limited to inspection.]

(4) *The buyer shall inspect* **only** *the goods on the dock.* [This means that the inspection is limited to the goods on the dock.]

(5) *The buyer shall inspect the goods* **only** *on the dock.* [This limits the location of the buyer's inspection, although it could also be construed as limiting the goods to be inspected, namely those on the dock.]

(6) *The buyer shall inspect the goods on the dock* ***only.*** [This violates the rule of construction, since the "only" precedes nothing. It was probably intended to limit the goods to be inspected, although like sentence (5) it might also be construed as limiting the location of the inspection.]

These examples suggest that the careful drafter should probably avoid the use of "only" altogether and express the idea in clearer, less ambiguous terms.

j. Truncated Passive

A normal passive voice sentence might state:

*All change orders over **$1,000** must be reported to the bank by the contractor within **10** days.*

Apart from its wordiness, nothing is substantively unclear or ambiguous. But in a truncated version of the passive voice, the actor disappears from the sentence altogether.

*All change orders must be reported to the bank within **10** days.*

Who has the conditional obligation to make that report? Is it the contractor or the owner?

k. "Which" and "That"

The choice between which and that is important, but not because the two words themselves have significantly different meanings. The choice is important, rather, because it can affect the syntax, structure, and meaning of the entire sentence. This is true, at least, when these words are used to introduce restrictive and nonrestrictive clauses.

A restrictive clause defines the noun it follows.

*The buyer shall inspect the goods **that are on the loading dock.***

The bolded clause is restrictive because it identifies and narrows the class of goods the buyer has a duty to inspect—namely a sub-class consisting of those that are on the loading dock. Restrictive clauses are not set off by commas.

A nonrestrictive clause, on the other hand, provides additional information about an already defined or identified noun.

> *The buyer shall inspect the goods,* ***which are on the loading dock****.*

Here, the bolded clause is nonrestrictive because it assumes the buyer already knows the identity of the goods to be inspected. The clause merely indicates where they are located. Nonrestrictive clauses are set off with commas.

Old-fashioned grammar purists vigorously insist on using "which" only in nonrestrictive clauses and "that" only in restrictive clauses, as in the above examples. While agreeing that "that" cannot be used to introduce a nonrestrictive clause, many modern style manuals allow the use of either "that" or "which" in restrictive clauses. The better drafting practice adheres to the old-fashioned approach. This is not just a matter of grammatical purity and proper style. In some instances the misuse of "which" and "that" creates ambiguity. Consider this sentence in a stipulation to arbitrate disputes under a construction contract.

> *The basement wall defects which cost less than $1,000 to correct shall not be submitted to this arbitration.*

Does this constitute an admission that none of the alleged defects in the basement wall will cost more than $1,000 to correct and that the parties are agreeing not to arbitrate them? If that is what was intended, the clause "which cost less than $1,000 to correct" should be set off with commas. This indicates that the clause is simply providing additional information about these defects. Under that construction, the owner demanding arbitration of some basement wall defects might be estopped from later claiming that these particular defects will cost more than $1,000 to repair. Alternatively, the sentence could merely mean that some of the defects in the basement wall (as yet undetermined) are being excluded from this arbitration—those that will cost less than $1,000 to correct. If that is what was intended, the drafter should have replaced "which" with "that." This provides the identity of the defects that are being excluded from the arbitration.

Finally, if a drafter can eliminate either "which" or "that" without creating an ambiguity, then do so in the interest of brevity. "The house **that** John built" can easily become "The house John built."

l. Plural Nouns

Drafted documents generally use the singular even when more than one entity is subject to the legal consequence being created.

*An applicant must file an appeal within **10** days after the day on which the application is denied.*

This applies to all applicants. The convention avoids ambiguities that sometimes arise when a drafter uses plurals. For example, consider the following:

> *Employees with children qualifying for coverage must file affidavits of eligibility from persons listed below:. . . .*

Does this apply only to employees with more than one child? Does it require more than one affidavit, presumably from all of the listed persons? These uncertainties can be resolved by using singular nouns and saying:

> *An employee with a child qualifying for coverage must file an affidavit of eligibility from a person listed below:. . . .*

Usually, "a," "an," "the," or nothing at all before a singular noun is sufficient to indicate that the sentence applies to everything within that noun class. However, if a sentence could be construed as allowing a duty to be discharged by applying it to a single member of the class or a right to be exercised by only one member of the class, then use "each," "every," or "all" plus a plural noun. The following sentence is capable of that construction:

> *A student with perfect attendance will be given a grade enhancement.*

Matthew, Mark, and Luke all had perfect attendance, but the professor gave only Matthew a grade enhancement, claiming that the rule required that this be done for "a student," which indeed has been done. To prevent such pedagogical duplicity, the sentence should say:

> *Every student with perfect attendance will be given a grade enhancement.*

m. Commas and Semi-Colons

Courts sometimes assert that punctuation is not a part of the statute. This non-deference to the grammatical implications of punctuation originated back when legislation was introduced orally. The punctuation was later added by clerks, who may or may not have understood either the intent of the legislature or the rules of punctuation. Today, almost all legislation is introduced in printed form. Along with the words that are used, the punctuation is one of the most important indicators of meaning. Drafters who ignore the significance of punctuation do so at their peril. Whether it is in legislation or private law documents, ambiguity can result from the misuse of commas and semi-colons.

Omission of the Serial or "English" Comma. The serial or "English" comma is the comma that follows the second to last word or phrase in a series joined by "and" or "or." The comma clearly identifies each unit in the series.

a. In a compound sentence composed of a series of short independent clauses the last two of which are joined by a conjunction, commas should be placed between the clauses and before the conjunction:

The attorney presented his closing argument, the judge instructed the jury, and the jury retired to consider the case.

b. In a series consisting of three or more elements, the elements are separated by commas. When a conjunction joins the last two elements in a series, a comma is used before the conjunction:

Small, Nelson, and Lee attended the conference.

The owner, the agent, and the tenant were having an acrimonious discussion.

Omission of this comma can sometimes cause ambiguity.

Dealer will maintain a supply of hats in the following colors: red, blue, orange and black.

Is the dealer obligated to maintain a supply of three kinds of hats or four? Putting a comma after "orange" makes it clear that the contract contemplates four kinds of hats, one in each color. To make the three-hat option clear, the drafter might say:

Dealer will maintain a supply of red hats, blue hats, and orange and black hats.

A series connected by more than one "and," but lacking the serial comma, can also be ambiguous with respect to which "and" creates a unit and which "and" links the series of units together. For example:

The Committee consists of one delegate chosen from each of the following four municipal areas: Able City, Bakersfield, Clarendon and Dover and Euclid.

Are Clarendon and Dover a unit? Or Dover and Euclid? A comma in the right place will resolve that ambiguity. The omission of a serial comma can also raise the question of whether it is a list of several units or one unit followed by a descriptive or defining phrase. For example:

The screening panel consists of five judges, two Democrats and three Republicans.

Does the panel consist of five judges, with the political affiliations as indicated? Grammatically, that is probably the most likely construction, although it could be made clearer by saying:

The screening panel consists of five judges, two of whom shall be Democrat and three Republican.

Or does the original sentence contemplate a panel containing 10 people, consisting of (a) five judges, (b) two non-judge Democrats, and (c) three non-judge Republicans? If that is what was intended, it should have been stated in just that form. A simple serial comma after "Democrats" (without the lettered parentheticals) would also support that construction, although less clearly.

The omission of the serial comma can also create ambiguities of modification, as in this example:

Tenant will not allow to remain on the premises overnight any persons not related by blood or marriage, minor children or pets weighing more than 25 pounds.

The omission of the serial comma suggests that the 10 pound infant who screams can stay all night. Similarly:

> *The Health Inspector may close a restaurant because of fire hazards, unclean facilities and rats.*

One certainly cannot tolerate dirty rats.

Even in situations where the omission of the serial comma would not create an ambiguity, an omission may nevertheless create confusion and misunderstanding.

> *The buyer must inspect all incoming rail shipments within **10** days of arrival, promptly notify the seller of any discovered defects or shortages and arrange for transportation away from the rail site.*

Here, the omission of the comma after "shortages" does not render the sentence ambiguous in any literal sense. The omission does, however, make the sentence difficult to understand and thus ambiguous in a loose sense, because it obscures the fact that the buyer has three distinct duties.

Finally, even if the omission of a serial comma will not create ambiguity or render the sentence obscure, the comma should always be included for the sake of consistency. Using the last comma will never be wrong, but omitting it may cause confusion. However, if you choose to forego the last comma, be consistent throughout the document and examine your result carefully to ensure your intended meaning is clear and legally precise.

Semi-Colons. Although a semi-colon can be used as either a strong comma (separating phrases in a series that are either very long or already contain internal commas) or a weak period (joining independent clauses), in either case in drafted documents each semi-colon unit is expected to have its own independent legal consequence or effect. But when that rule of construction is at odds with the sense of the sentence, an ambiguity results. Suppose that a statute prohibits the sale or use of Class III fireworks, but further provides:

> *Nothing in this Act is intended to prohibit a resident wholesaler's sale of Class III fireworks for which a permit has been granted by the Department of Public Safety; or the sale of any kind of fireworks for shipment directly out of state; the use of Class III fireworks by railroads; or the use of Class III fireworks as maritime signal flares by boats in distress.*

Sam Pyro, a retailer, sold $100 worth of Class III fireworks to Betty Popp who immediately shipped them to her brother out of state. Is Pyro's sale within the exceptions to the prohibition? If the phrases separated by semi-colons have an independent legal consequence or effect, the answer is yes. The first phrase thus applies to wholesalers. The second phrase applies to anyone, including Pyro. The third phrase applies to railroads. And the fourth phrase applies to boaters in distress. But if the harm to be avoided is the possession within the state by actual or potential users of the fireworks covered by the Act, then one would conclude that Pyro is not covered by the exception. Rather, the sense of the statute is that the direct shipment exception was intended to apply only to wholesalers. If that is what was intended, as is likely, then the second phrase should not have been set off from the first phrase with a semi-colon.

In a series consisting of three or more elements that are themselves either clauses or sub-series, use a semi-colon in place of a comma for the highest level of the list. For example, "the available color combinations are red, white, and blue; yellow, green, and tan; and gold, red, and purple."

CHAPTER 13

DRAFTING STYLE AND USAGE

The appropriate style of legal drafting is dictated by its function, which is to establish legal relationships—unambiguously, concisely, clearly, and simply.

A. CONSISTENCY

Ambiguity is the most egregious form of inconsistency. Other forms of inconsistency are the result of bad style. Good style requires the following:

1. CONSISTENT TERMINOLOGY

There is no place in legal drafting for the English composition and literature practice of "elegant variation," a term coined by Henry Watson Fowler in his *Dictionary of Modern English Usage* (1st ed., 1926). The practice consists of the unnecessary and often misleading use of synonyms or close synonyms to describe the same thing in different passages of a writing in order to avoid repetition. Although potentially useful in lyrics and poetry, it has no place in legal drafting.

Always use the same term to refer to the same person, thing, entity, or concept; always use different terms to refer to different persons, things, entities, and concepts. The prior sentence is not saying the same thing twice. One could consistently use "premises" to refer to each individual apartment within the complex, but also use that word to refer to something else, such as common areas—adhering to the first component of the rule, but violating the second. Or, one could never use "premises" to refer to anything except the individual apartments, but also refer to the apartments by other names, such as "leasehold"—adhering to the second component, but violating the first. So, follow both aspects of the rule. This is not only necessary to prevent reader confusion; a violation of the rule can also lead to a judicial interpretation that may be different from the intent of the drafter. For example, the drafter may have intended for both "premises" and "leasehold" to refer only to an individual apartment. However, once a court determines that "premises" refers to the individual apartment, the court is likely to conclude the term "leasehold," must necessarily refer to something else, such as all tangible property-related entitlements under the lease, including use of common areas.

2. CONSISTENT GRAMMATICAL STRUCTURE

Drafters frequently write sentences containing multiple phrases. Each phrase must have the same—or parallel—grammatical structure. Consider the following regulation:

> *Producers of toxic chemicals have the following options: (1) require purchasers to assume responsibility for subsequent spills, (2) depositing money in a damages escrow fund, (3) termination of production, or (4) a conspicuous disclaimer of liability on every container.*

The phrases in this list are not grammatically parallel. The producer's options are variously described with a verb, "require"; a gerund, "depositing"; a nominalization, "termination"; and a noun, "disclaimer." This is an awkward and confusing regulation. With the four phrases put into parallel grammatical form, the regulation reads as follows:

> *Producers of toxic chemicals have the following options: (1) require purchasers to assume responsibility for subsequent spills; (2) deposit money in a damages escrow fund; (3) terminate production; or (4) post a conspicuous disclaimer of liability on every container.*

Consistency between the items in a series also requires that the introductory word or phrase tie in grammatically with the language of each item in the series. The following provision is defective in that regard.

> *Buyer may accept the goods without inspection, authorize the shipper to hold the goods pending inspection, accept the goods and reserve a right of later inspection, or the provisions of section 6 dealing with acceptance will otherwise control.*

The introductory word, "may," is appropriate for the first three phrases. But it makes no sense to say, "Buyer may . . . the provisions of section. . . ." For the last phrase to be parallel, it should read, "or otherwise proceed under the provisions of section 6 dealing with acceptance."

When the various parts of a multi-phrase sentence are enumerated and tabbed under the introductory phrase, drafters tend to forget that this is still a single sentence. The grammatically consistent structure of the sentence is then destroyed when the drafter attempts to bury another sentence within that structure, as in this example:

The recipient of Title IX funds may—

a. use the money to fund day care centers directly,

b. channel the money to day care centers through a tax-exempt charity. ***The charity's articles of incorporation must list this as a purpose of the charity.***

c. fund college scholarships for students majoring in pre-school educational and child care programs, or

d. sponsor funded research into preschool education and child care programs.

The bolded sentence breaks the larger sentence cleanly in half. The defect could be cured by referring to "a tax-exempt charity whose articles of incorporation list this as a purpose."

3. CONSISTENT DOCUMENT STRUCTURE AND APPROACH

A reader can more easily understand how a statute or contract operates if everything in the document is organized in a consistent or parallel fashion. For example, if the internal sequence of section A is chronological, stay with the chronological approach in the following sections unless the subject matter compels a different sequence.

Internal headings and numeration should likewise be consistent. If section A is,

A. Heading

  1. Heading

    a. Heading

      (i) Heading

Organize section B of the same document the same way.

The point is to establish a rhythm that allows the reader to anticipate and more easily understand the logical structure and legal consequence of each provision. Doing the same thing in different ways disrupts that rhythm, promotes reader uncertainty, and may lead to misunderstanding.

B. CONCISION

After the avoidance of ambiguity and inconsistency, being concise is the next most important objective of the drafter. Concision can be achieved by addressing the following.

1. UNNECESSARY CONTENT

Chapter 9 dealt with the substantive content of a document, breaking it down into what is: (1) required by externalities; (2) essential given the nature of the transaction; (3) extremely important given the peculiarities of the transaction; (4) and optional. Anything beyond that is unnecessary and its omission will enhance the concision of the document.

The problem arises often in complex multi-party contracts where one or more of the players, for example an escrow agent or an architect, is agreeing only to certain provisions. If that is the case, use a separate signature page for that party, indicating what provisions he or she is agreeing to.

2. CROSS-REFERENCES AND SECTION/ PARAGRAPH REFERENCES

Cross-referencing can help cut down on repetitive provisions. It is usually better to cross-reference to articles, sections, and paragraphs rather than pages, since pages change in the drafting process. A good general rule is to use the word "section" to refer to separate provisions of a formal agreement and the word "paragraph" to refer to separate provisions of an informal letter or letter agreement. The key is to be specific and consistent. Remember to proofread cross-references at the very end of the drafting process to make sure they remain accurate. Some drafters prefer to leave the section or paragraph reference blank until the last draft, *e.g.*, "section ___," essentially forcing themselves to proof the cross-references.

3. REPETITIOUS SUBSTANCE

Avoid repetition; say what needs to be said and say it only once. Consider this lease provision:

> *Landlord's acceptance of rent payments in arrears does not otherwise affect any right Landlord has under this lease. An acceptance of late rent payments does not constitute a waiver of*

> *Landlord's right to insist upon timely rent payment in the future. Landlord's failure to call an immediate lease forfeiture when rent is late does not preclude Landlord from calling such forfeiture at any time before payment is tendered.*

That provision says the same thing three times. It could be stated once, as follows:

> *The non-enforcement of any provision of this contract does not constitute a waiver of the right to enforce the provision in the future.*

Similarly, formbook boilerplate often follows a pattern of unnecessary terms, consisting of a word of total inclusiveness, followed by redundant paraphrases and then some examples, as in the following:

> *During liquidation, the court-appointed trustee shall distribute all [a word of total inclusiveness] of the Petitioner's assets, of any kind or character, tangible or intangible [paraphrasing "all"], whether in the form of cash, real estate, movable property, inventory, equipment, accounts receivable, securities, goodwill, or anything else of value [examples], in strict compliance with the terms of subparagraph 89(b)(16).*

In most contexts, a simple reference to "assets" will cover "any and all" of them, regardless of "kind or character," and will include both the "tangible" and the "intangible." The list of examples adds nothing to that, and in some cases these example lists have been construed as words of limitation. It could probably be stated as follows, without any danger of ambiguity or vagueness:

> *During liquidation, the court-appointed trustee shall distribute Petitioner's assets in strict compliance with the terms of subparagraph 89(b)(16).*

Whether this is adequate or the longer version is necessary is a question of law that must be resolved by the drafter before the stylistic aspects are addressed.

4. REDUNDANT COUPLETS, TRIPLETS, AND OTHER CHAIN SYNONYMS

Avoid legal doublets and triplets.

These are those famous repetitious chains of words that are part of the hoary legal chant that has come down through the ages. Examples include: "null and void;" "settlement and compromise;" "swear and affirm;" "right, title and interest;" and others listed below. Ask: do I really need each of these terms? Will fewer do? Will listing these terms leave the provision vulnerable to the doctrine of *expressio unis et exclusio alterius*—the rule that when a document lists certain things this creates an inference that the list is exclusive? (See Chapter 4 for more discussion.) If *expressio unis* may be a problem, consider using a more general term that contains within its meaning all desired alternatives.

Further, tucking a general reference such as "etc." or "and the like" at the end of a list to cure the *expressio unis* problem may invoke the dangers of the doctrine of *ejusdem generis* ("Of the same kind").

At one time in English legal history, generally following the battle of Hastings in 1066 A.D., Norman French, Middle English, and Latin all competed to become the dominant or authoritative language of the law. The same legal concept could be expressed in three different languages. Cautious lawyers used the words from all three languages, to ensure that they achieved the desired legal consequence. Even after the words evolved into English as we know it today, lawyers continued to use these chains—as if they were some religious talisman that would guard them against a claim of malpractice. Of note, early document drafters, called "scriveners," were paid by the word.

The most common couplet and triplet phrases are unnecessary. The drafter should pick the simplest word of the group and drop the others. Here is a partial list of these traditional phrases:

acknowledge and confess	act and deed
adjust, compromise, and settle	advice, opinion, and direction
agree and covenant	aid and abet
all and every	all and singular
alter or change	annul and set aside
any and all	assign, transfer, and set over

assumes and agrees

attorney and counselor at law

authorize, direct, and empower

bear, sustain, or suffer

bind and obligate

build, erect, or construct

business, enterprise, or undertaking

by and with

cancel, annul, and set aside

cancel and terminate

cease and desist

cease and come to an end

cease and terminate

chargeable or accountable

changes, variations, and modifications

confessed and acknowledged

conjecture and surmise

consolidation, amalgamation, or merger

contract, agreement, covenant, and understanding

convey, transfer, and set over

costs, charges, and expenses

covenant and agree

cover, embrace, and include

deem and consider

do, execute, and perform

documents, instruments, and writings

due and owing	due and payable
each and all	each and every
engage, hire, and employ	entirely and completely
evidencing or relating to	excess and unnecessary
fair and equitable	fair and reasonable
false and fraudulent	final and conclusive
finish and complete	fit and proper
fit and suitable	for and during
for and in consideration of	for and on behalf of
force and effect	fraud and deceit
free and clear	free and unfettered
free and without consideration	from and after
full and complete	full force and effect
furnish and supply	give and grant
give, devise, and bequeath	goods, chattels, and effects
good and sufficient	have, hold, and possess
heed and care	hold and keep
if and when	in and for
in and to	in my stead and place

in truth and in fact	indebtedness and liabilities
initiate, institute, or commence	just and reasonable
keep and maintain	kind and character
kind and nature	known and described as
lands, tenements, and hereditaments	last will and testament
legal, valid, and binding	let or hindrance
levies and assessments	lien, charge, or encumbrance
loans or advances	loss or damage
lot, tract, or parcel	made and entered into
made and provided	made, ordained, constituted, and appointed
make, declare, and publish	maintenance and upkeep
meet and just	mend, maintain, and repair
mentioned or referred to	mind and memory
modified and changed	nature or description
nominate, constitute, and appoint	null, void, and of no force and effect

obligation and liability
obey, observe, and comply with
observe, perform, and carry out
of and concerning
ordain and establish
order and direct
order, adjudged, and decreed
over, above, and in addition to
pardon and forgive
part and parcel
pay, satisfy, and discharge
peace and quiet
perform and discharge
performance or observance
place, install, or affix
possession, custody, and control
power and authority
release and discharge
relieve and discharge
remise, release, and quitclaim
represents, warrants, and covenants
representations, understandings, and agreements
rest, resident, and remainder
revoked and annulled
right, title, and interest
rights and remedies
rules, requirements, and regulations
save and except
seized and possessed
sell, transfer, alienate, and dispose of

shun and avoid	signed, published, and declared
situate, lying, and being in	sole and exclusive
stipulate and agree	suffer or permit
suit, claim, or demand	supersede and displace
term or covenant	terminate, cancel, or revoke
then and in that event	true and correct
truth and veracity	type and kind
understood and agreed	unless and until
vacate, surrender, and deliver possession	void and of no effect
void and of no force	void and of no value
within and under the terms of	

Examine lists of synonymous terms and rank them in a hierarchy. Are they all of the same rank? If not, this is an indicator that *expressio unis* and *ejusdem generis* problems may be lurking in the list. Consider eliminating lower rank words and using fewer words of a higher rank.

On the other hand, do not indiscriminately delete pairs or triplets. They may exist for a reason and not simply as a list of synonyms. For example, in a real property sale agreement, the seller should be under a duty to "execute *and* deliver" the deed to the property. Execution without delivery (and vice versa) is ineffective to transfer title.

5. OTHER REDUNDANT EXPRESSIONS

The statements made in this section are general ones, and you must evaluate in each instance whether the general advice should be followed. In drafting agreements, concentrate especially on whether your chosen word has the correct level of specificity. Overdressing one's writing makes it harder to read and does not demonstrate education or sophistication. Education and sophistication are shown by drafting that makes its meaning clear with little effort on the reader's part. Still, reasonable minds can differ on matters of word choice. Use the following suggestions as a guide, but, as with most legal drafting, it is best for you to make up your own mind as to what is appropriate under the circumstances.

Avoid compound prepositions:

Avoid	Use Instead
the question as to whether	whether (the question whether)
all of the issues	all the issues
at that point in time	then
in the nature	of like

Avoid overly showy words:

Avoid	Use Instead
additionally	also
adequate number of	enough, sufficient
adjacent	next to (specify distance?)
aforesaid	previous, prior
any and all	any
at the time	when
approximately	about
at [the] present [time]	now
by means of	by
cease and desist	stop, cease
circumstances in which	when, where
commence	begin
contained in	in
contiguous	next to
due [to the fact that]	because
eventuates	occurs, happens
facilitate	help, assist
has a negative impact	harms
including but not limited to	including
inquire	ask

null and void	void
notify	tell, inform
permit	let, allow
penultimate	second to last
request	ask
retain	keep
ultimate	last
utilize	use

Some things are implicit in certain words, making it unnecessary to state them expressly. Implicit in "three hours" is the notion of a time period. The expression for a "time period of three hours" is redundant. In the following examples, the bracketed portion is or may be implicit in the remaining term and can therefore be deleted.

[a distance of] two miles	[a period of] a week
all [of the] materials	alongside [of]
appreciate [in value]	ascend [up]
[as to] whether	[at a] later [date]
[close] scrutiny	combine [together]
[completely] destroyed	depreciate [in value]
descend [down]	[different] kinds
during [the course of]	during [the month of] July

each [and every]	each [separate] provision
eradicate [completely]	few [in number]
[foreign] imports	join [together]
[general] public	[local] residents
merged [together]	never [at any time]
off [of]	postponed [until later]
[rate of] speed	recur [again]
refer [back]	regress [back]
revert [back]	[separate] entities
5 p.m. [in the afternoon]	

6. LEGALESE

A lay person might erroneously think that the chains of words discussed above are necessary, and thus admire their lawyer's attention to detail. Still, most lay persons know that the "wherein's," "aforesaid's," and "hereinafter's" are unnecessary. Indeed, nothing has contributed more to the bad reputation of legal writing than these archaic terms. Do not use them, or, if you must, use them sparingly. A partial list of legalese:

above-mentioned	aforegranted
aforesaid	before-mentioned
behoove	foregoing
forthwith	henceforth

hereafter	herebefore
hereby	herein
hereinabove	hereinafter
hereinbefore	hereinto
hereinunder	hereof
heretofore	hereunder
hereunto	herewith
hitherto	inasmuch
insofar	notwithstanding
nowise	saith
thence	thenceforth
thereabout	thereafter
thereat	thereby
therefore	therefrom
therein	thereof
thereon	thereto
theretofore	thereunder
thereunto	therewith
to wit	under-mentioned
unto	whatever
whatsoever	whence
whensoever	whereas
whereby	wherefore
wherein	whereof
whereon	wheresoever

whereupon	whosoever
whilst	within-named

Another form of legalese consists of antique phrases like the following:

Being first duly sworn, Sam Jones deposes and says:

Further affiant [or deponent] sayeth not.

In witness whereof I have hereunto set my hand and caused my seal to be affixed.

Know All Men By These Presents:

To All To Whom These Presents Come, Greeting:

WITNESSETH:

All of these phrases can be eliminated. Use common English in their place.

The words "said," "same," and "such" are another form of objectionable legalese, even if the usage is grammatically correct. Never use "said" as an adjective. Delete it or replace it with "the," "that," "this," or an appropriate pronoun.

Director shall grant or deny said application within 10 days,

becomes

Director shall grant or deny the application within 10 days.

Do not use "such" as an adjective before a singular noun; replace it with "the," "that," or "this." However, "such" may be used as an adjective before plural nouns, without running afoul the rule against the use of legalisms, to mean "of this kind, nature, or degree," as in "such acts of misconduct will not be tolerated."

Do not use "same" or "such" as a pronoun.

Director shall review the application within **10** *days and grant or deny same [or such]*

becomes

Director shall review the application within **10** *days and grant or deny it.*

Or consider this use of "such" as a pronoun:

While on duty, employees shall not drink alcoholic beverages, take illegal drugs, or smoke controlled substances. Such [replace with "these actions"] are grounds for immediate termination.

7. COMPOUND PREPOSITIONS AND PREPOSITIONAL PHRASES

A preposition is a word or phrase that expresses the relationship of one word with another. In "payment is due **after** delivery," the word "after" expresses the temporal relationship between "payment" and "delivery." Compound prepositions (also called prepositional phrases and complex prepositions) consist of two or more words that function as a single-word preposition would. Henry Fowler, author of *A Dictionary of Modern English Usage* said that compound prepositions "are almost the worst element in modern English, stuffing up what is written with a compost of noun-y abstractions." Most compound prepositions can be replaced with a single word that is clearer and more direct.

The more common compound prepositions, together with their replacements, are:

Compound Preposition	Replacement
along the lines of	like
as a consequence of	because of
as to	about
at that point in time	then
as the present time	now
at the time at which	when
at this point in time	now
be of help to	help
be means of	by
by reason of	because of
by virtue of	by, under
during such times as	when
during the course of	during
during the time that	while
for the duration of	during
for the purpose of	for, under
for the reason that	because

Compound Preposition	Replacement
from the point of view of	for
inasmuch as	because
in a manner similar to	like
in all probability	probably
in addition to	besides
in accordance with	by, under
in association with	with
in back of	behind
in case of	if
in close proximity	near
in connection with	by, from, about, at
in excess of	more than, over
in favor of	for
in lieu of	instead of
in order to	to
in receipt of	received
in regard to	about, concerning
in spite of the fact that	although
in terms of	at, in, for, by, with
in the absence of	without
in the case of	if
in the course of	during

Compound Preposition	Replacement
in the event that	if
in the midst of	amid
in the nature of	like
in the immediate vicinity of	near
in view of the fact	because, considering, that
notwithstanding the fact that	although
on account of	because
on the basis of	by, from
on the grounds of	because of
on the part of	by, among
prior to	before
similar to	like
subsequent to	after
the manner in which	how
under the provisions of	under
until such time as	until
with a view to	to
with reference to	about, concerning
with regard to	about, concerning
with respect to	about, with, on, concerning, for, in

Compound Preposition	Replacement
with the exception of	except
with the object of	to
with the result that	so that

8. "THE FACT THAT"

This wordy idiom usually appears in dependent clauses. A dependent clause is a group of words that contains a verb but does not qualify as a complete sentence. Dependent clauses are often used to fill the slot in a sentence that calls for a noun. A dependent clause containing "the fact that" can function as any of the following:

(1) **A subject:** "The fact that the buyer fails to inspect constitutes waiver."

(2) **A direct object:** "Upon delivery, the shipper must note on the invoice the fact that the buyer failed to inspect."

(3) **An indirect object:** "The consequences of the fact that the buyer fails to inspect are that buyer waives all defects."

(4) **An object of a preposition:** Under paragraph (c), the buyer may recover for defects that were not discovered because of the fact that the seller made timely inspection impossible.

The drafter can avoid these obtuse constructions by replacing the dependent clause with a true noun or noun clause, as in these revisions to the above sentences:

(1) "The buyer's failure to object constitutes waiver."

(2) "Upon delivery, the shipper must note on the invoice the buyer's failure to object."

(3) "The consequences of the buyer's failure to object are that buyer waives all defects."

(4) "Under paragraph (c), the buyer may recover for defects that were not discovered because the seller made timely inspection impossible."

9. RHETORICAL AND TRANSITIONAL WORDS AND PHRASES

Certain transitional words and phrases common in a brief or memorandum serve no purpose in a normative document and should be omitted. These words and phrases include:

admittedly	again
also	although
accordingly	as a result
because	besides
but	consequently
despite	even if
even though	for example
for instance	furthermore
granted that	hence

however	in addition
instead	likewise
moreover	nevertheless
next	nonetheless
on the other hand	similarly
still	so
therefore	too
to the contrary	thus

The relationship between the various components of a drafted document should be evident from the organizational scheme of the document and the numbered/lettered heading that it contains.

Their use, however, is arguably appropriate in two situations. First, the Recitals (or Background) in a contract and Findings (or Preamble) in a statute are usually expository in form and transitory words enhance the readability of these portions of the document. Second, if a document is intended minimize the harsh legalities of a relationship—an employment manual, for example—then transitory words will contribute to that tone of informality.

10. THE PHRASE "OF THE . . ."

This phrase can be either deleted or made into a possessive with an apostrophe. So, instead of saying,

All ***of the*** *applicants must attach a current photograph to the visa application,* say,

All applicants must attach a current photograph to the visa application.

Instead of saying,

*Children **of a** resident alien must be listed on line 4 of Form 459,*

say,

A resident alien's children must be listed on line 4 of Form 459.

11. UNNECESSARY "WHO'S," "WHICH'S," AND "THAT'S"

Eliminating these words will often make the sentence leaner and more efficient. Instead of saying,

*Voters **who** are registering to vote absentee must file within 30 days,*

say,

Voters registering to vote absentee must file within 30 days.

Instead of saying,

*The goods, **which** are sold only in bulk, are warranted against insect infection,*

say,

The goods, sold only in bulk, are warranted against insect infection.

Instead of saying,

The inspection ***that*** *the buyer conducts is subject to section 3(a),*

say,

The inspection the buyer conducts is subject to section 3(a).

Do not delete these words for style's sake, however, if this will create an ambiguity. For example, in the sentence "The buyer will inspect the goods on the loading dock," it is unclear whether the location relates to the identity of the goods to be inspected or indicates where the inspection will take place. If it relates to identity, then "the goods **that are** on . . . " would make that clear. If it relates to the location of the inspection, convert it into a dependent clause—"goods, which are on the loading dock." Alternatively, this might be an appropriate place for the passive voice, "The buyer's inspection of the goods will be conducted on the loading dock."

12. SUBSTANTIVE NUMBERS AND REDUNDANT NUMERATION

Lawyers commonly present numbers in both the Arabic and written form.

This section is subject to the four (4) exceptions contained in section 8.c.

One-half (1/2) of the payment is due on delivery.

Seller will deliver thirty (30) crates.

It is common practice that numbers used in legal agreements are both spelled and represented in numerals to avoid confusion and make later alteration more difficult. For example, "the sum of five-thousand, five hundred dollars ($5,500) will be paid at closing." This is wordy and serves no rational purpose other than making later document alteration difficult (justified in the case of say, a check or other negotiable instrument). The reader knows what "thirty" means, knows what "30" means, and knows that they mean the same thing. It is not necessary to say it twice.

Leading commentators on modern formal use of English disfavor writing out numbers in words. Unless concerns about alteration of the document are strong, drop the double form of expression and use numerals exclusively. Alternatively, write out the numbers one through ten in words and use numerals for 11 and up. Either system makes documents easier to proofread and prevents the opportunity for words to conflict with numerals, eliminating another source of ambiguity.

A combination of the numerical and the written version of a number should, however, be used when dealing with figures in the million range that end with a triplet of zeros. Rather than saying "$25,000,000" or "$25,400,000," say "$25 million" or "$25.4 million."

13. EXPLETIVES

In the grammatical sense, an expletive is a word without substantive content; it is a surrogate noun used merely to satisfy the grammatical requirement that the sentence have a subject. For example, in "There are six residential units in each pod," the grammatical subject of the sentence is "there." The word refers to nothing, however, and serves no function other than to provide the proper syntax for the sentence. The intended subject of the sentence is "residential units." With the expletive deleted, the sentence reads, "Six residential units are in each pod." The most common expletives found in drafted documents are "it is," "there is," and "there are."

Notice how much clearer and less wordy the non-expletive version is in comparison with the expletive version.

Expletive:

(1) It is the intent of Congress for this Act to prohibit all forms of obscenity.

(2) There is included in every lease subject to this Act an implied covenant of good faith and fair dealing.

(3) There are **6** *requirements for the job.*

Expletive Deleted:

(1) Congress intends for this Act to prohibit all forms of obscenity.

(2) Every lease subject to this Act contains an implied covenant of good faith and fair dealing.

(3) The job has **6** *requirements.*

14. NOMINALIZATIONS

Unbury verbs. Nominalizations contribute enormously to the wordiness of most drafted documents. Nominalization is a fancy term for turning an ordinary verb into a country-club noun, and then tacking on another verb to satisfy syntactical requirements. The simple "pending" becomes "during the pendency of." Nominalizations in a drafted document should nearly always be converted back into their simpler verb form.

The most common nominalizations and their verb replacements are as follows:

Nominalization	**Verb**
draw a conclusion	conclude
file a complaint	complain
give consideration to	consider
give recognition to	recognize
has pertinence	pertains
have knowledge of	know
have need of	need
in agreement with	agree
in collision with	collide with
in the determination of	to determine
is applicable	applies
is dependent on	depends on
is in attendance at	attends

make a contribution	contribute
make an appointment	appoint
make application	apply
make payment	pay
make provision for	provide
render a decision	decide
submit a payment	pay
suggestive of	suggests
take action	act

As these examples show, nominalizations can often be identified by their endings, such as: -al, -ancy, -ant, -ence, -ent, -ion, -ity, -ive, -ment.

15. PASSIVE VOICE

In an active voice sentence, the subject acts upon the object in some fashion, as in "The Seller [subject] warrants [verb, indicating what action the subject is performing] the goods [object]." Contract clauses should be drafted in the active voice whenever possible. Test your sentence by looking for a subject-verb-object structure (SVO), specifying *who* is doing *what* to *whom* (or *what*). To avoid the passive voice drafters should make the subject of the sentence a person or entity that acts, rather than a thing or a concept.

In a passive voice sentence, the subject of the sentence is being acted upon by something else, as in "The goods [subject] are warranted [verb, indicating an action upon the subject] by the Seller." To spot a passive voice construction, first look for an actual "by" prepositional phrase following the verb, as in that example.

In the truncated passive, however, this "by" phrase is merely implied, as in "All change orders must be reported to the bank [read *by owner* or *by contractor* and it could be either, hence the ambiguity], as the case may be, within 10 days." In addition to the ambiguity of the truncated passive discussed in Chapter 12, wordiness is the other principal defect of the passive voice. An active voice sentence is nearly always more concise than its passive voice counterpart.

However, the passive voice does have some legitimate uses in drafted documents. For example, it can be used if the intent is to put the emphasis on what must be done rather than on who must do it. This is accomplished more effectively with "Applications must be filed by each candidate before July 12" than with "Each candidate must file an application before July 12." Although other techniques are also available, the passive voice can be used to avoid gender-specific pronouns. Instead of saying, "An attorney must file his personal affidavit as an attachment to the motion," one might say, "An attorney's personal affidavit must be filed as an attachment to the motion."

16. "TO BE" VERB FORMS

Most forms of "to be" in drafted documents are "was," "is," "are," "were," and "been." A "to be" verb should be used only to define or identify, as in "the seller is a resident of Texas." When a "to be" form of the verb is used in other way, the resulting prose is wordy. If the drafter replaces the "to be" verb with an active verb, the sentence will be shorter and more direct. Consider this "to be" verb-laden paragraph.

> *If a subcontractor* ***is*** *in breach of the agreement, then the security bond* ***is*** *voided. If there* ***are*** *any suppliers of goods or materials who* ***were*** *in expectation of receiving payment, then the general contractor* ***is*** *expected to reimburse them out of the escrow funds which* ***are*** *held by the owner. [51 words.]*

Below, the "to be" verbs are replaced with active verbs:

> *If a subcontractor breaches the agreement, this voids the security bond. If any suppliers of goods or materials expected to receive payment, the general contractor must reimburse them out of the escrow funds held by the owner. [38 words.]*

"To be" verb forms often occur in connection with expletives, nominalizations, and the passive voice—as well as in sentences where the drafter has not used the proper word to create a particular legal consequence. Eliminating the errant to be verb is an indirect way of correcting these other mistakes. The to be verb phrases that drafters tend to use most often, and their replacements, are:

"To Be" Verb	Replacement
is able to	can
is authorized to	may
is binding upon	binds
is empowered to	may
is unable to	cannot
is directed to	shall
is required to	shall
it is the duty to	shall

C. CLARITY AND SIMPLICITY

A document free of ambiguity, inconsistency, and excessive wordiness is a clearer and simpler document. Lists, enumerations, and tabbing, which are discussed in Chapter 16, also promote clarity. In addition, these objectives are served by the following rules of style:

1. SHORT SENTENCES

An average sentence length of 26 words is an admirable objective for a drafted document. The closer the drafter comes to that objective, the clearer the document will be. Look for places to divide longer sentences into two or more.

2. SIMPLE SENTENCE STRUCTURE

Draft the way people think:

> *Someone [noun] does something [verb] to something [direct object].*

The normal, active voice word order in English is *subject, verb,* and *object.* If you wish to change this order for emphasis, remember that the strongest places in the sentence are the beginning and the end. Generally, stick to subject, verb, object (SVO) order. The best contract clauses follow this order; they tell the reader *who* is to do *what* to *whom, when,* and *what will happen* if they do not do so.

Try not to separate the noun from the verb or the verb from the direct object with dependent clauses, ideas buried between parentheses, or other intrusive asides. These are called "gaps." A single sentence can carry only so much substance. Let several sentences share the load. In the following provision, the bolded portions show verb/noun and noun/object gaps that make the sentence convoluted and confusing.

> *Buyer,* ***upon receipt and inspection of the goods,*** *will,* ***provided they are found to be in compliance with the contract and otherwise as warranted,*** *immediately notify,* ***per section 6 of this contract,*** *the seller of acceptance.*

Consider this alternative:

> *Upon receipt of the goods, buyer will inspect them. If buyer finds that the goods comply with the contract and are as warranted, buyer will immediately notify seller of acceptance. Seller's*

notification must satisfy the requirements of section 6 of this contract.

Avoid inserting clauses between the subject and the verb, particularly if the clause can be transferred to the beginning or end of the sentence.

Avoid	**Use**
The borrower, in its notice of borrowing, should specify the method for computing interest.	The borrower should specify the method for computing interest in its notice of borrowing.

Keep modifiers next to the word they modify.

Avoid	**Use**
The weak lawyer's contract.	The lawyer's weak contract.

This, of course, assumes that "weak" is intended to modify "contract," not "lawyer."

Do not insert adverbs between the component parts of verbs unless done for emphasis. This is particularly true for infinitives ("to clearly write"). The "unless done for emphasis" exception to this rule is more widely accepted now than in the past, but take care to know what your audience prefers. Split infinitives tend to *really* bother traditionalists.

Keep objects close to verbs.

Avoid	**Use**
The local court has repeatedly interpreted incorrectly that line of cases.	The local court has misinterpreted that line of cases repeatedly.

The overuse of dependent clauses set off by commas, parentheses, and dashes can be confusing and often indicates that a single sentence is being employed to do too many things. Instead, use separate sentences. So instead of this:

Tenant (unless Landlord has agreed in writing in advance) shall not keep or allow the presence of pets (including dogs, cats, rabbits, birds, hamsters, gerbils, or reptiles of any kind) in the Leased Premises (as defined in paragraph 6(b)(7)), and any violation of this provision is a material breach (justifying immediate termination of the lease).

say this: *Tenant shall not keep or allow the presence of pets in the Leased Premises. Landlord may waive this provision in advance in a signed writing. For the purpose of this provision, "pets" includes dogs, cats, rabbits, birds, hamsters, gerbils, and reptiles of any kind. A violation of this provision is a material breach of the lease, justifying immediate termination.*

3. PRESENT TENSE

Draft in the present tense. A contract or statute is said to be constantly "speaking." Drafted documents assume that whatever they are dealing with is currently happening, not that it happened yesterday or is going to happen tomorrow. The use of past tense, present tense, and future tense in the same document promotes confusion.

> *If seller's inability to deliver on time* ***is*** *[not* ***was*** *or* ***has been****] caused by circumstances beyond seller's control, buyer* ***is*** *not [not* ***will not be****] entitled to cancel.*

4. SIMPLE, ORDINARY WORDS

Do not use the fancy version of a word, or collection of words, when the simple, ordinary counterpart is more easily understood by the average reader.

Word	**Replace with**
accommodate	adapt, fit, suit
accomplish	perform, do
accorded	given
accumulate	collect, gather
acknowledge	recognize, admit
acquire	obtain, or buy
adequate number of	enough
adjacent	next to, near
admit of	allow
advantageous	good
afforded	given
allocate	divide

Word	**Replace with**
alternative	choice, option
appropriate (verb)	take
approximately	about
ascertain	determine
assist, assistance	help
attempt	try
cease	stop
commence	begin, start
complete	finish
conceal	hide
consequence	result
contiguous	next, adjoining
determine	decide, find
donate	give
duplicate	copy
during such time as	while
during the course of	during
effectuate	carry out, cause
eliminate	remove
employ	use
endeavor	try
eradicate	remove, erase
evince	show
execute	sign

Word	**Replace with**
exceptional	rare, unique
expedite	hasten
expeditiously	immediately
expend	spend
expiration	end
feasible	possible
finalize	complete
forthwith	immediately
frequently	often
fundamental	basic
furnish	give
heterogeneous	mixed, unlike
homogeneous	same, alike
horizontal	level, flat
immaculate	clean
immovable	fixed
impact on	influence
in arrears	late
indebtedness	debt
indicate	show
inform	tell, report
infrequent	rare
initiate	begin
inquire	ask

Word	Replace with
institute	establish, begin, start
intelligible	clear
interrogate	question
locality	place
locate	find
magnitude	size
manner	way
maximum	most, largest, greatest
minimum	least, smallest, fewest
modify	change
necessitate	require
obliterate	erase
obtain	get
occasion (verb)	cause
peruse	read, review
portion	part
possess	have
preserve	keep
prior	earlier
prior to	before
proceed	go
procure	obtain, buy, get
proficient	skilled
promulgated	issue, publish

Word	Replace with
proximity	nearness
purchase	buy
purchaser	buyer
recompense	reward, compensate
redundant	extra, unneeded
remainder	rest
remuneration	salary, compensation, pay
render	make, give
request	ask
require	need
retain	keep
specified	named
state	tell, give
subsequent	after, later
suffer	permit
sufficient	enough
summon	call, send for
terminate	end, finish
transmit	send
transparent	clear
unavailability	lack
utilize	use
verify	prove

5. TERMS OF ART

As discussed in Chapter 8, a word or phrase may qualify as a term of art because the law requires that it be used to achieve a particular result; because it is a defined term expression for a complex legal concept; or because its legal meaning is different from its conventional meaning. Terms of art may facilitate communication among lawyers, but they are a total mystery to lay readers of drafted documents. Thus, terms of art defeat a primary objective of drafting, to be clear to everyone within the intended audience.

Yet, many lawyers resist giving up the use of terms of art, asserting this will cause confusion and precipitate needless litigation. This fear is largely without foundation. First, most terms of art are not as precise and fixed in legal meaning as their defenders contend. Consider, for example, the multiple meanings that the courts have given to "appurtenances," "fixtures," and "tenantable"—words that real estate lawyers consider sacrosanct terms of art, but that have proved not to be. Second, some terms of art have a fixed meaning, but one that is so general that it is virtually worthless in a drafted document. For example, all lawyers know that a "right of first refusal" creates an option and regard that is a term of art. Certainly, that is its fixed, generalized meaning. But for an option to be enforceable, it must specify the details of the transaction. The option is an option to buy what, at what price, and subject to what payment, delivery, and other terms? That is what an actual contract must focus on, and a glib "Jones has a right of first refusal" is insufficient, even if that is an esteemed term of art. Third, specific words or phrases that absolutely must be used to achieve a particular legal result are relatively rare. Most terms of art can be expressed in other words—words that are both more familiar to the lay reader and that provide the precision and specificity required.

6. TECHNICAL AND TRADE TERMS

The drafter should also take care when using technical, scientific, commercial, and other terms with specialized meanings. If the context suggests that a word is being used in a specialized sense, the courts will construe it accordingly. If the specialized meaning is not what is intended, then the drafter must select a different word. For example, although a tomato is scientifically a fruit in the produce world, among consumers it is regarded as a vegetable. Defining the term can eliminate the ambiguity.

7. FOREIGN WORDS AND PHRASES

Unless it is a true term of art, like "*per stirpes*," avoid foreign words and phrases. These are usually Latin or French. Even commonly recognized words like "*bona fide*" can be replaced by their English counterpart, like "good faith." The most commonly abused foreign words and phrases, often found in old formbooks and file documents, and their more suitable replacements are as follows:

Foreign Word or Phrase	Replacement
ad infinitum	indefinitely
causa mortis	approaching death
exempli gratia (*e.g.*)	for example
fructus fundi	produce of the land
id est (i.e.)	that is
inter alia	among others
inter se	among themselves
lex loci	law of the, jurisdiction
mutatis mutandis	with the necessary, changes in detail
non compos mentis	not of sound mind
per annum	a year
pro rata	proportionately
pari passu	of the same priority
seriatim	separately
vis-a-vis	in relation to
viva voca	orally

8. WORDS ENDING IN "-EE" AND "-OR"

Even lawyers sometimes get confused over the identity of the lessor and the lessee, the mortgagor and the mortgagee, and the vendor and the vendee. When describing the parties, use dissimilar, plain English terms, like "landlord" and "tenant," "borrower" and "lender," and "seller" and "buyer."

9. COMPOUND ADJECTIVES AND NOUN PHRASES

Limit your use of hyphens. Generally, hyphens should be used to form compound adjectives:

The short-term loan agreement contained a cross-default clause.

A compound adjective is two adjectives, with the first adjective modifying the second adjective and the two adjectives combined then modifying the following noun, thus creating a noun phrase. Use a hyphen to signal the reader that the adjectives function as a unit: "one-owner vehicle." Hyphenation is even more important if the phrase contains three adjectives: "a year-round container supply." No amount of hyphenation will save extensive noun chains, however. Do not refer to a Research-and-Development-Department-approved rotor-wheel-abrasion-removal device. Refer to it as a device for the removal of abrasions on rotor wheels that has been approved by the Research and Development Department.

There are, however, exceptions. Nonpayment, intercompany, and *pro rata* (which can be replaced with "proportionately") should all be written without hyphens. Even if omitting a hyphen results in a double letter, a hyphen should generally not be used to attach a prefix to a word. However, if the result would cause confusion or mispronunciation (such as in the case of co-op or re-lease), a hyphen is justified. When in doubt as to the use of a hyphen, write the word as one unit. To be accurate, consult the most current unabridged or legal dictionary available to determine the preferred modern usage for your requirements.

In some cases hyphens are helpful in distinguishing use of a word as a verb (no-hyphen) or a noun (hyphen). Verb: " . . . *the bank is entitled to set off any deposit. . . .*" Noun: " . . . *the bank is entitled to a set-off in the event. . . .*" But the drafter can achieve the same effect by using an article to indicate the noun, as is also done in this example with the indefinite article "a."

10. UNCONVENTIONAL CAPITALIZATION

Eighteenth Century drafters often capitalized important nouns, a practice probably derived from German. Unfortunately, this practice is still followed in certain types of contracts. It would not be unusual, for example, to find something like this in a construction contract:

> *All Bills of Lading will be kept on file at the Construction Site. . . . Change Orders must be approved in writing. . . . The anticipated Completion Date of Construction is. . . .*

This is unnecessary and distracting. Capitalize only proper nouns, including defined terms.

11. POSITIVE VERSUS NEGATIVE EXPRESSION

If something can be said either positively or negatively, say it positively. This is clearer because people think this way. Instead of saying,

The curfew does not apply before midnight,

say,

The curfew applies only after midnight.

Double negatives are especially confusing. Instead of saying,

This section does not apply to applicants with no dependent children,

say,

This section applies only to applicants with dependent children.

12. EXCEPTIONS

Try not to draft in terms of a larger class from which certain members are then excepted; draft in terms of the targeted subclass directly. So, instead of saying,

All applicants ***except*** *those who are 40 years old or older must complete Form 647,*

say,

All applicants who are less than 40 years old must complete Form 647.

On the other hand, when drafting directly in terms of the excepted subclass would leave a substantive void with respect to what happens to the larger class, then the exception approach is necessary. For example, "Charleston, Richland, and Greenville Counties are not entitled to emergency relief funding" fails to create a positive entitlement by the other counties to receive the funding. Thus, one should use the exception approach, saying, "All counties, except Charleston, Richland, and Greenville, are entitled to receive emergency relief funding."

13. PERSONAL PRONOUNS

One of the objectives of the plain English movement was to make documents readily understandable by lay readers, especially consumers. Drafters were thus encouraged to use personal pronouns like "you", "I", and "we", on the theory that this made the document less formidable and more comprehensible. Drafters also sometimes use these pronouns to establish a tone of informality in documents like employee handbooks and application instructions. Although these pronouns serve a useful purpose in a limited class of documents, they should never be used at the expense of clarity and precision.

The principal dangers are as follows. First, the reader may misunderstand who is "I," who is "you," and who is "we." Second, the danger is compounded if the transaction involves multiple documents and they are not all written from the same point of view. The consumer may be "I" in one document, but "you" in another. Third, using personal pronouns can be more confusing than helpful in transactions involving more than two parties.

Pronouns are not the precise drafter's friend. As a general rule, identify the parties by name, title, or status and a defined term—not with a personal pronoun.

D. SOME BASIC RULES OF GRAMMAR RELEVANT TO DRAFTING

1. FORMING THE POSSESSIVE

a. Form the Possessive Singular of Nouns by Adding " 's"

The court's ruling.

The possessive is *not* used when specifying a time period, such as a notice period. For example, it is "20-days notice" (compound adjective form) rather than "20 days' notice" or, worse, "20 day's notice" (incorrect possessive forms).

An apostrophe followed by an "s" is often used to form the plural of letters, single-digit numbers, and symbols. While this form looks like possessive form, it is merely plural. It is incorrect to pluralize names with an apostrophe followed by "s". For example, "the Brown's" is the incorrect plural form. The correct plural form is "the Browns" with no apostrophe.

b. Form the Possessive Plural by Adding an Apostrophe

The lawyers' presentations.

c. Its, It's, His, and Hers

"Its" is the possessive form of "it."

"It's" is a contraction for "it is."

"His" and "hers" are possessive and have no apostrophe.

2. USE OF THE SEMICOLON VERSUS THE COLON

a. The Semicolon

When joining two or more grammatically complete (independent) clauses without a conjunction, use a semicolon. Think of its use in this fashion as representing a weak period.

The attorney's argument was compelling; he persuaded the jury.

Apart from being used to separate items in a list that are themselves long or compound, this punctuation mark has limited relevance to contracts and transactional documents. If you find that you are using semi-colons in transactional documents other than as part of a list, examine your use carefully.

b. The Colon

A colon directs the reader to what follows. It usually follows an independent clause and can be used to introduce a variety of related statements: a list of particulars, a quotation, an appositive, an illustration, or an amplification. Even two independent clauses can be joined with a colon if the second interprets or amplifies the first.

It is not necessary to use a colon every time a list is introduced. For example, "The model you like is available in red, blue, white, and ochre" takes no colon. Overuse of a colon with lists is cumbersome.

Commentators are split on whether the first letter of the word that follows a colon is capitalized. Most agree, however, that if that word is the first in a list of multiple items, each item begins with a lower case letter.

3. SLASHES

The slash should not be used in legal writing because of the ambiguity involved. The slash could indicate "and" (conjunctive) or "or" (disjunctive), thus creating unnecessary ambiguity. The only acceptable use for a slash in legal writing is for dates (03/13/20) and fractions (½).

4. SUBJECT AND VERB AGREEMENT

Subject and verb must agree in number.

a. The number of the subject determines the number of the verb. This is true even if other nouns are connected to it by "with" or "no less than."

The statute, as well as the regulation, favors a strict construction.

On the other hand:

Both the statute and the regulation favor a strict construction.

The statutes favor a strict construction.

b. Plural vs. Singular nouns.

A. When "none" means "no one" or "not one", use a singular verb. If "none" suggests more than one thing or person, use a plural verb.

B. Remember—forum, memorandum, datum, and criterion are singular; fora, memoranda, data, and criteria are plural.

C. Singular verbs should be used with "either" and "any" and, in its usual form, "neither . . . nor."

5. PARENTHESES

A sentence containing a parenthetical expression is punctuated outside the parentheses exactly as if the parenthetical expression were absent. The parenthetical expression itself is punctuated as if it stood by itself, except that the final or "terminal" punctuation mark is omitted unless it is a question mark or an exclamation point:

Payments of interest should be made quarterly (on the first business day of each quarter), but will be compounded daily.

The defendant protested (and why should we doubt his word?) that he had delivered the goods as specified.

(When a wholly detached statement is contained in parentheses, the final punctuation comes before the closing of the parenthesis, as here.) If the point is to make the statement stand out (rather than be concealed) a pair of dashes is probably the better tool.

6. QUOTATION MARKS

The placement of quotation marks in relation to other punctuation marks (commas, periods, colons, semi-colons, question marks, and exclamation marks) is a matter of some disagreement in the English speaking world. The British practice differs in significant respects from the American practice. But just as British spelling is not favored in documents drafted in this country, neither is the British practice with respect to quotation marks. The American practice is as follows:

- Always put commas and periods within the quotation marks.

  Unless referring to a specific individual, author will not use any gender specific terms in the text, including "he," "she," "him," "his," or "her."

- Always put colons and semi-colons outside the quotation marks.

  When shipping packages containing hazardous materials, seller shall clearly mark them as "hazardous materials"; all of the materials listed in section 302–b are considered "hazardous."

- Put exclamation and question marks inside the quotation marks if they are actually part of the quoted material; if they are the drafter's own addition, place them outside the quotation marks. Although exclamation and question marks are rarely used in drafted documents, the drafter may need to use them in correspondence relating to a drafter document.

Allow me to say this in response to your question, "Why does the contract not contain a liquidated damages provision?" [Also note the absence of a terminal period.]

Were you serious when you suggested that we change the reference in the statute from "bars" to "jook joints"?

The legal drafter, however, should deviate from these conventions when drafting amendments. Periods and commas should be outside the quotation marks unless they are intended to be a part of what is being amended. Colons and semi-colons should be inside the quotation marks if they are intended to be a part of the amended language.

- *Section 7. Section 499(c)(4) is amended by striking the word "children" and inserting "dependent minors".* [In the original, the word "children" was in the middle of a sentence and had no punctuation following it; the amended term must also be devoid of punctuation, thus requiring the terminal period to come after the quotation mark.]
- *Paragraph 64 is amended by inserting "territory already assigned to another agent;" after "Agent may not solicit sales in any of the following areas:"* [Insert is added at the beginning of a list that is separated by semi-colons.]

7. SPACING AFTER SENTENCES

The traditional rule is that two spaces are used after a sentence's terminal punctuation and the first word of the next sentence. This aids the reader when skimming or speed-reading the document by providing the eye with a double space to identify the beginning of the next sentence.

This rule has eroded in recent years, due to the rise of proportional spacing. The modern trend appears to be use of a single space after terminal punctuation.

Whichever of these conventions is adopted is up to the individual draftsperson, but consistency is desirable.

E. MISUSED AND ABUSED WORDS AND EXPRESSIONS

Effect/Affect. "Effect" as a noun means "result" or "appearance." As a verb it means "to bring about" or "to accomplish." "Affect," a verb, means "to influence" or "to simulate."

Farther and Further. Use "farther" when distance is involved and "further" when referring to time or quantities. My dog chases balls "farther" than other dogs. Attorneys often pursue a subject "further" than others.

Fortuitous. This word refers to something that happens by chance. It is not limited to fortunate or lucky happenings.

In Regard to. It is incorrect to use "in regards to." "As regards" is correct, and means the same thing. "Regarding" is preferred.

Irregardless. Use "regardless" rather than "irregardless."

Fewer/Less. "Fewer" refers to number; "less" refers to quantity. *My troubles are* less *than Rebecca's because she has* fewer *clients.*

Like. Often incorrectly used for the conjunction "as." "Like" is a preposition that compares nouns and pronouns; "as" is a conjunction used to introduce subordinate clauses (which generally contain a verb). This distinction has seen some erosion in recent years but is still drawn by purists.

Wrong	Right
like an expert.	*as an expert would.*

Loan. "Loan" is a noun. "Lend" is the verb, as in "I shall lend you $50."

Nor. Use "or" after negative expressions rather than "nor" to avoid unintentionally communicating a double negative.

Principle and Principal.

a. "Principal" is an *adjective* meaning the most important or the base amount of an investment (the "principal sum, plus interest"). It is also *a noun* meaning "one with controlling authority."

b. "Principle" is a *noun*, meaning a fundamental law, doctrine or assumption upon which all things are based or which guides conduct.

Secondly, Thirdly, etc. Consistency would lead one to begin with "firstly." It is preferred to use "first," "second," "third," etc. If you choose to use "secondly," "thirdly," and the like, begin with "initially" to avoid the awkwardness of "firstly."

F. GENDER-SPECIFIC LANGUAGE

A drafted document that offends, annoys, or even distracts a member of the intended audience is a less effective document.

Many writing devices exist for avoiding gender specific words without being conspicuous. These techniques are as follows:

Eliminate Unnecessary Pronouns. An agency regulation might read:

An employee of the Department of Health may elect to file under section 327 and ***he*** *may obtain the proper form for doing this from Payroll.*

The "he" is totally unnecessary and can be deleted.

Reword. A provision in an insurance policy might read:

If he fails to report the injury within ***10*** *days, the Insured forfeits coverage.*

This could be rewritten as follows:

*The Insured must report the injury within **10** days or forfeit coverage.*

Repeat the Noun. Instead of using a noun and then a gender-specific pronoun, simply repeat the noun. This alternative is more palatable in drafted documents than in briefs or memoranda, where fluidity is important.

*If a distributor fails to. . . . That distributor [rather than **he**] must then. . . .*

Use a Shortened Form of the Noun, a Synonym, or a Defined Term.

*The Director of the Department of Health must certify that all imported poultry is parasite free. The Director [rather than **he**] has the discretion to either refuse entry to poultry that contains parasites or order it destroyed.*

Some drafters might also use a synonym here—"This official," for example. Although this violates the rule about using the same word to refer to the same person, entity, or concept, it is safe enough if no ambiguity would result.

Change the Pronoun to "the," "a," or "this."

*If Buyer exercises the [rather than **his**] right of first refusal,. . . .*

Use "It."

*If any animal in the zoo escapes from its [rather than **his**] cage, all personnel shall immediately. . . .*

Use "One."

If one [rather than ***he****] elects to file under section 335,. . . .*

Use "You." Subject to the constraints on the use of personal pronouns discussed earlier, in some cases using the second person "you" may be a viable alternative to a male pronoun. In a set of course instructions, instead of saying:

A student must supply ***his*** *own computer,*

say,

You must supply your own computer.

Use the Imperative Mood. In a set of work rules directed at employees, instead of saying,

Each employee shall stay at ***his*** *work station until relieved by an employee on the next shift,*

say,

Stay at your work station until you are relieved by an employee on the next shift.

Replace "he" with "he or she." Because it is so wordy, the "he or she" phrase is not a particularly desirable alternative. However, it is better than the alternatives of "he/she," "s/he," using "he" and "she" alternatively, or other linguistic abominations. Although consistently putting the "he" first may seem sexist, most people find alternating it with "she or he" to be extremely distracting.

Use Plural Subjects. In discursive writing, lawyers often avoid gender-specific pronouns by using a plural subject and referring back to it with "they," "them," or "their." Since drafted documents normally use singular subjects, this option may not be available often. It can, however, be used occasionally. Instead of saying,

> *A candidate for county council must pay a $500 filing fee.* ***He*** *must also provide a list of contributors,*

say,

> *Candidates for county council must pay a $500 filing fee. They must also provide a list of contributors.*

Some drafters use the singular noun and the plural pronoun, as in "An investor must notify their broker within 10 days." Others consider this to be grammatically wrong and logically incoherent in a drafted normative document. The drafter must decide to which camp they belong. Above all, be consistent.

Use the Passive Voice. This is also an option of last resort. But, instead of saying,

> *When an applicant files Form 207,* ***he*** *must attach a photograph,*

say,

> *A photograph must be attached when an applicant files Form 207.*

Use Gender-Neutral Descriptive Terms. Many words ending in -man can be replaced with gender-neutral terms. For example:

councilman becomes council member

crewman becomes crew member

draftsman becomes drafter

fireman becomes fire fighter

meterman (or -maid) becomes meter reader

policeman becomes police officer

salesman becomes sales associate

watchman becomes guard

Drop the "-man" or Replace It with "-person." "Chair" instead of "chairman" and "anchor" instead of "anchorman" have become acceptable usage. But for other terms, the convention is to replace the "-man" with either "-er" or "-person." "Spokesman" has, thankfully, thus become "spokesperson," rather than "spoker." But, again thankfully, "draftsman" has become "drafter" rather than "draftsperson." Some "-man" terms, however, have become terms of art, like "journeyman" in collective bargaining agreements, and their usage still persists to some extent.

A Note on Gendered Pronouns. Pronouns may have serious implications for erasure of the identity of an individual, such as with transgender or nongender-binary individuals. In the employment context, contracts that stipulate as to what may be considered harassment in the workplace, especially based on gender identity, may not include the type of harassment received by a person who is transgender. Consider the issue of a family law contract, such as in a nuptial agreement or parenting plan, where one parent comes out as transgender and their identity and pronoun use changes. Using a traditional "he" default pronoun or even switching between "he" and "she" throughout the document may not address these issues and may only serve to confuse the issue.

Use Defined Terms to Eliminate Gender. In most commercial contracts, the matter of gender neutrality is best resolved by adopting a gender neutral defined term in the first paragraph. For example, Samantha Conboy (the "Tenant"), or Gerald Cummins (the "Borrower"). Essentially, this act of defining a term creates a new pronoun for purposes of the contract at issue and focuses the language upon what the contract is about, the legal capacities and relationship of the parties, not their gender. This removes gender from the equation entirely, at least on paper.

CHAPTER 14
DEFINITIONS

A. GENERAL PRINCIPLES OF USAGE

Definitions tell the reader what a particular word or phrase means. Well drafted definitions promote clarity, brevity, and consistency. Definitions are properly used:

- To resolve an ambiguity in terms that have more than one possible meaning.
- To clarify terms that have a dictionary meaning, but a vague one.
- To add to or subtract from a dictionary meaning.

Definitions are powerful medicine, and drafters should use them with care. A badly drafted definition will infect every portion of the document where the term is used. The drafter should keep the following considerations in mind when creating definitions.

Overly broad or narrow definitions can inadvertently introduce ambiguity or reallocate benefits and burdens. Defined terms can also be used to intentionally cloud meaning. The less-than-careful reader will often assume that a term has its ordinary, lay meaning and will not refer to a definitions section for clarification. Consider a contract that provides that refund claims submitted to a local company "will be Paid In Full within 90 days of Receipt." The initial-capped terms are defined, many pages away, as meaning "compensated in lawful money of [name of non-domestic country or state], calculated at the then prevalent exchange rate" and "when received by the Claims Processor [itself defined as a company in China]," respectively.

Be careful—if you define a term, it must *only* be used in the defined sense in the document. If not, ambiguity crops up. This is closely related to the practice of elegant variation from English composition classes. Those courses often encourage the use of different words for the same concept to avoid repetitive prose. The rule is different in legal drafting. *Use the same words for the same meanings every time.*

To protect against inadvertent use of defined terms that may create ambiguity, many drafters adopt a standard form of defined term that varies the normal rules of format, capitalization, and the like. Examples include: Initial Caps, ALL CAPS, *italics*, **boldface**, or underlining.

The predominant form appears to be Initial Caps. Initial capitalization drapes the defined term in the mantle of a proper noun. This is appropriate because within the document the term essentially becomes a proper noun. This book places the defined term in parentheses and quotes when it is initially defined, *e.g.*:

. . . June 7, 2020 ("Due Date").

When the defined term is later used, it is in Initial Caps, but without quotes, *e.g.*:

" . . . on the Due Date, the Payer shall . . . "

Finally, take care to make the definition either inclusive or exclusive. For example, consider whether trade secrets constitute Intellectual Property under each of these definitions:

> Inclusive: *"Intellectual Property" means intellectual property as that term is generally used and includes all patents, copyrights, and trademarks. (Yes).*
>
> Exclusive: *"Intellectual Property" means patents, copyrights, and trademarks. (No).*
>
> Ambiguous: *"Intellectual Property" means and includes patents, copyrights, and trademarks. (Maybe?).*

Party definitions can be tricky. For example, "Big Financial Co." is defined in a mutual settlement and release agreement to be "Big Financial Co., Inc., and all of its subsidiaries, parent corporation, officers, directors, employees, attorneys, and accountants." This definition gives these Big Financial Co. related individuals the benefit of the release of all claims granted by the other side. However, does this mean that Big Financial's release of the other party also includes a release by all the related entities defined as part of Big Financial?

1. TERMS WITH ESTABLISHED MEANINGS

Do not define a term that already has a perfectly adequate dictionary meaning. Consider, for example, an unnecessary definition found in a federal regulation:

"Form" means a piece of paper containing blank spaces, boxes, or lines for the entry of dates, names, descriptive details, or other items.

Before defining a term, check an English dictionary and a legal dictionary. The drafter can determine from these sources whether it is necessary to create a new definition.

2. TERMS OF ART AND TECHNICAL TERMS

Although legal terms of art and other technical terms have established meanings, the drafter may choose to repeat these definitions. This is especially true if the intended audience of the document includes persons who might not know what these terms mean or suspect that they have a special meaning. Documents used in consumer transactions often include this type of definition. A loan agreement, for example, might appropriately contain the following definition.

"Mortgage" means a charge or lien on real or personal property owned by Borrower to secure repayment of the loaned amount.

3. HUMPTY-DUMPTY DEFINITIONS

Do not define a term in a way that is totally at odds with its commonly accepted or dictionary meaning. This is called a "Humpty-Dumpty definition," in honor of the Lewis Carroll character who opined as follows:

> "When *I* use a word," Humpty Dumpty said, in rather a scornful tone, "it means just what I choose it to mean—neither more nor less."
>
> "The question is," said Alice, "whether you *can* make words mean so many different things."
>
> "The question is," said Humpty Dumpty, "which is to be master—that's all."

For example, consider this Humpty-Dumpty definition taken from a federal statute:

> "September 16, 1940" means "June 27, 1950."

Humpty-Dumpty definitions involve more than mere foolishness. First, the drafter who has defined "up" to mean "toward the center of the earth" may later forget this counter-intuitive definition and use "up" in its more conventional sense later in the document, thus creating a contextual ambiguity.

Second, the ordinary reader is even more likely to forget this strange definition and thus be misled by the contract. Indeed, when the defined meaning of a term is so at odds with its conventional or dictionary meaning, and when the defined meaning would work to the significant disadvantage of the party who did not draft the contract, a court might refuse to enforce the contract, on grounds of unconscionability.

Third, Humpty-Dumpty definitions deprive the appropriated term of its conventional meaning, thus leaving the concept without an easy referent. If the word "up" has been defined to mean what we normally think of in terms of down, how is one to refer to the concept of moving from the center of the earth toward the sky? Perhaps the perverse drafter of "up" would then define the word "down" to refer to what we normally think of in terms of up.

Finally, consider the ethical implications of using defined terms to obfuscate or mislead.

4. CIRCULAR DEFINITIONS

A definition should never define the term by reference to itself. This is a circular definition:

> *"Harass" means a course of conduct directed at a specific person which seriously alarms, annoys, or harasses the person.*

Some drafters recognize an exception to this rule when a compound expression is consistently used to refer to the operative concept and only one word in the expression requires definition. For example, a statute might repeatedly refer to an "underinsured motorist," with only "underinsured" requiring substantive clarification. To maintain the unity of the concept, some drafters thus define the entire phrase as a subclass of the broader category of motorist.

> *"Underinsured motorist" means a motorist whose personal liability coverage is under $25,000 per individual per accident.*

Other drafters would adhere to the rule and provide only a definition of "underinsured."

> *"Underinsured" means having personal liability coverage under $25,000 per individual per accident.*

5. ONE-TIME DEFINITIONS

Definitions are useful primarily because they avoid the need to repeat a lengthy chain of words every time a concept is referenced in the document. The definition provides a defined-term way of expressing that concept. If the corporate buyer's authorized agents consist of ten named individuals, it would be cumbersome and wordy to repeat their names every time the concept of an authorized agent arises. Defining authorized agents in terms of these ten individuals and then using that term achieves an economy of words.

On the other hand, a definition that is referenced only once in the document does not achieve an economy of words.

> *A corporate officer shall annually disclose to the Board of Directors any stock ownership of or financial dealings with any business in direct competition with Acme Industrials. For the purpose of this provision, "corporate officer" means the President, Vice President, Secretary, and Treasurer of Acme Industrials, but does not include the General Counsel.* [53 words]

> versus

> *The President, Vice President, Secretary, and Treasurer of Acme Industrials shall annually disclose to the Board of Directors any stock ownership of or financial dealings with any business in direct competition with Acme Industrials.* [34 words]

However, a one-time definition may be justified when the concept being defined is complex and when incorporating it into the substantive provision would create a sentence of unwarranted length.

> *An employee may be immediately terminated for (1) theft of company property valued at $50 or more, (2) driving a company vehicle or fork lift while under the influence of alcohol or drugs that impair reaction time, or (3) engaging in any conduct involving unwelcome touching, patting, pinching, caressing, intentional and unnecessary brushing against another's person's body, other sexually suggestive physical contact, explicit sexual propositions, suggestive comments, sexually oriented kidding, practical jokes involving sex or excretory functions, sexually-oriented jokes, comments and questions about sexual attributes or activities, foul or obscene language or gestures, display of foul or obscene pictures or printed material, indecent exposure, and attempts to invade the sexual privacy of another person.*

The substantive prohibition set out after (3) would be better worded in terms of sexual harassment, followed immediately by a definition of that term in a separate sentence. Moreover, this would allow the use of the defined term (rather than its full explication) in other documents, such as a supervisor's disciplinary report.

6. DEFINITIONAL MAZES

When a definition uses a term that itself is the subject of a definition—with that definition also including a term that is subject to a further definition, and so on—the reader enters a maze that may be abandoned before completed. This frustrates the communication function of the document. Consider the following definitions section of a statute, with emphasis added to illustrate the maze:

> *(1)* ***"Underinsured motorist"*** *means an* ***owner,*** *operator, passenger, lessor, or person with the right to direct the control of a motor vehicle who. . . .*
>
> . . .
>
> *(6)* ***"Owner"*** *includes the person in whose name title is held, a lessee, a bailee for hire, and* ***a holder of a security interest*** *in a motor vehicle.*
>
> . . .
>
> *(9)* ***"Holder of a security interest"*** *means a* ***"lienholder"*** *as defined in Code Section 14B:167–3(a).*

The reader then goes to the cross-referenced statute and discovers:

> *3(a)* ***"Lienholder"*** *includes . . . , and any other person with a non-possessory* ***property interest*** *in the goods.*
>
> . . .

3(q) ***"Property interest"*** *includes . . . an* ***equitable interest*** *in the goods.*

B. SUBSTANTIVE MATTERS

Definitions give meaning to words; they should not serve as vehicles for substance. Burying a substantive provision in a definition can have devastating consequences or be used to intentionally cloud meaning. The drafter might forget it is there and later draft an inconsistent provision in the main body of the document, creating a contextual ambiguity. The parties, who often think it is unnecessary to read definitions carefully, may inadvertently act in an inconsistent manner and incur significant liability. Conversely, courts sometimes treat substantive provisions that are incorporated into definitions as being without significance. This is because these provisions rarely use the proper terms to create rights, duties, and the like. Is the substance permissive or mandatory? Is it a duty or a condition? To whom is it addressed? And what are the consequences of noncompliance? Definitions containing substance rarely answer any of these questions.

Definitions containing substantive terms are not, however, uncommon. For example, the Civil Rights Act of 1964 defines "religion" as follows:

The term "religion" includes all aspects of religious observance and practice, as well as belief, unless an employer demonstrates that he is unable to reasonably accommodate to an employee's or prospective employee's religious observance or practice without undue hardship on the conduct of the employer's business.

In other words, if it cannot be reasonably accommodated, then it is not religion. The "unless" clause provides an exception to the substantive prohibition against religious discrimination and should be included in that portion of the statute, not buried within a definition of "religion" itself. Similarly, this Act includes pregnancy within the meaning of the term "sex," but then makes discrimination on that basis illegal only if similarly situated non-pregnant employees are treated differently. Again, that is a substantive limitation on the scope of the prohibited discrimination. It should not have been buried in a definition. It is perhaps not entirely coincidental that the meaning of these substantive provisions, which are buried in the definitions section of the statute, have been among the most heavily litigated with respect to what they mean.

Substantive terms sometimes creep into contract definitions as well.

"Place of delivery" means seller's warehouse, where appropriate loading equipment will be made available and used to avoid damage to the goods.

The "where" clause apparently imposes a duty on the seller and should be in the substantive portion of the contract. If a loading dock confrontation occurs and the parties refer to their contract to resolve the dispute, neither of them may ever think of looking in the definitions section. And even if they did, the passive voice construction leaves it unclear who has the duty of providing the equipment.

Finally, substantive requirements in definitions sometimes create unintended gaps in coverage:

> *"Vendor" means a person, licensed by the Director of the Department of Parks, who offers for sale food, drinks, souvenirs, or other merchandise.*

The intent, apparently, is to require that vendors be licensed, which is a substantive provision. Assume that another section of the regulation then prohibits vendors from operating in certain areas of the park. Sophia, who has not been licensed, is selling hot dogs in one of the identified areas. However, because she is not licensed, she also does not fit within the definition of a vendor. Consequently, she is not violating the regulation.

C. DEFINITIONS INCORPORATED BY REFERENCE

Legislative drafters sometimes borrow definitions from other statutes and incorporate them by reference into a new statute. This is bad practice. First, the borrowed definition may have been drafted with a particular problem in mind. The new statute may involve an entirely unrelated set of legislative circumstances, for which the former definition ultimately proves inadequate. For example, one might define a "healthcare facility" one way in a statute dealing with certification and another way in a statute creating tax exemptions.

Second, courts may later interpret the definition in the first statute in a way that is appropriate for the first statute but inappropriate for the one that incorporates it by reference. If the interpretation follows the incorporation, as is often the case, chaos may result.

Third, the first statute may be amended or repealed, with the legislature not realizing the effect of this on the statute that incorporates the definition by reference. Does the definition still have the force of law for the purposes of the second statute? Even if it does, when a new edition of the code or compiled statutes appears, the incorporated definition may be time consuming to locate electronically.

Fourth, when the text of a definition is buried in another statute, it is apt to be forgotten. The drafter may then draft something elsewhere in the document that is inconsistent with that definition. Similarly, persons affected by the new statute may ignore it altogether, to their disadvantage.

Private-law documents that incorporate a statutory definition are subject to the same problems. Drafters of these documents should incorporate statutory definitions only when the law requires that the term have the same meaning in the document as it does in the statute to which the reference is made. Articles of incorporation and by-laws are sometimes subject to this requirement.

The better practice for drafters of legislation and private-law documents is to repeat the statutory definition verbatim rather than incorporate it by reference, on the theory that the reader of the document should not be forced to go to another source to find out what critical terms mean.

D. TYPES OF DEFINITIONS AND TERMINOLOGY

1. DEFINED TERMS

If the document is a short one, if definitions are not numerous, or if it makes sense for some other reason, definitions can be introduced in the first place they occur, including in the preamble, introductory paragraph or the recitals. For example:

> *This ASSET PURCHASE AGREEMENT AND ESCROW INSTRUCTIONS (the "Agreement") is entered into and effective as of March* **10, 2007,** *at Seattle, Washington, by and between ______ ("Seller"), and______ ("Buyer"), on the basis of the following facts and constitutes (i) a contract of purchase and sale between the parties and (ii) escrow instructions to ______ ("Escrow Agent"), the consent of whom appears at the end of the Agreement.*

Defined terms used in only one section may be defined when used. If defined when used and a definitions section is included, the term should be included in the definition section as well, stating "defined as stated in section ___" for its definition. The idea is to ensure that, if the definition is changed, the change will ripple through the document automatically to avoid ambiguity that could be caused by revising one appearance of the definition and not another.

This is the most common form of definition and is used in all forms of legal writing. It provides the defined term that the document will subsequently use to refer to a party or concept. For example:

> *James Madison ("Seller") and Alexander Hamilton ("Buyer") enter into this contract for the sale of Blackacre Estates of Dinwiddie ("Property").*

In defining terms, do not lapse into legalese and say, "Hereinafter referred to as 'Seller.' " Some drafters prefer to delete the quotation marks. Some drafters prefer to put the defined term definition in all capital letters and sometimes also in bold face type. They will then use that same typographical convention whenever the term is used in text. Other drafters, however, view this as unnecessary and distracting, particularly the all caps format.

Give a person, entity, or concept only one defined term definition, not two. Do not say, "This is a contract between Jim Beam ("Buyer" or "Beam") and. . . ." Once a term has a defined term definition, use that abbreviation consistently in the remainder of the document. Do not start using the full term again. Moreover, do not create a defined term definition unless the defined term is actually used again later in the document. "Commencement Date" and "Termination Date" sometimes fall into this category.

2. FULL DEFINITIONS

This is the first of the more conventional forms of "defined terms." A full definition—also sometimes referred to as a "stipulative definition"—provides the complete and exclusive meaning of the term. It has fixed boundaries and courts are bound to construe it literally, thus disallowing the addition or deletion of referents by implication. Since a full definition is both complete and exclusive, it must be drafted carefully and with all the possibilities in mind. The word "means" signifies a full definition.

> *"Vehicle" means an automobile, bus, trolley, tram, or electrically driven cart.*

Under this definition, a horse-drawn carriage would not be included. This might be a significant omission if the drafter were drafting an ordinance dealing with traffic congestion around Central Park in New York City or the French Quarter of New Orleans.

Although two unrelated words should never be given the same full definition, this is not true of a word and its derivative forms. For example, a document may use both "writing" and "written." If the drafter intends for them to mean the same thing, then this form of definition would be appropriate:

> *"Writing" means the recording of words on paper, and "written" has a corresponding meaning.*

A full definition is appropriate in a variety of contexts. For example, a document may use a term that has no dictionary definition.

> *"Oceanside condominium property" means ...* [whatever the referents are going to be].

Similarly, the drafter may want to use a term that has a useful connotation but whose dictionary meaning is too vague to be used safely.

> *"Industry standards" means the product standards promulgated by the National Association of Widget Manufactures as of the date of this contract, which are attached as Exhibit A.*

Full definitions are also used to limit or provide new meaning to, and thus replace, the dictionary definition.

> *"Apartment" means unit number 6-B of the Fairview Apartment complex, 6216 Wilson Road, Sandy Beach, South Carolina.*

Finally, full definitions are often a by-product of the conceptualization process discussed in Chapter 10. For example, an attorney for a school district might be asked to draft a rule prohibiting students from possessing weapons on the school grounds. Upon further inquiry, the drafter determines that the weapons in question definitely include knives, sword canes, straight razors, guns, stun guns, mace, blackjacks, brass knuckles, and the other common paraphernalia of urban warfare. The drafter considers conceptualizing the problem and wording the prohibition in those terms, with an appropriate "and other" clause tacked on at the end. However, the drafter also discovers that students have used a sock containing a pool ball, hot pepper juice in a squirt gun, and a knotted rope in assaulting each other, teachers, and administrators. The drafter worries whether those objects would be covered by the "and other" clause.

In addition, the drafter discovers that students have used staplers, scissors, ball point pens, compasses, and rulers with a sharpened metal edge—objects one hardly thinks of as weapons, but objects the school superintendent wants the rule to deal with anyway. These items seem to have little in common, but after much thought, the drafter conceptualizes the intended objective of the prohibition in terms of an abstraction and defines the word accordingly—"things that are capable of causing injury to others and that are in the possession of a student who intends to use them in that capacity." In this case, the drafter has included intent—a substantive term in the definition. Or, the drafter may come up with some other complex and novel conceptualization of the problem. Whatever the resulting concept, the drafter will incorporate it into a definition.

3. PARTIAL DEFINITIONS

A partial definition takes the dictionary meaning of a word as the point of departure and clarifies its boundaries, by inclusion or exclusion of specific referents.

a. Enlarging Definitions

To ensure that a particular concept is included within the meaning of a term with a conventional dictionary definition or to add to that definition something the term would not otherwise encompass, drafters use the term "includes." Although "but is not limited to" is unnecessary, many drafters add the phrase to ensure that the list is not construed as being exclusive. Consider the following examples:

"Employee" includes, but is not limited to, persons working on a part-time or temporary basis. [Ensuring inclusion.]

"Apartment" includes, but is not limited to, the hallway, stairways, and other common areas. [Adding something probably not within the conventional meaning.]

The drafter of enlarging definitions must also take care not to be like Humpty Dumpty. Consider the definition contained in an old English statute:

"Cows" includes horses, mules, asses, sheep, and goats.

b. Limiting Definitions

The term "does not include" is used to ensure that something that might be within the conventional definition is excluded or to exclude something that otherwise would clearly be included. For example:

"Automobiles" does not include taxicabs.

The drafter, however, should take care not to exclude something that goes to the core of the conventional meaning, as in:

"Potable liquid" does not include water.

Water is the very essence of a potable liquid.

Often, a drafter could use either a limiting or a full definition to accomplish the same objective.

"Employee" does not include persons performing services for the company for less than 40-hours a week.

versus

"Employee" means persons providing services to the company for 40-hours a week or more.

The drafter should think about the purpose of defining "employee" before deciding which approach to take. Although drafting in terms of exceptions is generally not favored, if the purpose is clearly to exclude part-timers, then the "does not include" approach would be best. But if the purpose is to include within the definition of "employee" persons who might otherwise be considered independent contractors or leased employees, then the "means" approach would be best.

4. COMBINING FULL AND PARTIAL DEFINITIONS

A partial definition may both include and exclude.

"Lake front property" includes property separated from the water only by a publicly-

> *owned road, but does not include property any portion of which fronts water that, for at least 50% of the shoreline, is less than one foot deep.*

Similarly, a full definition can be further clarified by a partial definition, through either inclusion, exclusion, or both.

> *"Headquarters personnel" means persons employed at the corporate offices in Chicago and includes persons working there for more than 30 days on temporary duty from another office, but does not include persons working as guards under contract with Strongarm Protective Agency.*

The terms "includes" and "does not include" must always, however, have a prior reference—either a dictionary or a stipulated meaning. A term cannot simultaneously mean and include the same thing:

> *"Corporate officers" means and includes the president, vice president, secretary, and treasurer.*

The "includes" assumes "corporate officers" has a dictionary meaning and purports to ensure that it covers the named officers; the "means," however, replaces that dictionary definition with what follows, making the whole thing redundant and circular.

5. EXAMPLES

Definitions containing examples are similar to the list of included items in an enlarging definition. However, the purpose is slightly different. The purpose of an "includes" list is to clarify either a dictionary or stipulative definition that is fuzzy at the edges, and to ensure that the items listed are included. Inclusion on the list beats whatever vagueness is inherent in the concept.

This is not true of examples. Here, the elements of the full or stipulative definition still totally control. The list of examples merely gives the reader an idea of what the definition might mean in more concrete terms.

Thus, a school regulation might contain a stipulative definition of "cheating." The definition, however, may be both complex and somewhat vague. A list of examples of conduct that will usually satisfy that definition—such as tearing pages out of a library book—assists the reader in understanding what is being prohibited. However, the administration could not punish a student for cheating for simply tearing the pages out of a library book; rather, it would have to prove that this particular tearing incident fell within the elements of the definition of cheating.

Drafters should use examples sparingly, because they are apt to be construed as being more definitive than intended. Use of an example is a technique of last resort. The better approach is to craft the definition in such a way as to make examples unnecessary.

E. METHODOLOGY

Various methods exist for creating definitions, including (1) using familiar terms, (2) using precise terms, (3) identifying components, (4) identifying specific referents, and (5) indicating relationship to a larger unit.

1. USE FAMILIAR TERMS

Although the term "commons" has meaning to property lawyers, it is a term that most lay persons are unfamiliar with. It could be defined in more familiar terms, as follows:

> *"Commons areas" means the condominium property open for use by all Owners and includes the grounds, driveways, the parking lot, the tennis court, the swimming pool, and the recreation center.*

2. USE PRECISE TERMS

Vague concepts can sometimes be clarified with scientific precision.

> *"Dangerously hot" means **150** degrees Fahrenheit or above.*

3. IDENTIFY COMPONENTS

An "automobile" could be defined by reference to the sum of its parts, but that would not be feasible because of the large number of parts. However, sometimes this approach works very nicely.

> *"Mix #3" means a mixture in equal parts of gravel pebbles, 1/2 inch crushed granite, and sand.*

4. IDENTIFY SPECIFIC REFERENTS

A term can also be defined by listing the term's intended referents. Indeed, this is probably the most common form of definition. For example:

> *"Appliances" means the refrigerator, stove, microwave, disposal, window unit air conditioners, washing machine, and dryer.*

The danger is omitting something crucial. If the landlord also intended to include the central vacuum cleaner system in the list of items that the tenant is responsible for repairing, this definition will not accomplish it. Adding "and other similar items" would probably cure that oversight, but the better practice is to force the client to think about these details and deal with them expressly.

5. INDICATE RELATIONSHIP TO A LARGER UNIT

Often, the meaning of a term hinges on its inclusion in an existing class of entities. The definition builds on that class membership and creates a subclass.

> *"Tax-exempt recreational personal property" means an item exempt from taxation under state, county, or municipal tax law that is used exclusively for non-income producing purposes.*

The existing class is "items exempted from taxation under other laws." The defined subclass refers to items used for a particular purpose. Similarly, definitions often focus on sub-classes whose identity relates primarily to what they are not, in relation to the larger classification.

> *"Fair share members" means unit employees who are not full or affiliational members of the Union.*

F. LOCATION OF DEFINITIONS

Statutes and complex private law documents usually contain a separate section dealing only with definitions. For reader convenience, this section is usually placed at the beginning or end of the document and the defined terms are listed in alphabetical order.

That sounds like a sensible approach to the location problem, and usually it is. But there are drawbacks. In a lengthy document with many defined terms, the reader is constantly forced to refer back to the definitions section to obtain a full understanding of what is being read—and when this proves to be too troublesome, the reader plows ahead and often ends up with an inadequate grasp of the substance.

To help avoid this, if a term is used in only one section of the document, the drafter should define the term in that section itself. This makes the document easier to read and understand. This is especially important in consumer-related documents, because the average lay person probably will not read a separate definitions section and may not even refer back to it when the term is encountered in the document.

G. WHEN TO DRAFT DEFINITIONS

Definitions can be, and usually are, drafted before, during, and after the substantive provisions have been reduced to writing.

First, the drafter may know from the onset that certain terms must be defined. If the intended legislation will apply only to business entities with 50 or more employees, then the drafter can write a definition of "employer" in those terms right at the beginning of the process.

Second, the need for definitions will most often occur to the drafter during the critical conceptualization stage. If the drafter is creating a new or hybrid concept, then the drafter will nearly always need to use a definition to capture the essence of that concept.

Third, during the post-drafting review of the document, the drafter may discover that a concept is fully stated several times in the document. The drafter would then decide to define the concept and use the defined term instead of its full explication whenever the concept appears in the document.

In sum, drafting definitions is a simultaneous and interactive process, not something that is always done at the same time.

H. TESTING DEFINITIONS

The drafter should take care to test a document's definitions. First, the drafter should go through the document and highlight every use of the defined term. This may reveal several things. For example, the drafter may discover that the term is not used at all in the document or that it is used only once. More importantly, the drafter may discover that the term is occasionally used in its conventional, rather than its defined sense. Finally, the drafter may discover that when the full definition replaces the defined term in the text, the result is linguistic and logical incoherence. Assume that a definition provides, " 'Representative' means being party to a written agency agreement with the Company." The substantive provision of the contract then provides, "Representatives shall report all sales monthly." If the term is replaced with its definition, the result would be: "Being party to a written agency agreement with the Company shall report all sales monthly." Representative should be redefined in terms of a person who has a written agency agreement with the Company.

The second way to test definitions is to look not for the use of the term itself, but for the defined and closely related concepts. For example, if "recreational activity" means hunting, fishing, and camping, then that term should always replace those combined concepts in the text. If nothing else, this will ensure that the defined term is being used consistently to replace the full description.

CHAPTER 15

TERMS CREATING LEGAL CONSEQUENCES

This chapter is about terms creating legal consequences. Not many words used by drafters have any real magic to them. Usually, the drafter can choose from a wide variety of words to produce identical results. Terms of art, document-defined terms, and terms creating specific legal consequences are exceptions to the general rule.

A. THE IMPORTANCE OF THESE TERMS

The primary function of a drafted normative document is to create legal consequences. Most of the words in a drafted document relate to the substance of the legal consequence—the identity of the boat, the price, delivery, warranties as to fitness, and the like. But how is the reader to know that the contract created a duty and a right, rather than mere discretionary authority to sell and buy? These legal consequences are significantly different. The words that create these different legal consequences are of critical importance.

B. IDENTIFYING AND CREATING THE APPROPRIATE LEGAL CONSEQUENCES

Providing the proper legal consequences in a drafted normative document is a three-step process. First, the drafter must fully understand the client's specific desires and broader objectives. Second, the drafter must then match those desires and objectives with the appropriate legal consequences. Third, the drafter must choose the appropriate words to express those consequences.

For example, at the initial interview the drafter may discover that the client wants a contract to purchase certain goods but the client probably wants these goods only if they can be delivered on or before June 1, 2020. After that date, the client may be able to obtain the goods from another source and will want to have the option of canceling the contract. The drafter would recognize that delivery on or before June 1, 2020, should be a condition of the client's duty to accept and pay for the goods. But the drafter would also recognize that the legal consequence that should flow from the failure of this condition is that the client will have the power or authority to cancel the contract. The drafter would then draft a provision expressing these client desires, as follows:

> ***If*** *Seller fails to deliver on or before June 1, 2020, Buyer* ***may*** *cancel the contract.*

In sum, the drafter has determined what the client wants, has translated that into a recognized legal consequence, and has used the proper words—"if" and "may", to create those legal consequences, thus meeting the client's desires. This is what drafting is all about.

C. THE SUGGESTED CONVENTIONS

Despite the importance of legal consequences and the significance of the differences between them, courts and legal drafting authorities are not in complete agreement over exactly what words should be used to create them. In the face of this diversity, the legal drafter should choose terms that are both lexicographically sound and enjoy the widest usage. The following are suggested conventions.

1. DUTIES

A duty consists of a legally enforceable obligation to do or refrain from doing certain things. The breach of a statutory duty subjects the breaching party to some kind of sanction—a fine, incarceration, disqualification, a cease and desist order, or something else. The nonperformance of a contractual duty makes the breaching party liable in damages to the other party or, alternatively, subject to a decree of specific performance; it may also excuse the other party's performance, temporarily or permanently.

a. Statutory Duties

"Shall" and "shall not" are the operative words of civil obligation and should be used in legislation to create duties to act or refrain from acting. These words express what legal positivists call the "command of the sovereign."

> *Sec. 34 (a). The owner of an animal classified as "dangerous"* ***shall*** *keep that animal in a wire mesh enclosure as defined in subsection 34(q) and* ***shall not*** *allow that animal outside its enclosure unless it is on a leash capable of restraining it or is being transported in a secure cage.*

This is the proper use of "shall" and "shall not."

Unfortunately, drafters use "shall" for too many other purposes. When "shall" is used other than to issue a command, it is called a "false imperative." For example, definitions often provide:

> *"Vehicle"* ***shall*** *mean. . . .*

The drafter, however, is not commanding that the term be defined in that fashion. The intent, rather, is to give the word that meaning. Definitions involve their own set of conventions, discussed in Chapter 14. Similarly, contracts often provide:

> *This option* ***shall*** *expire at noon on March 1, 2020.*

Again, the drafter is not commanding the option to expire on that date. Rather, the drafter's intent is to create that legal consequence directly. Words other than "shall" are appropriate for doing that.

Contracts and statutes also often use the duty-creating word "shall" erroneously to create rights, other duties, or discretionary authority to act.

> *The tenant* ***shall*** *have the right to immediate occupancy of the premises.*

> *Buyer* ***shall*** *have the duty to make payment within 10 days of delivery.*

> *The union* ***shall*** *have the authority to initiate grievances in its own name.*

Since the term "shall" means "has a duty," then these provisions say that the tenant has a duty to have the right, that the Buyer has a duty to have the duty, and the union has a duty to have the authority.

A minority of drafters favor "must," as the proper term for creating duties. The primary drawback of this convention is that it disqualifies the word "must" from being used to create conditions, thus forcing drafters to find yet another word or phrase to accomplish that legal consequence.

b. Privately Created Duties

Although "shall" and "shall not" are used most often in legislative drafting, drafters also use them frequently in private law documents when one entity is essentially commanding another entity to do or refrain from doing something. A party creating a trust, for example, is imposing duties on the trustee.

> *Trustee **shall** distribute the earned income from the trust in the manner provided in section 8(d).*

Private law documents also use "will" to create duties. The term "shall" is preferable because "will" is also used to refer to events that will occur in the future—after execution of the contract or other private law document. What is essential, however, is that the drafter pick one term ("shall" or "will") to create a duty and use it consistently throughout.

2. NEGATION OF DUTIES

If the existing legal relationship between the parties involves an express or implied duty on the part of one of them, then another drafted document might operate to negate that duty. The legal consequence, in other words, is to eliminate a pre-existing legal consequence. Use the phrase "is not required to" to negate the existence of a duty, of either the statutory or contractual variety. For example, if a statute imposes a general reporting duty and the administrative agency is also given authority to waive that requirement, an agency regulation might read as follows:

> *A source* ***is not required to*** *file annual discharge reports under section 8–009.1(b) of the Clean Water Act if the amount of pollutant discharge is less than. . . .*

Or suppose that a general common law rule requires employees to perform reasonable overtime work when requested. An employment contract might negate or limit that duty, as follows:

> *Employee* ***is not required to*** *perform any overtime work on that employee's day of religious observance (such as Saturday or Sunday) unless Employer is unable to use other employees without these religious convictions to do the work on those days.*

Similarly, a statute or contract may first create a broad duty and then immediately limit its scope.

> *Landlord shall maintain the premises in a habitable condition, but Landlord* ***is not required to*** *bear the expense of correcting habitability defects that have been created by Tenant's own use or abuse of the premises.*

This states the general duty and then a limitation on the scope of that duty.

The negation of a duty can also be expressed in terms of an exception, discussed below, although that approach is not favored for stylistic reasons.

3. RIGHTS

Rights are the converse of duties. A rights-possessor is the party to whom the duty is owed. The right entitles that party to invoke the power of the state in the enforcement of the duty, whether the duty is of a statutory or contractual nature, and the state may often invoke the right on behalf of the rights-holder. Use the phrase "is entitled to" to create a right to do something or refrain from doing something.

> *The prevailing party in litigation under this contract* ***is entitled to*** *recover attorney's fees and expenses from the other party [and also implicitly creating a duty to pay].*

> *A registered voter* ***is entitled to*** *review the County Election Board's roster of eligible voters [and also implicitly creating a duty to make the roster available].*

The legal consequence of those two examples could also be created by imposing the duty directly, thus making the right implicit. Many times, conceptualizing the consequence in terms of a duty makes more sense than conceptualizing it in terms of a right. It would be counterintuitive, for example, to conceptualize payment of the sales price in terms of the buyer's right to receive the payment.

Finally, what many drafters attempt to treat as a right is often better conceptualized as a privilege or the creation of a discretionary authority to act. Examples of this are given in the discussion of privileges, below. This distinction may be fading and many drafters take the position that one may use either "may" or "is entitled to" to create both rights and privileges. If one adopts that view, one should choose one formulation and use it consistently throughout the document.

4. NEGATION OF RIGHTS

A legal relationship between the parties may involve the possession of a right by one of the parties, created by the common law, a statute, a prior private law document, or even the existing document. A later document or provision might then operate to limit or extinguish that right. Use the phrase "is not entitled to" to limit or negate the preexisting right. Suppose, for example, that the state's landlord-tenant statute generally requires reasonable notice before eviction, but allows a lease to abrogate that right in some situations. A provision in the lease might read as follows:

> *In case of an eviction under the terms of this paragraph, Tenant* ***is not entitled to*** *any prior notice.*

Similarly, a document may create a broad right and then immediately limit or qualify it.

Buyer ***is entitled to*** *[creating the right] require Seller to open for inspection and reseal shipping cartons when they arrive at the Port Authority, but Buyer* ***is not entitled to*** *[qualifying that right] require Seller to open any cartons that have been shipped under seal from the Port of Canton.*

Alternatively, this could be conceptualized and expressed in terms of an exception to the general duty, " . . . all cartons . . . except. . . ."

5. SURRENDERING RIGHTS OR CAUSES OF ACTION—WAIVER AND RELEASES

A statute may create a right but also provide for the forfeiture of that right in some situations. A person may have a statutory or contractual right but be willing to give it up for some reason. Or, the law may have created a duty that has been breached; a right has been violated and a cause of action now exists but the parties want to settle. These arrangements involve extremely important legal consequences to both parties and they must be worded with care.

When dealing with the forfeiture of rights, the operative term is nearly always "waives."

By requesting an administrative review of the claim, an aggrieved party ***waives*** *the right to seek immediate judicial review.*

In consideration of Buyer's payment of an additional $20,000, Seller ***waives*** *its right to* *charge a retail sale origination fee for goods sold in California.*

When litigation is threatened or in progress, the parties often enter into a settlement agreement. The wording of these agreements varies. One approach focuses on the asserted claim the potential plaintiff is giving up, an approach that shields the potential defendant of any implication of an admission of wrongdoing. This approach favors the word "waives." Another approach shifts the focus onto the putative wrongdoer, by emphasizing that the liability this person is avoiding is through the beneficence of the would-be plaintiff. This approach favors the word "releases." The defense bar prefers the first approach and the plaintiff's bar prefers the second. The difference, however, is more cosmetic than real, and some settlement agreements use both words to accomplish this legal consequence.

In return for $10,000, Jane Smith ***waives*** *her rights under the Workplace Safety Act and* ***releases*** *the Blunder Corporation from any liability that it might have for existing violations of the Act.*

6. PRIVILEGES

A privilege creates a discretionary authority to act. Use the word "may" to create a privilege.

A privilege differs from a right in that the other party has no corresponding duty other than honoring or accepting the choice made—shipping by rail or terminating the lease. Even if the effect on someone else is merely to refrain from interfering with the act or from imposing some detriment on the actor, that should be expressed in terms of "right" or "duty." For example, the privilege against self-incrimination is more properly thought of as a right we have, with the government having a duty not to coerce confessions and to not treat silence as an admission of guilt.

On the other hand, the only effect that the existence of a privilege has on others is that they are legally bound to accept or be bound by the actor's choice.

> *Seller* ***may*** *ship by air, truck, or rail.*

This simply means that if the seller ships by one of these methods, the buyer's duty to pay for the goods, which has been created separately, comes into play. The buyer is bound by the seller's choice in this regard.

A contract or statute may also give an individual the discretionary authority to unilaterally create a direct legal consequence.

> *Either party* ***may*** *cancel this contract by giving notice in advance by certified mail.*

If either party does that, then the contract comes to an end, whether the other party likes it or not. In other words, the exercise of this privilege cancels or terminates the other party's rights under the contract, which is why the converse of a privilege is said to be a "no-right." If the seller cancels, the buyer has no right to continue to insist on performance under the contract.

Something may be both a right and a privilege.

> *Tenant* ***will*** *pay* ***$1,550*** *rent on the first of every month [creating a Tenant duty to pay and an implied landlord right to obtain payment, the breach of which would give rise to an action for damages] and Landlord* ***may*** *immediately terminate the lease upon non-payment within* ***10*** *days after a payment is due [also giving Landlord discretionary authority to create that legal consequence].*

7. NEGATION OF PRIVILEGES

If a privilege would otherwise exist, a legal consequence of a particular provision might be to negate that privilege. Use the phrase "may not" to deny or limit the existence of a pre-existing discretionary authority to act. Assume that under the law of agency a landlord's resident manager would have the presumed authority to alter the terms of the lease and the effect would be that the landlord is bound by the modification. To negate that privilege, the lease might provide:

> *Landlord's resident manager* ***may not*** *alter the terms of this agreement without the express written approval of Landlord.*

8. IMMUNITY

An immunity exempts the immunity-bearer from liabilities that would otherwise attach. To create an immunity, either use the term "immune" (more commonly done in statutes) or express the legal consequence directly (the usual contract approach).

Officers acting under the provisions of this Act are ***immune*** *from criminal prosecution and civil liability.*

Tenant ***is not responsible for*** *any damage to the premises caused by third-party invitees of the Landlord.*

9. CONDITIONS

a. Definition and Types

A condition is something that must be satisfied before some other legal consequence attaches. Express conditions are the mechanisms that control how a transaction progresses in that the condition states what will happen, or will not happen, should a particular event occur in the future. Non-satisfaction of a condition means that the legal consequence does not come to pass. A condition thus differs from a duty in that the party charged with satisfying a condition is not liable in damages for a failure to do so.

A constructive condition has both promissory and conditional aspects, as in:

Buyer shall pay for the goods prior to delivery.

What this means is that Buyer has an express duty to pay, the breach of which will result in liability. But payment also appears to be a constructive condition of the seller's duty to make delivery.

Similarly, something may be both an express condition and a duty.

> *Builder shall install plumbing pipes of the Reading brand [creating a duty]. If Builder fails to install Reading Pipes, Owner's obligations under this contract, including the obligation to pay, are suspended until the defect is cured and if they are not cured within a reasonable time, Owner may terminate the contract and is relieved of all duty, express or implied, to compensate Builder [also making this an express condition].*

There are several types of conditions. A condition may relate to the conduct of the parties. For example, a seller may have no duty to ship the goods until the buyer has paid in full. Or, a condition may relate to external events. These events are sometimes referred to as "contingencies." Thus, a seller may have no duty to ship until an embargo ends.

When the condition relates to the occurrence of an event outside the control of the parties (death, calamity, effectiveness of a government regulation, a cost of living change, etc.), the condition adjusts the transaction to the change in the "outside" world. For example, a lease may contain a rent escalator clause that increases the rent based upon increases in the cost of living (the condition).

In most contract negotiations, one party will seek to include many conditions, especially conditions to closing or another event when they must part with consideration, and the other only a few. For example, in a purchase and sale agreement, the seller will try to limit the conditions to closing as few *objective* conditions as possible, such as any necessary third party approvals and the lack of any prohibitory injunction or other adverse ruling by governing bodies. By doing so, the seller is seeking to lock the buyer into the deal.

The buyer, on the other hand, will want to build in as many conditions and to keep these conditions as *subjective* and dependent upon the buyer's own judgment as possible. By doing so, the buyer can more easily walk away if due diligence reveals that things are other than as expected, or enjoy the opportunity to later renegotiate terms in exchange for a waiver of the condition. For example, buyers may seek to include as a condition that its due diligence will conclude with satisfactory results (as judged by the buyer in its sole discretion). This sort of condition can also be framed as "lack of material adverse change" condition to closing. Pay careful attention to what "lack of material adverse change" means, and who determines whether the condition has been met. Buyers, keep it as subjective as possible and attempt to maintain control over the determination that the condition has been met. Sellers, keep it as objective as possible. Also, consider including a materiality threshold to define a material adverse change.

Conditions must be carefully drafted and integrated into the rest of the contract. First, you must take care to draft the condition so its terms are clear. Take care to define the standards to be used and the identity of the person that will make the determination as to whether the condition has been met. Conditions generally trigger duties ("shall" clauses) or privileges ("may" clauses). The reader must be able to determine when the condition is satisfied and, if not, what consequences follow. Word choice is key.

Another common condition is that of one party obtaining financing and final written approval by all internal and external entities with any jurisdiction over the transaction. Again, the buyer is motivated by two desires: (a) the ability to back out of the deal if it is no longer interested in proceeding for whatever reason, and (b) the ability to threaten to back out in order to gain more favorable terms.

Consider the benefits of linking your client's material duties to the condition that the other party use its best reasonable efforts to perform either all or an enumerated list of duties under the contract. This is especially worthwhile in the case of parties with unequal economic or bargaining power in which the weaker party's success is dependent upon the other party's performance. In those circumstances, a best- or reasonable-efforts clause is to the weaker party's advantage. Examples include construction agreements, distribution agreements, and intellectual property agreements.

A duty to use "best efforts" in contract cases usually arises in one of three ways. First, the contract itself may specifically require that the promisor put forth his or her "best efforts." Second, the contract language might specify a result, and this may be interpreted as imposing a duty of best efforts. Finally, a court may impose a duty of best efforts based simply on the facts and circumstances surrounding a contract.

There appears to be no firm rule as to what constitutes adequate or sufficient best efforts. In general, each case turns on its particular facts. Some cases suggest that best efforts requires the same amount of effort under a contract as that expended under other similar contracts where the quality of effort has not been questioned. Others imply that the promisor should merely avoid manifestly harmful conduct. The duty to act "reasonably," like a duty to employ "best efforts," or to act in "good faith," is not reducible to a fixed formula—unless the contract itself provides the formula or an objective measure.

A duty of best efforts is distinct from the duty of good faith. Good faith is a standard with a moral component that has honesty and fairness at its core, and that is imposed on every party to a contract. The best efforts standard focuses on diligence in performance or attempted performance.

Case law demonstrates that inclusion of a "best efforts" clause may give rise to an almost fiduciary level duty on the part of the burdened party. Even without a best efforts provision, one may be implied into an agreement like an exclusive license. Inclusion of a "best efforts" clause should cause concern unless the contract defines "best efforts" and provides an objective measure (such as dollars or time spent) for when the standard is met. The prudent approach is to include a standard for performance, such as best efforts, and then define the standard, including any limitations intended (*e.g.*, contractor shall only be required to expend $50,000 in attempt to . . .).

Conditions can be either subsequent or precedent. A condition precedent must be satisfied for the legal consequence to arise. The legal consequence is often the creation of a duty, as in the above examples. The party to whom the duty is owned (the right-holder) generally has the burden of proving a condition precedent. A condition subsequent operates to terminate an existing legal consequence, again usually a duty. The party possessing the duty generally has the burden of proving a condition subsequent. Most conditions can be expressed as either precedent or subsequent. But given the difference in the allocation of the burden of proof, the difference can be significant. A provision favoring the buyer could be worded as:

> *Buyer will purchase the cotton contained on the ship Lady Adams, but* ***only if*** *this ship arrives at Nantucket Roads on or before July* ***14, 2020.*** *Otherwise, ...*

A provision favoring the seller could be worded as:

> *Buyer will purchase the cotton contained on the ship Lady Adams unless this ship arrives at Nantucket Roads on or after July* ***15, 2020.***

If the arrival time of the *Lady Adams* cannot be proved conclusively either way, then the buyer wins under the first provision and the seller wins under the second.

You must confront the fact that parties and courts often ignore or waive conditions. Contracts are often full of clauses providing that a party's failure to act or enforce a right shall not be deemed to be a waiver of that right, and that any waiver of a current right shall not be a waiver of any other right or a future incidence of the same right. The litany of the non-waivable continues: time is of the essence; non-severability; no amendment or waiver by conduct; all amendments and waivers must be in writing; recitations that both parties have been represented by counsel, or at least had the opportunity to consult with counsel, have read the agreement and understand it.

All these provisions are attempts by the parties to avoid having a court later refuse to enforce a condition by finding that it was waived by conduct, was unconscionable, would otherwise lead to a forfeiture, and the like. A determined court can often find some way to excuse a failed condition should it choose to do so, and can usually do so in a ruling that is so fact-based that it is largely immune on appeal. The drafter can best guard against this result by (a) drafting the consequences of failure of a condition into the condition, not just leaving it to the default and remedy provisions of the agreement; (b) employing good boilerplate to document the parties' intention that all the terms of the document be strictly construed; (c) explicitly stating the reason that the condition was included; and (d) explicitly stating that the condition was a fundamental inducement for one or more of the parties to enter into the transaction.

One specific provision relating to covenants and conditions should be mentioned: "time is of the essence." Generally speaking, the law is that time is not of the essence and delayed performance will be found to constitute substantial performance rather than material breach unless the parties make time for performance an express condition. Thus, the inclusion of the venerable "time is of the essence" clause, often in the boilerplate section of the contract.

These are not magic words that fix the problem, however. Cases are legion in which courts have found that they are "mere boilerplate" and are contradicted by other words in the contract or the parties' actions. So, what is to be done? The solution lies in making it clear that the parties agreed that time of performance was material to their deal. To this end, reference to the time of performance and the reason for its importance belong in the recitals of the contract. A covenant of timely performance also belongs in the consideration section along with all the important economic terms. Finally, an argued consequence of untimely performance such as notice, an opportunity to cure (or not), and a remedy should be provided. One cannot handcuff a determined judge or jury, but one can make it harder for them to dismiss a boilerplate five-word statement of such an important condition.

b. Terminology

Conditions must be carefully drafted and integrated into the rest of the contract. First, you must take care to draft the condition so its terms are clear. Conditions generally trigger duties ("shall" clauses) or rights ("is entitled to" clauses). The reader must be able to determine when the condition is satisfied and, if not, what consequences follow. Word choice is key. If the condition is in the form of someone's conduct, use "must" or "if." Use "must" when satisfaction or non-satisfaction of the condition affects the actor's entitlement to something

> *Buyer* ***must*** *give notice of intent to cancel by no later than the 30th day prior to the anniversary date of this contract.*

Use "if" when satisfaction or non-satisfaction of the condition triggers a duty on the other party.

> ***If*** *Buyer discovers and reports defects in the goods within* ***10*** *days after delivery, Seller will immediately replace the goods.*

When a condition requires the occurrence of an external event to trigger the duties of one or more of the parties, use "if," "when," or "after."

> ***If*** *the United States lifts the trade embargo with China before December 1, 2020, Seller will deliver six carloads of. . . .*

Use "when" or "after" if the occurrence is relatively certain, but the timing is not.

> ***When*** *the bank submits its credit report, Seller will immediately arrange for. . . .*

> ***After*** *receiving the EEOC notice of a right to sue, the charging party must. . . .*

Term	Use
Shall	Use "shall" to create a duty.
Will	"Will" may be used to create a duty but "shall" is preferable.
Must	Use "must" to create a condition precedent.
May	Use "may" to create a privilege or an option. Use "may not" to negate a privilege.
Entitled	Use "is entitled to" to create a right. Use "is not entitled to" to negate a right.
Waive	Use "waive" to indicate a forfeiture of a right.
If	Use "if" when satisfaction or non-satisfaction of a condition triggers a duty.

c. Objective Versus Subjective Conditions

Objective conditions can be thought of as "true" or "false," "off" or "on"—something either exists or has occurred or it has not. This is perhaps an overly simplistic view of the matter but is given for illustrative purposes. A few common examples of *objective* provisions include, "in the event of a labor strike . . . ," "in the event that [x party] petitions for relief under the bankruptcy code . . . ," or "in the event that the Consumer Price Index rises above [x numerical level]. . . ."

Subjective conditions are typically more open ended, such as, "in the event of a harmful price change . . . ," "in the event that [x party] deems itself insecure . . . ," or "in the event of a labor dispute. . . ." Notice that some of the conditions can be left more open-ended than others, for example, the above noted "in the event of a 'harmful price change." In this case it is unclear which party is being "harmed," to what degree they are being "harmed" and, perhaps most importantly, what does "harmful" mean anyway? Though a degree of subjectivity can often be beneficial for one party, the drafter must always take care to ensure that subjectivity does not cross over into the realm of ambiguity.

D. COVENANTS

Covenants are the parties' promises and duties under the agreement. They should be contained in provisions that are clearly labeled and structured as covenants and should include a specific consequence for failure to perform.

Covenants should be drafted in the active voice—subject, verb, then object—and should be based on the convention of using "shall" to designate duties, "entitled" to designate rights, and "may" to designate privileges. For example, "Seller shall deliver the deed to Blackacre to Escrow Agent no later than December 1, 2020; failure of Seller to do so shall be cause for Buyer to terminate this agreement under section 10.08."

Covenants should clearly state what party is to do what, for whom, when, and the like.

E. REPRESENTATIONS, WARRANTIES, RELEASES, GUARANTIES, AND INDEMNITIES

Contracts frequently use representations, warranties, guaranties, and indemnities. Each is a different type of provision, and it is important to select the proper type to generate the proper legal effect. Perhaps more than any other set of provisions, these provisions highlight the litigation or default planning aspects of transactional practice and contract drafting. Each of these provisions gives rise to a particular set of causes of action in the event of breach or error.

In particular, representations, warranties, guaranties, and indemnities are interrelated and reinforce each other. A represented fact will induce a party to enter into negotiation and documentation of a transaction. If it is false, a misrepresentation action will support recession or damages. That representation will likely be converted into a warranty as to that fact that may survive closing. The surviving warranty provides a strict liability breach of warranty cause of action that can support an award of damages. Finally, to the extent that the non-warranting party has been damaged by the breached or incorrect warranty, an indemnity or a guaranty creates a route for damage recovery from the counter-party or a third party.

When thinking about these sorts of clauses as a drafter, you should approach the problem from the desired *remedy* first. This is unlike the way you were probably taught to analyze a set of facts for tort, contract, or property claims—element by element, with damages or other remedies last. For example, if certain facts are misstated, what remedy do you wish to seek? Possibilities include rescission pre-closing, rescission post-closing, or consequential or liquidated damages from the other party or from a credit-worthy third party. Then select the type of provisions that will produce a cause of action for your client that is ripe when needed, lies against the appropriate defendant, and provides the desired remedy.

1. GENERAL RULES AND TECHNIQUES: TYPICAL REPRESENTATIONS AND WARRANTIES

A contract may require a party to "represent" that they are authorized to enter into the agreement and "warrant" that they will fulfill their obligations under the agreement. Also, a party may "warrant" that they are authorized to enter into the agreement and "represent" that the goods delivered conform to certain specifications. Each of the general rules regarding representations and warranties can be altered by language of the contract itself, so none can be drafted or interpreted in a vacuum.

Typical representations and warranties include (1) the party is duly organized, in good standing, and authorized to enter in the transaction, (2) the transaction is not a breach of any other agreement and does not violate the law, (3) a seller or lessor has good title to all assets being sold or leased, and those assets are free of liens and encumbrances, and (4) all material facts have been disclosed. Each is often phrased as "except as disclosed on schedule *X* to this agreement, [representation or warranty]"—an example of a "carveout." As noted above, this structure makes the provision more than just a representation or warranty—it becomes a due diligence tool that shifts the burden of finding and discussing exceptions to the statement to the representing and warranting party. Representations and warranties of this type are often combined with a covenant to defend against claims that are adverse to any of the representations and warranties, and an indemnification (see next section) against losses caused by inaccurate representations or warranties.

An important method of reducing the scope of a representation or warranty, and any covenant or indemnity linked to it, is a knowledge limitation. For example, "the representations and warranties of section *X* below are limited to facts of which *a, b,* or *c* [people] have actual knowledge on the date of this agreement." This is a fair limitation, as long as the appropriate persons are specified: those who would naturally have the knowledge sought. Do not stop at the senior executive level—as knowledge there is generalized—but delve down to cover the knowledge of middle management and even the operations level of a business, as appropriate. Carveouts, *e.g.*, "except as listed on schedule 2.4," and materiality thresholds—also called "baskets"—*e.g.*, "except that Seller may dispose of inventory in the ordinary course of its business consistent with past practice," can also be used to limit the scope of a provision.

2. REPRESENTATIONS

Classically, a representation is a statement of presently existing facts—that is intended to induce reliance and action by a party, such as entering into a contract. An incorrect representation will support an action for rescission or damages sounding in contract (and tort, if fraud is present).

Unless otherwise specified, the representation speaks as of the execution of the document in which it is contained. The cause of action is, therefore, generally ripe as of that time, which may be pre-closing. Pre-closing representations may terminate at closing by operation of law unless the contract specifies that they survive the closing. Check governing law in your jurisdiction on this point and address the matter specifically in the contract with a survival or cancellation clause.

Representations are meant to give one party some reassurance that the other party's statements of fact are true. In this sense, they shift the risk that a stated fact is untrue to the representing party. Typical subjects for representations include the accuracy of financial statements; due formation and compliance with laws; and the existence of adverse claims, breached or defaulted contracts, liens, encumbrances, and legal actions.

Representations are also used to shift the burden and cost of investigation and disclosure in the due diligence process. For example, assume that your client wishes to purchase a business but wants to know if there are any claims or lawsuits against the business. You and your client could search relevant court records, perhaps nationwide. You could also dig through all of the business records looking for evidence of claims. These are burdensome and expensive activities. Alternatively, you could insert a representation into the purchase agreement in which the seller states that, except as disclosed on an attached schedule, no claims or lawsuits have been asserted against the company. This sort of blanket statement is known as a flat or unqualified representation. It shifts the burden of investigation and disclosure back to where it belongs, on the seller, which is the entity that is in the position of the least cost, the provider of the information.

Typically, the seller's counsel would respond with the suggestion that the representation be qualified, often by narrowing it to relate to claims or lawsuits of a certain type or over a certain size (a "materiality threshold") or known to certain specific individuals (a "knowledge limitation"). Depending on the circumstances, this may be acceptable to your client. If so, make sure that either limitation is not overbroad. Materiality thresholds, sometimes referred to as materiality qualifiers, should be set at levels that sound appropriate alarms, but filter out the noise generated by immaterial claims. A common issue here is the meaning of "material." When contracting parties disagree on whether something is material, a court might have to decide for them. Multiple courts have held that something is material if knowledge of it would affect an individual's decision-making process. Thus, it is best for the drafter to define "material" in the agreement, instead of leaving your client's fate to the courts.

Knowledge limitations, sometimes referred to as knowledge qualifiers, should specify persons who are likely to know the *details* involved; rarely will it be sufficient to limit knowledge to that of the uppermost tier of management. In this way, the burden of necessary investigation and disclosure can appropriately be shifted to the sellers. The inclusion of a knowledge qualifier has the effect of shifting the representations from those of the facts themselves to *awareness* of the facts. A party may justify its need to include a knowledge qualifier by arguing that it should not be required to make an assertion that it does not know to be the truth. If a party has incomplete knowledge, or if the truth of a fact is fairly immaterial and difficult or costly to obtain, a knowledge qualifier may be appropriate. On the other hand, if the fact is based upon something within the party's control or is one that the other party wishes to rely upon in deciding whether to proceed with the transaction, a knowledge limitation is inappropriate.

Representations are generally drafted in the form:

> *[Buyer, Seller, other defined term] represents [representation carefully stated as to scope and substance].*

Representations should almost always be drafted in the present or past tense, not the future tense, to prevent them from being interpreted as covenants.

A representation is often combined with a warranty, in which case the form is:

> *[Buyer, Seller, other defined term] represents and warrants [representation and warranty carefully stated as to scope and substance].*

This combination ensures that a cause of action will lie post-closing if the representation has terminated as of closing but the warranty survives or as part of an overall "belt and suspenders" approach.

3. WARRANTIES

Classically, a warranty is a statement made about certain facts whereby the warrantor promises that those facts are as stated. A breached or incorrect warranty will support a strict liability cause of action for damages sounding in contract, and the cause of action is ripe as of the closing of the transaction and survives closing unless the contract provides otherwise or, in the case of traditional real estate law, the warranty is not reflected in the deed as well as the purchase agreement. Since the law is not uniform with regard to survival, the best practice is for the contract to explicitly address the issue.

Warranties are generally drafted in the form:

> *[Buyer, Seller, other defined term] warrants that as of [date or dates, certain or referent] [warranted facts carefully stated as to scope and substance].*

Like representations, warranties should almost always be drafted in the present or past tense, not the future tense, to prevent them from being interpreted as covenants.

4. GUARANTIES AND INDEMNITIES

A guarantor is one who promises that if another party does not perform a duty, the guarantor will.

The word "guarantee," when used in the colloquial sense of a warranty (on your microwave oven, for example) has one spelling, and "guaranty," when used in its formal legal meaning (a promise to perform a third party's obligation) has a different spelling. *There should be no double-e guaranties in your contracts.*

5. INDEMNITIES

An indemnity is a collateral contractual obligation where one party (the indemnitor) engages to hold another (the indemnitee) harmless from losses to third parties. An indemnity agreement essentially shifts financial risks and burdens from one party to another. A common indemnity is one that covers any losses from a breach or inaccuracy of any representation or warranty in the agreement. The indemnitor need not be the other party to the contract. Like guaranties, indemnities are only as good as the net worth or liquidity of the indemnitor.

The basic issues that arise with indemnities are related to scope. Scope of indemnification is defined or limited by (1) the time period during which claims can be asserted; (2) the time period during which the event underlying the claim occurred; (3) the minimum and maximum amount of any claim or of all claims in the aggregate, or over a particular period of time; (4) the damages covered (actual pecuniary loss to third parties, consequential damages, punitive damages, liquidated damages); and (5) the mechanism for presenting claims and solving disputed claims.

6. RELEASES

A release of a right, claim, or privilege is a cancellation of the right to assert a right, claim, or privilege.

A similar result may be achieved by assignment of the claim. However, an assignment of the claim can have other effects that are useful in creatively structuring a transaction, such as maintaining the subordinate priority of other claims or one party's judgment-proof status.

7. CONCLUSION—CAUTIONARY PROCEDURES

At the outset, consider including a master provision that eliminates or disclaims as far as legally possible, all express or implied representations, warranties, indemnities, and releases except as expressly provided in the contract. This is an attempt to wipe the slate clean of common law and statutory implied provisions such as the UCC's warranty of merchantability or fitness for intended use. *But see* UCC § 2–316(1) (disclaimers of express warranties in conflict with apparent warranty will be inoperative if that construction is unreasonable); 2–316(2), (3) (disclaimer of implied warranties with specific disclaimers, general disclaimers, buyer inspections, and course of performance). A disclaimer of warranties may be subject to different, peculiar drafting requirements that seem to indicate hostility to overreaching disclaimers and releases obtained by economically dominant parties. Include a merger or integration clause to trigger the parol evidence rule to exclude evidence of any statements that could be construed as agreements, representations, warranties, covenants, etc., made during negotiations or earlier rounds of documentation.

The use of the wrong type of provision can result in the provision working in unintended ways, limiting a party's rights, or giving rise to unintended consequences. For example, since warranties concern the present existence of facts, the characterization of a covenant as a representation or warranty may prevent the covenant from applying to a future breach of the obligation. Likewise, the characterization of a covenant as a representation or warranty may create fraud or misrepresentation tort liability, including potential punitive damages, for the promisor's breach, but that breach should only be a contract claim (limiting damages to compensatory ones in most jurisdictions), if a true covenant is used.

To disclaim all warranties outside the four corners of your agreement, include a prefatory clause in the warranty disclaimer that preserves only the explicitly stated warranties in the agreement. For example, "EXCEPT FOR THE WARRANTIES

SPECIFICALLY PROVIDED IN THIS AGREEMENT. . ." and then disclaim all other warranties, express or implied. Absent an exclusion of these implied warranties, a seller might impliedly warrant to the buyer that the goods are both merchantable and fit for a particular purpose. But be careful, some courts may be wary of enforcing broad disclaimer provisions, others are not. Thus, a drafter must never be too cautious. Including the language "as is" or "with all faults" is, at best, a start to disclaiming implied warranties, but such language by itself might not be enough. (See UCC § 2–316(2) & (3).

Claims of breach or inaccuracy accrue and statutes of limitations run at different times depending upon the type of provision used. A claim for misrepresentation can arise at the time of signing a purchase and sale or other agreement. A breach of warranty claim generally arises at the time of the closing or sale. A breach of covenant claim accrues when the party does not honor the covenant, which may be in the distant, post-closing future.

If an indemnity is used to cover a warranty claim, the indemnitee may not have a claim if the indemnitor can limit its liability to true indemnitor liability. This includes only reimbursement of the indemnitee for its liabilities to third persons. Self-sustained and remedied damages are not included. This limitation can be drafted around in many jurisdictions by expressly including otherwise excluded damages.

An indemnity against liability becomes collectible immediately when the indemnitee become liable to a third person. An indemnity against anything else (such as claims or damages) becomes collectible only after the indemnitee has paid the third person.

Finally, an indemnity may not be effective if the indemnitee's own negligence contributed to its obligation to a third party. Generally, an indemnitee can recover in these circumstances only if the indemnity expressly provides for recovery under those circumstances. Draft carefully.

F. EXCEPTIONS

Drafted documents often create exceptions to or limitations on the rights, duties, privileges, and immunities that they otherwise create. In the past, these exceptions were often worded in terms of "provided further, that no. . . ." Modern drafters should avoid these archaic provisos, although their usage is still widespread. Some use "except that" language for simple exceptions.

> *The Executor may disburse the remainder of the estate as her discretion dictates,* ***except that*** *she may distribute no funds to any political party.*

Although "unless" is a potentially ambiguous term, some drafters use it to express exceptions.

> ***Unless*** *expressly bequeathed to a specific individual under the terms of this will or a written and attached memorandum, my estate goes to. . . .*

For longer and more complicated exceptions, the approach can be even more direct.

> *This section does not apply to (1) . . . ; (2) . . . ; and (14). . . .*

Exceptions can also be conceptualized as and worded in terms of conditions:

> *Seller will continue to deliver buyer's monthly requirements of widgets at $10.00 per ton, but this obligation terminates if the Canadian embargo ends [creating an exception to the duty to deliver].*

> *If the wholesale price of okra goes over $1.50 per pound before the delivery date of June 30, 2020, Buyer will pay an additional. . . . [creating an exception to the contract duty to pay at another price level].*

G. EVENTS OF DEFAULT AND REMEDIES

Law students study common law rules regarding remedies—from limits on damages to the availability of specific performance and other equitable remedies. However, the principle of freedom of contract also allows parties the opportunity to tailor their own remedies, drafting them to best suit a particular client or a particular deal. As a contract drafter, you need to plan your way into or around these common law rules to allow your client to recover as much as possible in the event of the other party's breach. Good drafters know the substantive law applicable to their transactions and then plan and structure transactions to take advantage of favorable law (*e.g.*, tax effects, validation of liquidated damages provisions, etc.) and to avoid, or "draft around," unfavorable law.

"Default," for example, is a broader concept than "breach of contract." The default and remedy section of a contract should begin with a listing of what actual events are "events of default." Although the enumerated events of default generally include events that would be a breach of the contract under the common law without a specific default section (for example, non-payment of rent under a real property lease) they can also include many things that would otherwise not be considered a breach, such as changed financial status as measured by financial ratios, a failure to maintain casualty insurance for collateral, and other insecurity provisions. Events of default or a declaration of default under one contract can also be a default or an event of default under another agreement, including an agreement involving a completely separate transaction and completely different parties. This is known as a "cross-default."

Events of default are selected for each transaction. Common events of default include:

- Failure to perform an obligation to the other party to the contract or a third-party.
- Failure to pay monies when due.
- Failure to maintain a certain status (membership, financial condition, etc.).

- Breach or inaccuracy of a representation or warranty.
- Bankruptcy and similar insolvency-related conditions and proceedings (although these are generally unenforceable if the contracting party is the debtor in a bankruptcy case).
- Default under another agreement.
- General insecurity of the other party.

The contract can make the occurrence of an event of default an automatic default under the contract entitling the non-defaulting party to exercise its remedies. Alternatively the contract may require the non-defaulting party to give notice that the event of default has occurred and declare a default. The latter form gives the non-defaulting party more flexibility, but also requires more careful monitoring of the other party, especially if non-monetary defaults are involved. Note that even if the occurrence of an event of default is automatic under the contract, as a practical matter, every jurisdiction will require some form of notice of the default prior to exercise of remedy. Remember, a notice of default or termination will generally not be effective if the defaulting party is in bankruptcy before the proper notice is given of an event of default.

Many default provisions include the concept of a right to cure—or fix—the default and avoid application of the remedies provided in the contract. Different cure periods can apply to different events of default, and the contract should specify when the cure period begins to run. In drafting, one of two approaches is used to provide cure rights. One either drafts a separate provision addressing the right to cure or builds the cure right into each event of default provision.

The provisions that establish a default are generally followed by provisions that specify (1) remedies, (2) whether those remedies are automatic or elective on the part of the non-defaulting party, (3) how the election of remedies, if any, is to be made, and (4) whether the remedies are mutually exclusive or cumulative. Consider the legality and enforceability of remedies as well. The most effective ones that you can imagine are often unenforceable or of limited enforceability.

The mutual foreseeability test of *Hadley v. Baxendale,* 9 Exch. 341 (Court of the Exchequer 1854), would limit liability unless the drafter used, among other provisions, a liquidated damage clause and a prevailing party attorneys' fee clause. Alternatively, the drafter could include recitals showing what damages were reasonably foreseeable by all parties. Similar issues arise in other areas, including provisions for acceleration of payment obligations, post-judgment attorneys' fees, interest, default interest, prepayment fees, or calculation of interest based upon an actual year or a 360-day accounting year. The drafter needs to assess all applicable issues, the limiting or expanding effect of otherwise applicable law, and possible draft-arounds available to serve the client's interests.

A final note about default and remedies: when an event of default has occurred, and it is time to declare the default, the notice of default (generally in the form of a letter) should be *drafted in unequivocal language and should track the language and requirements of the contract exactly*. There is no need to be either overly kind or insulting in tone. A neutral description of the contract, the pertinent provisions, the event of default that has occurred, a declaration of the default, an election of remedies, if needed, and any demand for action will suffice. The notice of default should be transmitted exactly as specified in the contract. Failure to strictly adhere to the contractual requirements will afford the defaulting party a defense to enforcement and may allow additional time to cure and reinstate the agreement.

H. WHEN NOT TO FOLLOW THESE CONVENTIONS

Although the above conventions enjoy wide usage and the drafting environment would be significantly improved if made universal, courts do not always follow them when construing documents. If the drafter is in a jurisdiction prone to its own idiosyncratic interpretation of words that create legal consequences, then the drafter will need to defer to the local law. This may involve using alternative terms or simply calling what is intended to be a duty a "duty," a right a "right," and so on.

> *Buyer* ***is obligated to****. . . . [if that is the preferred usage for creating duties].*

> *Buyer's* ***duties*** *under this contract are as follows:. . . . Seller* ***has the right*** *to require Buyer to. . . . Buyer's duty to pay the contract*

> *price on June 30, 2020,* ***is expressly conditioned on*** *Seller's delivery of the goods on or before that date. . . . Buyer* ***has the power and authority to*** *terminate this contract upon* ***10*** *days notice to Seller. . . . [stating the intended legal consequence directly].*

> *Tenant* ***must*** *give notice of intent to vacate at least one month in advance. This is an express condition and failure to give this notice results in forfeiture of the security deposit. [Using the conventional term but also stating its intended meaning and legal consequence].*

The object is to express the intent of the parties in such a way that the courts, when construing the document, will give effect to that intent. Keeping the unique rules of interpretation of that state well in mind, the drafter should use whatever words are necessary to do that, regardless of how artless they may seem to be.

CHAPTER 16

DOCUMENT TYPOGRAPHY AND LAYOUT

The objectives of transactional and legislative drafting are: (1) to establish legal relationships, and (2) to state those relationships in ways readily understandable by all users of the document. Everything discussed in the previous chapters contributes to those objectives—determining client desires, careful legal and factual investigation, precise conceptualization, impeccable organization, and clear and concise expression. This chapter focuses on making documents easily readable in appearance and format.

A. PHYSICAL APPEARANCE

One of the plain English movement's points was that the physical appearance of drafted documents should enhance even the least literate user's understanding of the substantive content of the document. Plain English proponents enlisted the aid of experts in the fields of typography (the appearance of printed words) and layout design. Their contribution to good drafting has been significant. The basic features and principles involve the following.

1. WHITE SPACE

The readability of the document is enhanced by lots of white space, referring to the spaces on the page where nothing is printed. The drafter should make a conscious effort to avoid producing a document that is densely filled with text.

2. TYPE SIZE AND FONT

The optimal type size and font is often debated. Indeed, each reader has individual preferences—which is why e-book readers such as Kindle and Nook devices have many choices among type size and font styles. The objectives in transactional and legislative drafting are to make type size and font style accessible to the widest possible audience.

The most important consideration in choosing type size in drafted documents is that the printed words should be *capable* of being seen by all or most readers. Some people are capable of and prefer reading small print. Others, however, cannot read small print without resorting to a magnifying glass or special glasses. Thus, generally, text in drafted documents should be no smaller than 12-point type.

Indeed, some appellate court rules require that briefs be in 14-point type, and contract drafters would be wise to emulate that rule in at least two situations. First, if the document will be frequently referred to during the term of the agreement, it should be in easily readable 14-point type. This is particularly the case with documents that will be used on construction sites or manufacturing plants. Second, an adequate type size is especially important in consumer-oriented documents, where easy readability may be a condition of enforceability. For example, one court held that a portion of an installment sales contract that was printed in 8-point type rather than the required 10-point type violated the Truth in Lending Act. Standard real estate contracts, which in many respects represent drafting at its worst, are often crammed into the seemingly mandatory two-page (front and back of a standard piece of paper), densely packed, tiny print format that defies reading or comprehension.

Similarly, choose a font style that is easy and comfortable to read in standard format, as well as when presented in *italics*, **boldface,** and ALL CAPS. This book is written in Century Schoolbook. This is a clear, easy to read font that is included as standard in most word processors. The objective is to ensure that the drafted document is accessible to the widest possible audience. Thus, avoid—

- `Courier`, which is a holdover from the days of typewritten legal documents.
- Sans serif typefaces—those that do not have small lines or "serifs" at the end of characters—like Arial and Tahoma. These may be considered more modern but tend to be fatiguing to the eye in lengthy documents.
- Any kind of script or cursive font, even in the heading to the document, because these are difficult to read.
- Old English type or any of the silly fonts found in a word processing program.
- Any font style that calls more attention to itself than the printed words themselves.

3. LIMITED USE OF ALL CAPITALS AND UNDERLINING

Type that is set in upper and lower case is easier to read than type set in all capitals, and underlined text is a strain to the eyes. Back when most contracts were typewritten, all caps and underlining were the only way to set off the headings and provide emphasis to select portions of the text. Hence, one might see something like this.

> T. DISCLAIMER OF WARRANTIES. Except as provided in paragraphs c, q, and r above, <u>THIS PECAN SHELLER IS SOLD WITHOUT ANY WARRANTIES, EXPRESS OR IMPLIED, INCLUDING THE WARRANTY OF MERCHANTABILITY AND OF FITNESS FOR ANY PARTICULAR USE AND ANY PRIOR REPRESENTATIONS BY SELLER, ORAL OR IN WRITING, TO THE CONTRARY ARE VOID</u>.

Today, in the absence of statutory requirements to the contrary, the better practice is to use **bolded headings** with a font-size two points larger than the rest of the text and **bolded phrases** for the critical words to satisfy conspicuousness requirements.

Using white space is also a way to make specific language conspicuous.

Another way to satisfy conspicuousness requirements is to put the required language in a text box like this one.

4. LINE LENGTH

Line length involves how long, in distance, a line of text is on the page, as well the number of characters in each line. Most legal documents are formatted for a standard 8 1/2 by 11 inch piece of paper, with one inch margins. This generally equates to a line length of 6 inches, although many people find a line length of 4–5 inches preferable. Text designers are not in agreement about the optimal amount of characters per line. Some suggest the most easily read line length is from 39 to 52 characters, while others opt for the 50 to 70 character range. Of course the type size and font style also affect the number of characters in a line. A line of 14-point Times New Roman text contains approximately 67 characters, while a 12-point line of the same font contains 78 characters.

The point is that drafters should make conscious choices regarding line length, both in distance and characters per line, in creating documents that are readily accessible to the widest possible audience.

Sometimes, using columns may make the document easier to read. For example, when the document, like a newspaper, contains many one- or two-sentence sections or paragraphs. These read more easily when they are in three or four short lines, rather than in a single line or two stretching across the page. Also, drafters who view line length as a major problem may elect to use two columns on a standard 8 1/2 by 11 inch piece of paper. However, columned text requires the reader to go to the bottom of the page, back to the top, and then down to the bottom again—a lot of eye muscle exercise for someone merely scanning the document.

Finally, the shorter the line of text, the shorter the tab (or first line indent) should be—no longer than 1/2 an inch for 6 1/2 lines and 1/4 an inch for 4 inch lines.

5. JUSTIFICATION

Some believe that full left and right justification makes the text look neater and makes paragraph breaks more distinct, thus contributing to the comprehensibility of the document. And many experts believe that a fully justified text is simply easier to read.

Not everyone agrees with that. One source of the disagreement is the Securities and Exchange Commission; drafters of documents with that agency as an audience should take note. Although it is only a recommendation, the SEC and many practicing attorneys believe left-only justified text is easier to read, because fully justified text has uneven spacing between the words. This can be minimized by the use of short words—a desirable trait in drafting, the automatic hyphenation feature of word processing software, and standard rather than column length lines. The jury is still out on this issue. But make justification a conscious choice.

6. LINE SPACING

Line spacing refers to the vertical space between lines on the page. In the typewriter age, the unit of measurement was limited to a single line—hence single space, double space, triple space, etc. Thus traditionally most transactional and legislative documents were single-spaced, while courts required briefs and other court filed documents to be double spaced. Generally, though, the most easily readable line spacing is 1.2 or 1.3 spacing between lines. This usually translates to line spacing that is about 120% to 130% of font size—which can be specifically set in most word processing programs.

Remember that line spacing is not equivalent to or a substitute for creating sufficient white space in drafted documents.

7. BLANK SPACES

Standard contracts are often printed with blank spaces for things like the date, the names of the parties, the identity of the property or goods, the price, and other terms and conditions. Unfortunately, the blank spaces are often not large enough, in either length or height, for the information that must be handwritten in. The length problem is easily solved by making sure the blank lines are long enough. However, a 12-point, single-spaced document still does not allow enough height for the handwriting of most people. And the 8-point or smaller type that is used in many commercially printed documents is simply impossible. The solution is to either use 14 point type or increased spacing between the lines, or both.

8. SECTIONS AND PARAGRAPHS

Check your sections and paragraphs for length—either too short or too long. Generally avoid one or two sentence sections or paragraphs. Check to see if the sentences should be combined with or folded into other paragraphs or sections, or if the very short paragraph should be further developed. Also check for paragraphs or sections that are longer than ¾ of a page. Ask if these should be broken into more than one paragraph connected by transitional sentences. Beware of the section or paragraph that tries to do too much or contains more information than the reader can assimilate.

Every sentence in a paragraph or section should (1) relate and support a single topic and (2) relate to the sentences around it.

Detractions include paragraphs without clear topics; sentences that do not relate to the topic identified; and paragraphs that are choppy or disconnected because of the sentences are not arranged smoothly and/or because transition words are needed.

B. TEXT

The text of a drafted document can be made more comprehensible in a number of ways.

1. TABLE OF CONTENTS

A lengthy document should contain a table of contents on the cover page. This enables the parties and other readers to find what they are looking for quickly. A table of contents may also be appropriate even in short consumer documents. The table of contents should contain all the headings and subheadings of the document, together with the page on which they appear.

2. NUMBERED PAGES

Even a short document should be page numbered. Usually, a simple "5" or "–5–" placed conspicuously on the page, *e.g.*, at the bottom center, is sufficient. But some drafters, exercising an excess of caution in important documents and to ensure that no page is later removed, use the "Page 5 of 100 pages" convention. These documents also often provide a space for the initials of the parties on each page. It would be pretentious, however, to use these conventions in short simple contracts.

3. HIERARCHICAL PARAGRAPH HEADINGS

Hierarchical, numbered, or lettered paragraph headings are the visual signposts of the document. They make it easy for the reader to find a particular provision, and they give the top-to-bottom reader an indication of what the next provision is about. A document without them provides the reader with a frustrating and tedious reading experience.

The headings and subheadings reflect the organization that the drafter has decided upon. Indeed, an inability to produce the necessary heading and subheadings—using a proper outlining structure with respect to the numbers or letters—is a sure sign of a faulty organization.

The clearest form of labeling hierarchical headings is using series of tiered numbers that corresponds to specific subject matter. For example:

§ 1 Seller's Obligations

§ 1.1 Delivery

§ 1.1.1 Mode

§ 1.1.2 Time

§ 1.1.3 Place

§ 1.2 Installation

This method clearly identifies and sets out the hierarchy among the sellers' obligations.

Some drafters still prefer this type of numbering and lettering format:

I. Seller's Obligations

A. Delivery

1. Method

2. Time

3. Place

B. Installation

With this method it is not as clear where an item is in the hierarchy.

With either method, the numbers or letters make it easier for the parties to refer to specific sections and allow for clear cross-reference within the document itself. However, after the document is complete, the drafter should double check all cross-references. In an early version of the document, the referenced material may have been in paragraph 1.1.2. In the final version of the document the material may appear in 1.1.3. Unless the cross-reference is changed, the document will be confusing, at best. An erroneous cross-reference could make the document ambiguous or produce totally unintended results. One may minimize the danger of an erroneous numerical cross reference by also including the paragraph heading in the cross reference, in the hope that the referenced subject matter will prevail over the referenced number. That, however, is no substitute for careful proofreading.

The headings must accurately reflect the content of the paragraph. For example, one should not bury a disclaimer of warranties in a paragraph marked "Warranties." Such a disclaimer may not even be legally effective due to lack of conspicuousness.

Some drafters are inclined to include a provision stating that headings are not part of the contract and should not be used to limit, expand, or interpret the substantive text. This is an admission of sloppy drafting. The better approach is to word the heading so that it is totally coincident with the substantive text that follows. The drafter's inability to do this easily may indicate a fundamental flaw in the conceptualization or organization of the document.

4. LISTS AND ENUMERATIONS

Lists and enumerations enhance readability and ease of reference when dealing with a number of items. Traditionally a list consists of an introductory sentence that expresses the nature of the relationship between the items in the list by indicating whether the items are cumulative or alternative, followed by the list of items themselves. The introductory sentence may end with a colon or a period, with each item in the list beginning with a capital letter and ends with a period. The items should be numbered, lettered, or introduced with a bullet or other visual representation. For example:

> ***B. Appliances.*** *Landlord will furnish all of the following appliances and maintain them in good working order:*
>
> 1. *Refrigerator.*
> 2. *Stove.*
> 3. *Disposal.*
> 4. *Washer.*
> 5. *Dryer.*

Unlike a list, an enumeration retains its single-sentence structure. The introductory clause may have no terminal punctuation at all, although dashes and colons are sometimes used. Each item in the enumeration is terminated with a comma or a semi-colon, except the last one, which takes a period. The nature of the relationship between the items in the series is indicated by an "and" or an "or" following the next to last item. A single "and" or "or" following the second-to-last item in the series is sufficient; it is not necessary to put the connective after each item in the series. The enumeration can be accomplished with parenthesized numbers or simple bullets. For example:

> *Agent's territory consists of*
>
> - All of South Carolina, except the counties of Greenville, Richland, Horrey, and Charleston;
> - All of Georgia, except the City of Atlanta; and
> - North Carolina.
>
> ***Q. Tenant's Duties Upon Termination of the Lease.*** *At the termination of the lease, Tenant will*
>
> *(1) restore the property to the same condition it was in at the beginning of the lease, except for changes caused by reasonable wear and tear;*
>
> *(2) arrange for the disconnection of all utilities for which Tenant is responsible;*
>
> *(3) return all keys to Landlord;*
>
> *(4) remove all furniture and personal belongings; and*
>
> *(5) vacate the premises by no later than 4:00 p.m. on the last day of the lease.*

Although, that is a 73-word sentence—far too long by conventional standards—the fragmentation of its parts into an enumeration makes it easy to follow. So, whenever a drafted document contains a series of items joined by an "and" or "or," the drafter should consider making using the enumeration technique.

Enumerations not only make complicated provisions easier to read and understand, but are also extremely useful in resolving ambiguities. If the contract states that "Seller is to provide red caps, jerseys, and pants," does this mean that all three items must be red? Or only the caps? It could be expressed as either

Seller will provide (a) red caps, (b) jerseys, and (c) pants,

or

Seller will provide red (a) caps, (b) jerseys, and (c) pants.

5. TABBING

Drafters also often use a device called tabbing or tabulator form to avoid ambiguities of modification. Tabbing joins sentences and related ideas by shortening the provision and facilitating reading. Tabbing allows the drafter to reformat long, convoluted sentences using identifying letters, numbers, indentation, and white space to show the relationship of each subpart to the sentence. In addition to increasing clarity, precision, and readability, tabbing long and complex sentences may help with comprehension as well. Consider the following provision written in conventional paragraph form:

A person who drives an automobile on a public road recklessly, negligently, or at a speed or in a manner posing a danger to others ***considering***

> ***the condition of the highway and the weather*** *is guilty of a misdemeanor.*

Does the bolded language only modify the dangerous manner of the driving? Or does it also modify "recklessly," "negligently," and "at a speed?" One court construed the phrase in a similar statute as modifying all four of the preceding expressions. However, this could have been expressed more clearly by the statute itself, through the tabbing device.

> *A person who drives an automobile on a public road*
>
> > *recklessly,*
> >
> > *negligently,*
> >
> > *at a speed posing a danger to others, or in a manner posing a danger to others,*
>
> *considering the condition of the highway and the weather, is guilty of a misdemeanor.*

By bringing the "considering" phrase back over to the margin, the drafter indicates that it modifies all four of the tabbed items.

6. CHARTS AND GRAPHS

Often, a chart or graph is the clearest way to present complex information. Consider, for example, how the following chart clearly and easily describes the treatment of claims in a workout agreement.

Class	**Description**	**Treatment**
Administrative	Trustee Fees	Paid in Full on Effective Date
Class One	Secured Claims	Paid in Full on Effective Date or Collateral Surrendered
Class Two	Tax Claims	Paid in Full within 60 days of Effective Date
Class Three	General Unsecured Claims	Paid in Full out of Net Income over 3 years after the Effective Date
Class Four	Equity	Retained by Partners

7. COMPUTATIONS

Computations can be presented clearly in two ways—by list and by formula. A list details the computation step by step.

To determine the Flesch-Kincaid Readability Index, by grade level:

a. Divide the number of words by the number of sentences to determine the average sentence length (ASL).

b. Multiply the ASL by .39.

c. Divide the number of syllables by the number of words to determine the average syllables per word (ASW).

d. Multiply the ASW by 11.8.

e. Add the results of steps b. and d.

f. Subtract 15.59.

The formula approach simply presents a mathematical formula for the computation.

The Flesch-Kincaid formula for determining the Readability Index, by grade level, is as follows: Grade Level = [.39 × (number of words – number of sentences)] + [11.8 × (number of syllables – number of words)] – 15.59.

Consider including an example of any specified formula in use. In other words, provide a step-by-step computation under a hypothetical set of facts.

CHAPTER 17

REVIEWING AND REVISING

The final step in the drafting process is to do a comprehensive review of the document and, on the basis of that review, to do one final revision. The review process also occurs when a drafter is asked to review and revise documents prepared by others, not only to bring these documents into compliance with the more modern conventions of good drafting style, but to satisfy legal requirements, fill substantive gaps, and cure ambiguities. Similarly, specific substantive changes usually provide the impetus for statutory revisions because of the difficulty and complexity of the amendment process. However, it is not uncommon for other types of legislation to be periodically reviewed and revised without any substantive changes. For example, as a result of Plain English legislation, an administrative agency may find it necessary to revise their rules and regulations.

The components of a comprehensive review and revision are similar, whether they involve a document the reviewer has just prepared or one that was prepared earlier by someone else.

A. PREPARE A FLOWCHART

One helpful technique is preparing a flowchart. A flowchart is a schematic diagram of a drafted document or portions of it. Doing a flowchart will accomplish four things.

First, if the drafter is reviewing an earlier contract or regulation, a flowchart will enable the drafter to master the substance of the document. Many of the documents needing revision are exceedingly dense. That is, the substance is hidden in a forest of bad drafting, rendering the document incomprehensible to the ordinary reader. The drafter must determine what the substance is before attempting to present that substance in a more palatable form. Making a flowchart will accomplish that.

Second, the rules of flowcharting impose a discipline that will force the drafter to identify and deal with substantive gaps, those created by "if . . . then" constructions, for example. The flowchart will illustrate the consequence when the "if" clause is identified, as well as what happens when it is not satisfied. The infamous UCC § 2–207, for example, which was supposed to resolve the battle of the forms, does not always do that. A flowchart of that section is not only enormously complicated, it also reveals that the framers did not think the process through thoroughly or provide answers to all the questions that can arise in deciding whether a contract exists and on what terms.

Third, if the drafter discovers that passage through the flowchart could arguably lead in two different directions (two "yes" exit doors from the same block, for example), this means that the provision in question is ambiguous and needs to be revised.

Fourth, if the logical analysis of a provision, as reflected in the flowchart, suggests that it should start at one point and the document, as written, starts somewhere else, then this will suggest a sequence problem that needs to be corrected.

The steps for creating a flowchart are:

- Reduce the document to its individual, component parts. This could consist of an action to be performed, a criterion to be applied, an element to be satisfied, or a procedure to be exhausted. Each component becomes a separate block in the chart.
- Express the component in the form of a question. "Has claimant filed form 285?"
- Identify the various ways in which each question can be answered. Usually, the choices are "yes" and "no." Sometimes, however, several answers are possible. For example, the question might be, "Which section is claimant filing under?"—for which there might be three possible answers, "§ 258," "§ 259," and "§ 260."
- Make each possible answer an exit gate from the block, with a path down which the analysis will flow.
- At the end of each path, identify the consequences of taking that path. Often, the consequence is that another component must be dealt with. In other words, the path will usually lead to another block, containing another question, and another set of exit gates and paths.

- Continue the chart until it reaches the ultimate conclusions. This could be something like, "Claimant qualifies for the benefit" and "Claimant does not qualify for the benefit." Or, other alternatives might exist, like "Claimant is required to file supplemental information within 30 days."

B. DOCUMENT REVIEW

1. REVIEW BY THE DRAFTER

Once the initial writing is over, put the draft away for at least a day, if possible. Although you will have revised and rewritten as you produced the first draft, you did so with the perspective of the writer organizing and putting thoughts down on the page. You need fresh eyes for the revising and rewriting stage of the drafting process, which is where you turn your draft into a quality document.

At this point the thinking process begins anew. Basically, the drafter must ask, "Is this document going to work?" That is, will it serve the client's objectives effectively, efficiently, and without the need to resort to litigation? The drafter should review the document several times, each from a different perspective.

- Substantively, does it cover everything that it needs to cover?
- Does it satisfy all the legal requirements?
- Does it contain ambiguities?

- Does it contain potential loopholes that a hostile reader could exploit?
- Is it internally consistent?
- Are the rights, duties, and other legal consequences clearly and unequivocally stated?
- Are the objectives of the document properly conceptualized?

Some of the items on this review list involve what is called "vertical review," requiring the drafter to look in depth at each provision in turn for hidden ambiguities and stylistic flaws. Other items on the list involve what is called "horizontal review," requiring the drafter to compare how a particular topic is handled in different provisions throughout the document. The drafter's search for inconsistency, for example, may require the drafter to track through multiple provisions to ensure that the person who is renting the property is always referred to as the "tenant."

a. Review for Content—a Ten Point Checklist

When reviewing documents drafted by others, and when critically examining your own drafting, use the following questions to focus your review:

1. Parties, Dates, Dollar Amounts, and Interest Rates

Does the document identify the correct parties in their proper capacities? Are the dates correct? Are all currency amounts and interest rates correct and complete? Never assume that any factual statement is correct. Trust, but verify.

2. Appropriate Structure

Does the document and the overall structure of the transaction suit your client's needs? Do you understand the deal that is at issue? Is there an alternative structure that is more desirable for your client, perhaps for reasons outside the immediate transaction, such as accounting and tax treatment? Does the document match your client's expectations? Does it match your client's earlier description of the deal to you?

3. Clear Expression of Duties, Rights, and Privileges

Does the document contain clear mandatory duty provisions regarding all performances by other parties? Are mandatory duties specified using the words "shall" or "must?" Are rights expressed in terms of "is entitled to" and privileges in terms of "may"? Do these provisions clearly state who does what to or for whom or what, when? Timing of performance is essential; do not neglect to specify the "when."

4. Representations and Warranties

Does the document contain representations and warranties running in favor of your client regarding all facts, statements, and assurances upon which your client is relying? Are any qualifiers such as knowledge, material, and thresholds, appropriate? If these representations and warranties prove false, is there a mechanism for recovering from a creditworthy entity, for rescinding, or for otherwise modifying the transaction? These mechanisms include a covenant coupled with an indemnity, an event of default coupled with a remedy, and a covenant and third party guaranty.

Does the document require your client to make broad or unnecessary representations and warranties? Can these be estimated, narrowed, or limited in temporal or geographic scope? Can a materiality threshold limiting the representation to things over a certain amount (*e.g.*, claims in excess of $25,000) be added to limit the breadth of the statement? Can a knowledge limitation be inserted so that a representation, especially as to the lack of something, is limited to the knowledge of a specific individual at a specific time?

Are the representations and warranties that your client is making factually correct? How about those of the other side? Are there any that you know to be false?

5. *Internal and External Consistency*

Does the document fit the desired structure? Is it complete and consistent, internally and with any other documents involved in the transaction? Defined terms and boilerplate should be consistent across all documents in a transaction to avoid confusion and potential ambiguity. Do all the documents contain a non-severability clause? Are they governed by the same integration, merger, choice of law, choice of forum, and alternative dispute resolution provisions?

6. *Substantive Understanding*

Do you understand each provision of the document? Review each of them until you understand it completely and its interaction with the other sections of the document and related documents. As a general rule, if you do not understand a provision, a sentence, or a paragraph after reading it a few times, flag it. If someone else explains it, require edits consistent with their explanation. If no one can explain it, strike it and redraft it as necessary. Do not make a habit of striking entire provisions from a contract. Err on the side of requesting clarification or edits, or redrafting.

7. *Hypothesize Performance*

Think through the life of the transaction and the document under various fact patterns. What will happen, moment by moment, if the parties comply with all the terms in a timely manner? Sometimes it is useful to think this life cycle through in reverse to determine if the final product is supported in all respects by the agreement's provisions. Are performances required in the proper order?

8. *Hypothesize Non-Performance and Default*

What if one or both parties fail to perform all or part of the agreement? Are the consequences of failure of conditions or failure to perform stated and closely linked to the performance required? Are there clear events of default and associated remedies? Does the document address other issues and problems that are likely to arise in the course of performance? Resolve issues and problems at the drafting stage, rather than waiting for the parties to reach the problem. It is likely that the parties will never be more amenable to working out details than they are at the inception of the deal. Capitalize on the opportunity to prevent trouble before it occurs.

9. Address Bankruptcy Risk

Analyze what will happen if one of the parties files a bankruptcy petition or becomes subject to a receivership. Will property or rights that are important to the other party become "property of the estate" under 11 U.S.C. § 541? Will performance be stayed or affected by the automatic stay of 11 U.S.C. § 362?

Will the document be considered an "executory contract" subject to assumption or rejection under 11 U.S.C. § 365? If so, will this assumption or rejection be possible independently from assumption or rejection of the other documents in the deal? If so, is there a way to structure the transaction so that this property or these rights are held by a third party that is unlikely or unable to be the subject of a bankruptcy case?

Can the document incorporate, or be incorporated into, other documents from which it should not be divisible? Do the recitals in the contract make clear what performances and property rights are important to each of the parties and what injury and damage they may suffer if they are deprived of them? Can you provide for a lien, security interest, or third party credit support, such as a guaranty or letter of credit, to secure the opposing party's payment and performance obligations?

10. Consider the Worst Case Scenario

Assume that the document is executed and the parties become openly hostile, seeking to undermine each other at every opportunity. Will the document provide sufficient guidance to govern the relationship? Will it provide sufficient guidance to a court interpreting the document or imposing remedies if the parties are locked into their dispute with no thought to the opportunity or litigation costs involved? Although this may be a worst-case scenario, that is the appropriate test for a well-drafted transactional document.

b. Review for Style and Usage

It is best that the drafter of the document not be the one to review it for style and usage. We all become blind to our own writing weaknesses and deficiencies, and this task is best performed by another competent drafter. Take this person's criticisms and suggestions to heart. In particular, if a reasonable reader thinks a provision is unclear, then that provision is, by definition, unclear. Do not argue. Revise it. However, if, another person is not available, then the drafter must make a conscious mental effort to change from a drafting persona to an editing persona.

In addition, the solo drafter should always use the style and grammar check programs that come with most word processing software. They will identify many writing deficiencies and make valuable suggestions for improvement. However, the drafter should only consider these suggestions and not follow them if good reasons exist for not doing so. For example, the drafter may have consciously decided to split an infinitive, use the passive voice, or enumerate a series of items in a sentence that is longer than the program thinks appropriate. The program may also suggest simplified substitutes for words that are terms of art or have special legal meaning. Thus, one should not follow the advice to replace "affirmative action" with "yes action."

A particularly valuable feature of style and spelling checkers is the document readability index it creates. Many of the techniques for achieving brevity, clarity, and simplicity discussed elsewhere in this text have been incorporated into these indexes. There are several of them. The Flesch-Kincaid index, which the United States Department of Defense uses for contractors producing manuals for the armed services, is very popular. The insurance industry relies on the Flesch index, and some states even require that insurance policies meet a certain readability standard.

Linguists and lawyers have debated the reliability and utility of readability indexes since they were first devised back in the 1920s. Most drafters regard them as useful tools, but also recognize their shortcomings. If a document has a poor readability index, it should probably be revised. An apartment lease need not have an index suggesting that it is comprehensible only to someone with a Ph.D. degree. On the other hand, a good readability index does not necessarily guarantee that the document is comprehensible. Factors other than sentence length, number of syllables in each word, and the commonness of the words are also relevant. For example, readability indexes do not measure whether the substance of the sentence makes sense. To borrow from a famous linguistic example: "Colorless green ideas sleep sharply" scores just as well on a readability formula as "Beautiful white houses sell quickly." Readability indexes also do not measure whether the document follows a logical sequence, nor do they take into account the grammatical structure of the sentence—both of which affect comprehensibility tremendously.

However, consider this provision from a form lease, which would presumably be read and used by lay landlords and tenants as the basic charter of their relationship:

> *If the leased premises, or the building of which they form a part, are partially damaged by fire or other casualty, not occurring through fault of Tenant, its agents, servants, or employees, and such damage can be repaired within one-hundred and twenty (120) days of the date of such occurrence, this lease shall remain in full force and effect, and the Landlord shall promptly repair such damage at its expense, and in that event there shall be a proportionate abatement of rent for so much of the leased premises as may be untenatable during the period of repair or restoration. If in the opinion of a registered Architect or Engineer appointed by the Landlord the leased premises are damaged by fire or other*

> *casualty, as aforesaid, to such an extent as to make them wholly untenantable for a period of sixty (60) days or more from the date of such occurrence and such damages cannot be repaired or the premises restored within said time, this lease shall terminate at the option of Landlord upon the written notice given within thirty (30) days after such occurrence. If twenty-five percent (25%) or more of the leased premises or the building of which they form a part, are damaged by fire or other casualty, as aforesaid, to such an extent that the same cannot be repaired or restored within sixty (60) days of the date of such occurrence, this lease may be canceled at the option of the Landlord upon thirty (30) days written notice from the date of such occurrence, even though the premises occupied by the Tenant have not become untenantable, and there shall be an adjustment of the rent to said date of termination. In addition, there shall be no obligation upon the part of Landlord to repair or rebuilt during the last three (3) lease years of the term of this lease agreement unless Tenant shall, within fifteen (15) days after such occurrence, exercise any option to extend the term of this lease agreement that may be afforded to Tenant under the terms hereof. Landlord's obligation to repair or rebuilt pursuant to this paragraph shall be limited to a basic building and the replacement of any interior work which may have originally been installed at Landlord's cost.*

This example of bad drafting has a Flesch-Kincaid index of 16, which means that one would need 16 years of education or a college degree to understand the document.

c. Prepare a Summary

This is not necessary or practical for all documents, but the practice is especially helpful for legislation and complex private law documents. Summarize the document provision-by-provision. This will accomplish several things.

First, if the drafter finds it difficult to summarize the content of the document, this suggests the document will be even more incomprehensible to a reader who is not already familiar with it. The problem may be one of inadequate conceptualization, poor organization, artless expression, or all three. In any case, this is a serious problem indicating that major revision is necessary.

Second, after preparing a summary and comparing it against the document, the drafter or another reader may discover discrepancies. The summary usually reflects what the drafter intended to say and also what the drafter thought he or she said. If this is not the case, then the document must be revised.

Third, after preparing the summary, the drafter may discover that its language is superior to the language of the document itself. The drafter should opt for the better language.

2. REVIEW BY OTHER PEOPLE

Drafting by committee can be frustrating. In its initial stages, drafting should be an individual endeavor. Substantively, however, the individual drafter is error prone, particularly if the document is subject to extensive legal requirements. It is too easy to omit a critical substantive term. This sometimes occurs with respect to a term that has not been the focus of the negotiations, such as a piece of critically important boilerplate, that will cause the transaction to flounder if omitted. Another person, well versed in these substantive requirements, should be asked to review the document with a critical eye. Similarly, this reader may be able to suggest alternative ways of dealing with the problem.

When someone reviews your work and marks it up or otherwise make comments, this is not a sign of failure. In fact, to the extent that the reviewer—be it client, supervising attorney, or opposing counsel—makes any comments at all, this expresses interest in the document and shows that you have the reviewer's attention. Receiving comments and mark-ups of your work is part of the drafting process . You should get used to it as soon as possible.

There are different considerations for each type of reviewer and review.

a. Your Colleagues and Supervisors

Especially when starting out, the first group to review your documents will probably be your colleagues and supervisors. These comments will be designed to improve the documents and your client's position. As such, you should receive them as what they are: constructive commentary from a different perspective, produced with the benefit of different experiences and knowledge that are meant to improve the final work product. They are *not* a personal indictment of your failure to grasp what needs to be done.

First, make any suggested changes that improve the document, then make the other ones that do not harm the document, which is much easier than explaining why you think they are unnecessary. Disregard, *with* explanation, the ones that harm the document. Even if you are in the unfortunate position of receiving comments that appear designed to undermine your confidence and sense of self-worth (which does happen from time to time), you should look for the constructive, beneficial points hidden within what may appear to be venom. Even comments that seem minor or purely stylistic are important. They should be internalized so that the next project involving that commentator incorporates the feedback from the last project in its first draft. Do not incorporate these changes into all your projects in the future, unless (a) you like them or (b) you are working with another client or colleague with similar style.

An effective technique to minimize your reviewer's time and effort and to focus attention on the areas that most require review is to use what is generally known as "track changes" based on the Microsoft Word feature of the same name. In a track changes revisions are indicated by using ~~strikeout~~ text to indicate deletions from a prior draft and underlining to indicate additions. The advantage of track changes is that, when reviewing successive generations of drafts, the reviewer knows exactly what is new and needs to be reviewed, the other material presumably having been approved earlier. Track changes may even be appropriate at the first draft stage if you are basing the document on an exemplar, especially one prepared by your reviewing attorney.

If you use track changes it must be accurate and complete. Inaccurate tracking of changes will establish your reputation as sloppy within your firm and with your client. With opposing counsel, it is likely to create distrust and concerns about your ethics.

It is also valuable to communicate to the reviewer what you need reviewed, when you need it back, and other contextual matters. Find out how they like to get this information, what information they like to get, and the best method for getting it to them.

To minimize comments about your work that may impact negatively upon your reputation, take great care to make your document as good as you can be *before* turning it over for review. Attorneys and clients are busy people for whom time and effort are valuable resources. Skilled practitioners can spot a misspelled or misused word, a grammatical mistake, or even an extra space from a mile away. These distractions impede their review of the substance of your prose.

Learn the rules of your supervising attorneys and follow them before turning in work for review. Although most supervising attorneys will clean up your grammatical and typographical mistakes, this is not their job. Forcing them to do so is not good for your career. Develop your eye for detail as early as possible.

Finally, especially for new attorneys, it is easy to find yourself in a cycle of endless revisions that are rather pointless. After a certain point, polishing results in no further material increase in quality. If you bill your client for the time spent on these rounds of revisions, your work product will be overpriced. If you do not bill for the time, you will be working without compensation. If you find yourself making endless rounds of non-substantial changes, such as changing all instances of "Seller's" to "of the Seller" or vice versa, and are making no meaningful changes, stop.

b. Review by the Client

No complex document should be submitted to the client on a "Here it is, sign where flagged" basis. Much may have been lost in the translation—from the client's desires, to the client's expression of those desires, to the drafter's understanding of those desires, to the specific words that are used to express those desires. The conscientious drafter will sit down with the client and review the document provision-by-provision, explaining what each provision means and ensuring that the document reflects the client's wishes. The summary merely serves as a written form of this review. In legislative drafting, the summary may also become a part of the legislative history.

The degree of depth of this client review depends upon your client representative's level of interest and training. Inside counsel and accountants can be expected to give the document a relatively thorough reading and rarely require extensive explanatory cover letters or transmittal email. For those without such detail-intensive backgrounds, you will want to highlight the most important points in the documents or this round of revisions to ensure that the client is "on notice" of these items and will pay attention to them during the review.

Some clients will not want to review the documents at all, or will be happy to review them at the same time that the other side reviews them. In this case, the documents should be transmitted with a cover letter or transmittal email to opposing counsel stating that the documents are subject to modification. It is important to make sure your client reviews the documents at least once prior to the final draft. You should take note of their comments and modify the documents accordingly. This ensures that you really do understand the directions your client has given to you.

Remember, clients rarely care if you fail to incorporate comments from the other side. They *do* mind when their comments—however minor, inconsequential, or wrongheaded they may seem to you—are not incorporated or at least discussed with them and discarded after that discussion.

c. Review by Opposing Counsel

You have transmitted the documents to the opposing counsel—is your review over? *No*. Take a break, so that your next review of the document will be conducted with fresh eyes. Then, without waiting for opposing counsel to get back to you, review the document one more time and note any corrections that appear to you. Things will be readily apparent to you at this stage that you could not see earlier. You will then be prepared to raise them in your first conversation with opposing counsel, thus avoiding protests based on notions of waiver, closure, or re-opening negotiations. Your changes will also provide you with a selection of trading points to use as consideration for changes requested by opposing counsel.

Encourage opposing counsel to provide you with a marked-up copy of the document showing specific line-edits that are desired, not vague comments like "we need an indemnity here" or "this won't work." It is usually a waste of time for this mark-up to be accompanied by lengthy commentary in the transmittal email explaining and justifying each change, and those letters are costly. They should be generated only when it is important to make a detailed record of the negotiations beyond what marked-up drafts would show. This may be the case in extremely large multi-party transactions where one attorney is collecting and synthesizing the comments of many lawyers; in situations when negotiations are going badly and may fall apart, perhaps precipitating lawsuits; or when they are required by clients who wish to receive this sort of costly narration and entertainment.

Comments from opposing counsel fall into one of four categories and should be responded to as follows:

<u>**Category of Comment**</u>	<u>**Response**</u>
Beneficial to all parties or to the document and the deal.	Make the changes, perhaps thanking opposing counsel for insight and contribution.
Matters of style of opposing counsel and that do no harm to the documents or your client's position.	Consider making the changes. It is less expensive than trying to negotiate out opposing counsel's pet peeves. But also consider how acquiescence across the board can affect the way you are viewed by opposing counsel and your colleagues. Acquiescence can be perceived as a sign of weakness. Sometimes you have to put your foot down and say "no" to a change that would not really matter to maintain your authority and credibility.

Category of Comment	Response
Harmful to either your client's position or the smooth operation of the document.	Reject the changes, with an explanation of the problem that they cause. If the effect opposing counsel was aiming for is evident, and you believe the effect may be desirable or merely neutral, consider suggesting an alternative method of reaching the same end without doing violence to your client's interests or the document.
Valid points for future negotiation.	Consider what, if anything, you would request in exchange for the change. You could also be tentative about making the change, perhaps inserting the requested change into the document as an alternative to the original provision, which is also retained. Make reference to the trade off, if any, or to keeping

Category of Comment	Response
	the issue open in your cover letter. *Do not acquiesce without receiving something in return unless you and your client have run out of points, issues, and comments. Once you give something away it is difficult or impossible to come back and try to charge for it.*

For each comment you receive from opposing counsel, or anyone else, think: What is the point of this comment? What substantive effect are they trying for? Then determine if that effect is acceptable to your client. This may require checking with your client and gaining authority for the change. If acceptable, ask yourself, "Is this the best way to gain this effect?" If it is not, respond with an alternative change that has the same effect, pointing out that it addresses the same issue, but is better because it is more elegant, will take less time to institute, will not affect other issues, is less costly, etc.

For example, a landlord's counsel may demand a large cash security deposit from a start-up tenant with little or no track record. This may be unacceptable or impossible for your client, but your client may be able to obtain a letter of credit from a reputable bank or provide a guaranty from a well-heeled shareholder. Either of the alternatives should satisfy the landlord's legitimate desire for some form of credit support. But, unlike the security deposit, they do not require your client to part with its cash at the present time. If the effect is unacceptable, you will have to respond by rejecting the comment or change and, if necessary, explaining why it is unacceptable.

After you have made the changes you and your client are willing to make in response to the opposing counsel's comments, go over the document one more time, looking for conforming changes. If the same language that was changed appears in other locations and it is appropriate to make the changes there as well, do so.

C. PROOFREAD THE DOCUMENT

After all the corrections and revisions have been made as a result of the review process outlined above and the document has been printed, it is still not final until it has been proofread one final time. Again, this is best done by someone other than the drafter. But it must be done by someone, because many mistakes occur in the very process of correction and revision. And a simple typographical error is capable of making the drafter, despite all the effort and expertise that went into the document, nevertheless appear incompetent and unprofessional.

APPENDIX

The following publications are among those that have influenced or contributed to the content of this book.

Adams, Kenneth A., *A Manual of Style for Contract Drafting*, ABA 2004.

Aitken, J.K., *Piesse, The Elements of Drafting*, 9th ed. 1995.

Brody, Susan L., Rutherford, Jane, Vietzen, Laurel A., Dernbach, John C., *Legal Drafting,* Little, Brown and Co. 1994.

Burnham, Scott J., *Drafting Contracts,* The Michie Co., 2nd ed. 1993.

Butterick, Mathew, *Typography for Lawyers,* O'Conner's 2015.

Child, Barbra, *Drafting Legal Documents, Principles and Practices,* West Publishing Co., 2nd ed. 1992.

Darmstadter, Howard, *Hereof, Thereof, and Everywhereof: A Contrarian Guide to Legal Drafting,* ABA 2002.

Dickerson, Reed, *The Fundamentals of Legal Drafting,* Little, Brown and Co. 1986.

Filson, Lawrence E., *The Legislative Drafter's Desk Reference,* CQ Press 1992.

Fox, Charles M., *Working With Contracts*, PLI 2002.

Garner, Bryan A., *A Dictionary of Modern Legal Usage,* Oxford University Press, 2nd ed. 1995.

Garner, Bryan A., *Advanced Legal Drafting*, LawProse, Inc. 1993.

Garner, Bryan A., *Advanced Legal Writing and Editing*, LawProse, Inc. 1993.

Garner, Bryan A., *The Red Book, A Manual on Legal Style*, West Group 2002.

Gentle Jr., Terry W., and Heminway, Joan MacLeod, *Bank Mergers in Tennessee: An Annotated Model Tennessee Bank Merger Agreement. Transactions: The Tennessee Journal of Business Law*, William S. Hein & Co., Inc., 2004.

Haggard, Thomas, R., *Legal Drafting in a Nutshell*, West Publishing Co. 1996.

Haggard, Thomas, R., *Legal Drafting: Practical Exercises and Problem Materials*. West Group 1999.

Haggard, Thomas, R., *UCC 2–207 A Suggested Analysis*, 10 J. LAW & COMMERCE 257 (1991).

Haggard, Thomas, R., *The South Carolina Rules of Statutory Interpretation*, SOUTH CAROLINA LAWYER, November/December 1991.

Haggard, Thomas, R., *Tips on Drafting and Enforcing a Policy Against Sexual Harassment*, 36 INDUSTRIAL MANAGEMENT, No. 1 (January/February 1994).

Haggard, Thomas, R., *The South Carolina Anti-Stalking Statute: A Study in Bad Drafting*, SOUTH CAROLINA LAWYER (March/April 1994).

Hayakawa, S.I., *Choose the Right Word, A Modern Guide to Synonyms,* Harper and Row, Publishers 1968.

Heminway, Joan MacLeod and McLemore, Timothy, *Acquisition Escrows in Tennessee: An Annotated Model Tennessee Acquisition Escrow Agreement.* 7 TRANSACTIONS: THE TENNESSEE JOURNAL OF BUSINESS LAW #2 2006.

Kuney, George W. and Lloyd, Robert M., *Contracts: Transactions and Litigation,* 5th ed. West Publishing Co. 2019.

Kuney, George W., *The Elements of Contract Drafting,* 5th ed., West Publishing Co. 2020.

Kuney, George W. and Looper, Donna C., *Mastering Legal Analysis and Drafting,* Carolina Academic Press 2009.

Kuney, George W. and Looper, Donna C., *Mastering Appellate Advocacy and Process,* Carolina Academic Press 2015.

Kuney, George W. and Looper, Donna C., *California Law of Contract,* University of California, Continuing Education of the Bar 2007.

Oates, Laurel C., Enquist, Anne, Kunsch, Kelly, *The Legal Writing Handbook.* Little, Brown and Co. 1993.

Ray, Mary B., Cox, Barbara J., *Beyond the Basics, A Text for Advanced Legal Writing,* West Publishing Co. 1991.

Ray, Mary B., Ramsfield, Jill J., *Legal Writing: Getting It Right and Getting It Written,* 3rd ed., West Group 2000.

Shertzer, Margaret, *The Elements of Grammar.* New York, NY: Macmillan Publishing Co., Inc. Copyright 1986.

Sjostrom, Jr., William K., *An Introduction to Contract Drafting,* West Publishing Co. 2013.

Stark, Tina L., *Negotiating and Drafting Contract Boilerplate,* ALM Publishing 2003.

Strunk, Jr, William, White, E.B., *The Elements of Style,* Macmillan Publishing Co., Inc., 3rd ed. 1979.

Swegle, Paul A., *Contract Drafting and Negotiation for Entrepreneurs and Business Professionals,* Business Law Seminar Group, LLC. 2018.

Temple-Smith, Margaret, & Cupples, Deborah E., *Legal Drafting, Litigation Documents, Contracts, Legislation, and Wills,* West Publishing Co. 2013.

Drafting Business Contracts: Principles, Techniques and Forms, University of California, Continuing Education of the Bar 1994, 1996.

INDEX

References are to Pages

ABSTRACTION/CONCRETENESS
Choice between, 18, 238

ABSURD RESULTS
Rule of interpretation, 108

ACCURACY
Defined, 4–6

ADJECTIVES
Compound, 362
Quality vs. identity, 312

ADMINISTRATIVE AGENCIES
Rule favoring interpretation by, 124

ADVERTISING
Ethical limits on, 136

AFTER/BEFORE
Use in indicating time spans, 282–83

AGES
Indication of, 288

AMBIGUITIES
Ages, 288
Commas, semi-colons, 309–10
Consequences of, 265
Dates, time spans, 279–81
Defined, 265
Homonyms, 271
Legalese, 290
Modifiers, 295
Negative pregnants, 300
Participles, 300

Plural nouns, 307
Prepositions, chain, 300
Pronouns, 294–95
Relational words, 288–89
Specific words
  After/before, 283–84
  Among/between, 293–94
  And, 273–75
  And/or, 277–79
  Because, 302
  Biennially/bimonthly/biannually, 286
  If/then, 301
  Now, 288
  Only, 303
  Or, 277–79
  Provided that, 289
  Shall, may, will, must, 291–92
  That/which, 305–06
  Unless, 302–03
Tabbing to avoid, 464–65
Truncated passive, 305
Types
  Contextual, 267–68
  Semantic, 271–72
  Syntactic, 294–95

AMONG
Use of, 293–294

AND
Ambiguity of, 273–75

AND/OR
Ambiguity of, 277–79

APPROPRIATIONS
In statutes, 98

ASSIGNMENT
Contract rights, 60–61

ATTORNEY-CLIENT PRIVILEGE
In drafting documents, 147–48

AUDIENCE
Accommodating various, 194–95
Characteristics, 193–94
Identity, 173, 165, 192–93
Legislative, 81–83
Overview, 81

***BECAUSE* CLAUSES**
Ambiguity of, 302

BETWEEN
Use of, 293–94

BETWEEN/AND
Ambiguity of, 279

BIMONTHLY/ANNUALLY
Ambiguity of, 286–87

CAPITALIZATION
Unconventional, 363

CARROLL, LEWIS
Humpty Dumpty, 384–85
Saying what you mean, 5–6

CHARTS
Use of, 465

CHECKLISTS
Commercially prepared, 218
Content, 273
How questions, 228–29
What questions, 222–24
When questions, 224–27
Where questions, 227
Who questions, 220–21
Document review, 473–74
Drafter prepared, 219–20
Legal, 209
Substantive term, 218–19

CHOICE OF LAW PROVISION
In contracts, 2, 208

CLARITY
Defined, 6–7
Drafting style and usage, 350–51

CLASSIFICATION
Rules for, 257–58

CLIENT OBJECTIVES
Basic questions, 184–85
Drafter evaluation of, 190–91
Overview, 183–84
Perspectives, 197–200
  Multiple-client, 183–84
  Other parties, 187–88
  Scope of use of document, 188–89

COMMAS
Ambiguities, 309–10

COMPUTATIONS
In drafted documents, 466–67

CONCISION
Cross-references, section/paragraph references, 320
Defined, 7–9
Drafting style and usage overview, 319–20
Expletives, 344–45
Expressions, redundant, 329–32
Legalese, 332–35
Nominalizations, 346–47
Numeration, redundant, 343–44
Of the phrases, 341
Passive voice, 347–48
Prepositions, compound and phrases, 335–39
Repetitious substance, 320–22
Rhetorical words, 340–41
Synonyms, redundant, 327–29
That's, 342–43
The fact that, 339–40
To be verb forms, 348–50
Unnecessary content, 319
Which's, 342–43

Who's, 342–43

CONDITIONS
Definition, 421–28
Objective vs. subjective, 430
Terminology for creating, 428–30

CONFIDENTIALITY
Attorney-client privilege, 147
Ethics requirements, 146
In drafting documents, 145

CONFLICT OF INTEREST
In drafting documents, 149–56

CONSISTENCY
Document structure and approach, 318
Drafting overview, 315
Grammatical structure, 316–17
Terminology, 315–16

CONTEXT
Factual, 198–200
Legal, 196–98
Overview, 195

CONTRACTS
Amending, 69–73
Other parties, 187–88
Parts of
  Appendix, 65–67
  Caption or heading, 48
  Date, 64
  Definitions, 53–54
  Housekeeping provisions, 57–62
  Introductory paragraph, 49
  Notarization, 65
  Recitals, 50–53
  Signature block, 62–64
  Statement of consideration, 54–55
  Substantive provisions, 56
Recurring problems
  Ambiguous terms, 44

Gaps, 43–44
Intended contracts that fail, 41–43
Unanticipated events,45
Unintended contracts, 39–41
Vague terms, 44
Role of drafter, 36–38
Types, 46–47

COSTS OF BAD DRAFTING
Client, 27
Drafter, 27
Social, 26

CRIMINAL CONDUCT
Drafting documents involving, 140–143

DAYS
Indication of, 284–85

DEFINED TERM DEFINITIONS
Use of, 394–95

DEFINITIONS
Circular, 386
Combining full and partial, 400–01
Definitional mazes, 389–90
Examples, 401–02
Full, 396–98
General precepts, 481–82
Humpty Dumpty, 384–86
Incorporated by reference, 392–94
Location, 405–06
Methods for creating, 402–03
Components, 403
More familiar terms, 403
More precise terms, 403
Relationship to a larger unit, 404
Specific referents, 404
One-time, 387–88
Overview, 53–54
Partial, 398–99
Enlarging, 399
Limiting, 399

Substantive rules contained in, 390–92
Technical terms, 384
Terms of art, 384
Terms with established meanings, 383
Testing, 406
When to draft, 406
Within a statute, 93
Writing the document, 174–75

DELEGATION
Contract duties, 60–61

DISCURSIVE WRITING
Defined, 10–11

DIVISION
Rules of, 253–55

DOCTOR
Ambiguity of, 271–72

DOES NOT INCLUDE
Use in definition, 399–400

DUTIES
False imperative, 412
Must, 429–30, 449
Negation of, 413–14
Overview, 411
Private-law documents, 413
Shall, 411–13
Shall not, 411
Statutory, 411–13
Will, 430

ECONOMIC ENTERPRISE
Drafting facilitates, 13–14

EFFECTIVE DATE
Housekeeping provisions, 95–96
In legislation, 226–27

EJUSDEM GENERIS
Rule of interpretation, 117–18

ENACTING CLAUSES
Overview, 91–92

ENUMERATIONS
Creation of, 461–62, 464

ETHICS
Communication with client, 144
Competence and diligence, 137–38
Confidentiality, 145
  Attorney-client privilege, 147–48
  Ethical requirements, 146–47
Conflict of interests, 149–50
  Former government lawyer/drafters, 156
  Imputed disqualification, 155–56
  Representation against current client, 150–54
  Representation against former client, 154
Dealing with third parties, 157
Fees, 144
Scope of representation, 138–39
  Criminal, fraudulent, and prohibited transactions, 140–43
  Objectives and means, 139–40
Solicitation, 136–37
  Advertising, 136
  Former clients, family, and friends, 137
  Mass mailings, 136
Unauthorized practice of law, 159–60

EXCEPTIONS
Creating, 261, 364–65, 443–44

EXPLETIVES
Avoidance of, 344–45

EXPRESSIO UNIUS EST EXCLUSIO ALTERIUS
Rule of interpretation, 115–17

FEES
Charging for drafting, 144–45

FINDINGS
In legislation, 92–93

FLOWCHARTS
Creation of, 469–72

FORCE MAJEURE CLAUSE
In contracts, 62

FOREIGN WORDS AND PHRASES
Avoidance of, 360–61

FORMAT
Overview, 176
Physical appearance, 451
  All capitals, 454
  Blank spaces, 457
  Justification, 456
  Line length, 455
  Line spacing, 456–57
  Type size and font, 452–53
  White space, 451–52
Text, 458
  Charts and graphs, 465–66
  Computations, 466–67
  Enumerations, 461–64
  Lists, 461–64
  Numbered or lettered headings, 459–61
  Numbered pages, 459
  Tabbing, 464–65
  Table of contents, 458

FORMBOOKS
Checklists, 218–19

FOUR CORNERS RULE
Rule of interpretation, 108–09

FRAUD
Drafting documents involving, 142–43

FROM/TO
Ambiguity of, 280

FROM SCRATCH DRAFTING
Need for, 29

GENDER SPECIFIC LANGUAGE
Avoidance, 374–79

GENERALITY/SPECIFICITY
Choice between, 239–42

HEADINGS
Creation of, 24, 176, 454, 459–66

HOMONYMS
Ambiguous nature of, 271–73

HOURS
Indication of, 286–87

IF/THEN
Ambiguity of, 301

ILLEGAL OR PROHIBITED CONDUCT
Drafting documents involving, 140–43

IMMUNITY
Creating, 420–21

IN PARI MATERIA
Rule of interpretation, 125–27

INCLUDES
Use in definitions, 400–01

INTERPRETATION, RULES OF
See Rules of Interpretation and specific rules by name

IS ENTITLED TO
Use in creating rights, 415–16

IS NOT ENTITLED TO
Use in negating rights, 417

IS NOT REQUIRED TO
Use in negating duties, 414

LAST MODIFICATION
Rule of, 121

LEGALESE
Ambiguity of, 290–91
Unnecessary use of, 332–335

LEGISLATION
Amending statutes, 98–99
  Changing judicial interpretation, 102–03
  Parts, 99
  What amendments do, 99–100
  When drafted, 98
Compared to private-law documents, 79–80
  Audience, nature and size, 81–82
  Factual data, 84
  Form, style, and usage, 89–90
  Legal limits, 86–87
  Legislative history, 88
  Policy considerations, 83
  Political considerations, 84–85
  Precision, 83
Function of drafter, 76–77
Parts of a statute, 90–91
  Appropriations, 98
  Definitions, 93
  Effective date, 95
  Enacting clause, 91
  Enforcement mechanisms, 94
  Findings, 92
  Housekeeping provisions, 95–96
  Preemption, 98
  Remedies or penalties, 95
  Repeals, 96
  Savings clause, 96
  Severability, 97
  Short title, 92
  Substantive provisions, 94
  Termination, 97
  Title, 91
Who drafts, 75

LEGISLATIVE HISTORY
Creation of, 88

LEX POSTERIOR DEROGAT PRIORI
Rule of interpretation, 128

LIBERAL CONSTRUCTION
Rule of interpretation, 115–16

LIMITATIONS PERIODS
Need for, 227–28

LIQUIDATED DAMAGES
In contracts, 61

LISTS
Creation of, 461–64

LITERARY EXERCISE
Drafting a form of, 20–24

LITIGATION-RELATED WRITING
Defined, 11–12

MAY
Use in creating privileges, 291, 419–20

MAY NOT
Use in negating privileges, 420

MEANS
Use in definitions, 139–40

MERGER CLAUSE
Defined, 60

MIDNIGHT
Ambiguity of, 287–88

MISCHIEF RULE
Rule of interpretation, 109–10

MODIFIERS
Dangling, 298–99
Items in a series, 295–97
Linkage problems, 298
Passive voice, used with, 299–300
Quality/identity, 297

Squinting, 299

MONTHS
Indicating, 284–86

MUST
Use in creating conditions, 291
Use in creating duties, 429–30

NEGATIVE PREGNANTS
Ambiguity of, 300

NO ORAL MODIFICATION CLAUSE
In contracts, 60

NOMINALIZATIONS
Avoidance of, 346–47

NORMATIVE WRITING
Defined, 10

NOSCITUR A SOCIIS
Rule of interpretation, 119–20

NOTICES
Contract provisions for, 61

NOUNS
Chains, avoidance of, 362–63

NUMERATION
Redundant, 343–44

ONLY
Ambiguity of, 303–05

OR
Ambiguity of, 275–76

ORGANIZATION
Classification, 257–59
Division, 253–57
Overview, 19–20, 172–73, 253
Sequence, 259
    Chronological, 259

Familiar before unfamiliar, 261
Frequency of occurrence, 261
Importance, 260
Rules before exceptions, 261
Substance before procedure, 262
What before *how*, 262

PAROL EVIDENCE
Merger clause, 60

PARTICIPLES
Ambiguity of, 300

PASSIVE VOICE
Overview, 347–49
Ambiguity of, 299–300
Use in avoiding gender specific pronouns, 376–79
Truncated, 305

PLAIN MEANING
Rule of interpretation, 108–09

PLURAL
Nouns, ambiguity of, 307–09

POSITIVE EXPRESSIONS
Preferred over negative, 363–64

PREEMPTION PROVISION
In legislation, 98

PREPOSITIONS
Chain, ambiguity of, 300
Compound, 329, 335–39

PREVENTATIVE LAWYERING
Purpose of drafting, 14–15

PRIVILEGES
Creation, 418–20
Negation, 420

PRONOUNS
Ambiguity of, 294–95
Gender specific, avoidance, 374–75

Personal, 365

PUBLIC
Ambiguity of, 271

READABILITY INDEXES
Use of, 466–67, 479–80

RECITALS
In contracts, 50–52

REDDENDO SINGULA SINGULIS
Rule of interpretation, 120–21

RELATIONAL WORDS
Indicating time, ambiguity of, 388–89

RELEASES
Wording, 417, 432, 440

REPEALS
In legislation, 96–97

RESIDENCE
Ambiguity of, 272

REVIEW AND REVISION
Client, 486–87
Opposing council, 488–92
Other persons, 482–83
Overview, 469
Summary of document, 482

RIGHTS
Creation, 415–16
Negation, 416–18

RULES OF INTERPRETATION
Agency interpretation, 124
Borrowed language, 123
Common law, 107–08
Construed against drafter, 111
Document read as a whole, 125
Ejusdem generis, 117–19

Expressio unius, 115–17
Handwritten typed prevails over printed, 121
In pari materia, 125–27
Intent controls, 107–08
  Mischief rule, 109
  Plain meaning or four corners, 108
Last modification, 121
Lex posterior derogat priori, 128
Liberal construction, 115
Noscitur a sociis, 119
Public policy, 129
Reddendo singula singulis, 120
Repeals by implication, 127
Specific prevails over general, 123
Statutory, 106–07
Strict construction, 112–116
  Common law, statutes in derogation of, 113
  Criminal statutes, 112
  Jurisdiction, statutes depriving a court of, 113
  Sovereignty, statutes in derogation of, 114
Validity, rule favoring construction, 121
Written amount prevails over numbers, 122

SANCTION
Ambiguity of, 272

SAVINGS CLAUSE
In legislation, 96

SELF-GOVERNMENT
Drafting facilitates, 13–14

SEMI-COLONS
Ambiguity of, 309, 313–14, 367

SEMIMONTHLY/ANNUALLY
Ambiguity of, 286

SENTENCES
Length, 350

SEVERABILITY CLAUSE
In contracts, 59

SHALL
Ambiguity of, 291–92
Use in creating duties, 413–14

SHALL NOT
Use in creating duties, 413

SHORT TITLE SECTION
In legislation, 92

SIMPLICITY
Defined, 9, 350

SINCE
Ambiguity of, 272

STATUTES
See Legislation

STRICT CONSTRUCTION
Rule of interpretation, 112–13

SURVIVABILITY
Contracts, 61

TABBING
Use in avoiding ambiguity, 464–65

TABLE OF CONTENTS
Need for, 458

TECHNICAL AND TRADE TERMS
Use of, 360

TENSE
Present preferred, 353

TERMINATION DATE
In legislation, 97

TERMS CREATING LEGAL CONSEQUENCES
After, 429
Conditions, 421–22
    Definition and types, 421–22
    Terminology, 428–29

Duties, 411–12
Negation of, 423–24
Private-law documents, 413
Statutory, 411
Exceptions, 443
If, 429
Immunity, 421
Importance, 435
Is entitled to, 442, 457
Is not entitled to, 443, 457
Is not required to, 414
Is not responsible for, 421
May, 419
May not, 420
Must, 429
Privileges, 445–47
Negation of, 447
Releases, 440
Rights, 441–44
Negation of, 443–44
Shall, 411–12
Shall not, 411–12
Surrendering causes of action, 444–45
Unless, 443
Waives, 417–18
Warranties, 438–39
When, 429
Will, 188, 313, 440, 457

TERMS OF ART
Defined, 384–85
Use of, 359–60

THAT
Which/that choice, 305–07

THE FACT THAT
Avoidance of, 339

TIME REFERENCES
After/before, 282–83
Between/and, 279

Bimonthly/annually, 286
Currently, 288
Days, 284–85
From/to, 280
Hours, 286
Midnight, 287
Months, 284
Now, 330, 336
Presently, 288
Semimonthly/annually, 286
Until, 280
Weeks, 284–85
Within, 283
Years, 284–85

TITLE
In legislation, 92

TYPOGRAPHY
Blank spaces, 457–58
Capitalization, 454–55
Justification, 456
Line length, 455
Line spacing, 456
Type size and font, 452–53
White space, 451

UNLESS
Ambiguity of, 302–03

UNTIL
Ambiguity of, 280

VAGUENESS/PRECISION
Choice between, 83, 243–44

WAIVERS
No-waiver-of-rights clause, 60
Waiver of rights, 56, 417–18

WARRANTIES
Overview, 438

WEEKS
Indication of, 284–85

WHEN
Use in creating conditions, 429

WHICH
That/which choice, 305–07

WHILE
Ambiguity of, 272

WILL
Use in creating duties, 292

WITHIN
Use of, 283

WORDS
-ee and *-or* endings, avoidance of, 360
Order, 340–41

YEARS
Indication of, 284